# Voices of the Voiceless

## Mulk Raj Anand and Jayakanthan

Social Consciousness and Indian Fiction

Celebrating Indian Literature

# Voices of the Voiceless

## Mulk Raj Anand and Jayakanthan

Social Consciousness and Indian Fiction

G. Dominic Savio

Prestige

*an international publishing house*

*Published by*
**Prestige Books**
3/28, East Patel Nagar
New Delhi 110 008
Ph. 9818755529

ISBN: 81-7551-167-2



Printed at Chaman Offset Press, New Delhi 110 002

# Contents

*for*

**my parents**

# Preface

My love for Comparative Literature dates back to the late Seventies when I was offered Comparative Literature as an optional subject for my Post Graduate Programme in the Department of English at the then Madurai University. My perception and understanding of the discipline grew sharper and more critical in the early Eighties when I was fortunate to do a course. 'Introduction to Comparative Literature,' for my M.Phil. degree at the same Department. Having been trained in this fascinating discipline it was but natural that I developed a desire to do my Ph.D. on a Comparative Literature subject.

I have always admired the trimurtis of Indian Writing in English epitomising one of the finest creative sensibilities in their literary works. My mental disposition has often failed to comprehend the metaphysical dimensions of Raja Rao. Nor has it found resonance with the rich comic mode of R.K. Narayan. Mulk Raj Anand's love of life, his passionate longing for freedom and his keen interest in fighting against social evils portrayed in his novels had an irresistible appeal to me. My reading of Jayakanthan goes back to the student days when he was considered the best living novelist in Tamil. His robust optimism, his love of human beings, his compassion and his crusade against the anti-human institutions impressed me to the extent of choosing him for a critical evaluation. As the common denominator between Anand and Jayakanthan is their social consciousness, I thought I could attempt a comparative study of these two novelists.

The stages involved in the preparation of this project required the co-operation and assistance of many persons. First and foremost, I am very grateful to Dr. P. Marudanayagam, Professor and Head, Department of English, Pondicherry University, Pondicherry for his constant encouragement and help. I am especially indebted to my teacher, Professor V. Sachithanandan, who first initiated me into this field of Comparative Literature.

I heartily thank Principal Dr. D. Peter Jeyapandian of The American College, Madurai, for enabling me to avail myself of one-year study leave under F.I. P. sanctioned by the U.G.C. under the Eighth Plan. I also extend my sincere thanks to Dr. Paul Love, P.G. Professor and Director, Advanced Study Centre for Indian Writing in English and Translations, The American College. The research library he has established and his Study Centre have always been of great help to me.

Finally, I express my gratitude to all others who helped me in the preparation of the present project: to authorities of the National Library, Calcutta, especially to Mr. Subramaniam, Editor, Tamil Division, Mrs. Kovy, Deputy Librarian and Mrs. Koshy, Assistant Librarian for making my two weeks' stay in September 1992 very useful; to the personnel of the several libraries where I sought source materials for this study: Central Library, Visva Bharati University, Santiniketan, Dr. T.P.M. Library, Madurai Kamaraj University, Library at the Institute of Correspondence Course and Continuing Education, M.K. University, Library at the Gandhigram Rural Institute (Deemed University), Gandhigram, Daniel Poor Memorial Library, P.G. Department Libraries in English and Tamil at American College, Romain Rolland Library, Pondicherry and Libraries in the Department of English and Comparative Literature and The School of Tamil Studies at Madurai Kamaraj University; to Dr. Premila Paul for the help and encouragement shown to me; to Prof. Chandramohan Nair; my dear colleagues in the Department; to Prof. V. Swaminathan of Tamil Department, The American College; to Dr. Thirumalai of the Department of Tamil and Comparative Literature, M.K. University; to Mrs. Guruvammal of Tamil Department, Gandhigram Rural University, Gandhigram; to my former teacher, Dr. N. Subramaniam, Professor and Head, Department of English and Comparative Literature; to my former teacher, Mr. Lakshmi Narayan of the same Department for sharpening my critical perception on seminal issues of religion and philosophy; to my friend and librarian, Mr. G.P. Reuben, The American College, for his invaluable service in procuring source materials for my study.

# Introduction

Though Anand and Jayakanthan belong to different linguistic backgrounds, they bear essentially the same social consciousness. These two novelists are primarily social realists who revolt against all man-made, anti-human establishments. Both of them evince keen interest in the eradication of social evils and their novels are nothing but artistic attempts to arouse the slumbering conscience of the people to activise them to remove these evils.

The study of Anand and Jayakanthan from a comparative angle, essentially analogical, is a rewarding experience. Their novels throw light on many complex aspects of modern life and their outlook is almost identical as humanists. The life of the poor people is the subject matter of most of their novels. Their understanding of society has Marxian overtones and the value of it lies in a plea for human justice and equality. They are also apostles of the creed of modernity with their basic faith in improving the quality of social life. Their art is an instrument for social transformation.

K.R. Srinivasa Iyengar in his comprehensive book, *Indian Writing in English*, has demonstrated to the readers the nature of the achievement inherent in Anand's works of art.[1] Professor M.K. Naik's study of Anand lays great emphasis upon the conflict between tradition and modernity in his novels. His study of The Lal Singh Trilogy is an excellent exposition of the clash between the ancient tradition and modern values. He offers a close critical paraphrase of the entire novels in a cryptic way in order to illustrate the basic conflict. He is close to Anand in spirit when he captures the theme of the novel, *The Old Woman and the Cow* in a synoptic sentence: "it is the transformation of a cow into a tigress."[2] This critical study of Naik is crucial in that he goes to the heart of Anand's major theme, namely, modernity.

Balarama Gupta's book *Mulk Raj Anand: A Study of his Fiction in Humanist Perspective* is a seminal one in Anand Criticism. The special significance of Gupta is that he has laid emphasis upon the humanist element which is the fundamental base of all his novels.[3] The author shows that Anand tirelessly attacks in all his novels people's belief in Karma and Fatalism. Gupta points out that Anand's humanism makes man "the master of his destiny uncontrolled by God."[4] The critic states that "Anand is mainly in the tradition of scientific humanism." (20) Gupta's study of the novel *Death of a Hero* is praiseworthy as it lays bare Anand's belief in secularism and human liberty. The best part of the book lies in the comprehensive account of the basic theme of all his novels.

Krishna Nandan Sinha's book *Mulk Raj Anand* is an illuminating study which captures the social conscience of the novelist. Sinha treats Anand's novels as novels of social responsibility and takes pains to show in an elaborate way the literary techniques of the novelist such as naturalism and symbolism which add poetic beauty to the novels. The main task of the novelist, according to him, is to show his deep passion for the welfare of the human race. Sinha says that though his novels make a reference to a local cultural place like Punjab, his concerns are universal and timeless in spirit.

Saros Cowasjee's book *So Many Freedoms* projects the multidimensional vision of Anand beginning with a biographical account of Anand's life and the help he has received from his literary friends in London. Cowasjee offers a profound analysis of the psychological predicament of Munoo, Eakha and Gangu and points out that Anand's theories arise from his conception of literature which is to reveal the complicated drama of human life in all its aspects. According to him the novelist's social impulse is conditioned by the Marxian dialectics. He says in his third chapter on 'The Trilogy' that "Bakha, Munoo and Gangu are not intellectually equipped to think in terms of revolution."[5] Their problem of survival rules out this need. This book throws light on the mind of the novelist in many ways in showing his shift from idealism to revolutionary socialism and finally to 'comprehensive historical humanism'. C.D. Narasimhaiah's assessment of Anand's achievement is primarily based on his study of Anand's novels, *Untouchable, Coolie* and *The*

*Big Heart*. He prefers these works of Anand "in the belief that they are fairly representative of Anand's art." (110)

Premila Paul's book, *The Novels of Mulk Raj Anand: A Thematic Study*, is an excellent work on Anand. She assimilates and synthesizes the essentials of the previous works and adds her fresh and new insights and findings. Human suffering in a hostile society is the major concern of Anand. It takes the forms of caste rigidity, class structure, religion and predicament of women, according to her. The book is perceptive in many ways tracing Anand's interest in the class struggle to his love of liberal humanism. She rightly feels that Anand exaggerates the evil of organized religion. Her analysis of the predicament of women reminds one of a feminist.

Marlene Fisher's book *The Wisdom of the Heart*, a close analysis of Anand's achievement as a novelist, examines the relationship between his life and experiences which have their origin from the agony of the human heart. The author points out the novelist's belief in modernity as a solution for increasing the possibilities of "one world." Marlene Fisher has an illuminating chapter on women which is bold, frank and forthright. This book is valuable as it is written out of deep personal contact with the author.

A.V. Krishna Rao's book *The Indo-Anglian Novel and the Changing Tradition* contains an interesting chapter, "Mulk Raj Anand and the Novel of Protest." The author says that "Mulk Raj Anand has established himself as the chief spokesman of the Indo-Anglian 'Literary Naturalist' with a proletarian bias."[6] He also points out that the chief aim of the novelist lies in the naturalistic projection of social reality, and traces certain typical naturalistic characteristics such as determinism, survival, violence and taboo. The value of the work lies in fixing Anand in the Indo-Anglian literary tradition. P.K. Rajan's book *Studies in Mulk Raj Anand* reveals the value of the content-form interaction within the novels. He takes Anand to be more than a socialist, a Marxist, a revolutionary humanist, a pacifist and a social realist.

Jack Lindsay's study of the novels of Mulk Raj Anand in his monograph, *The Elephant and the Lotus* identifies the significance of Anand in relation to Tagore and Premchand. He says that Anand assumes importance because of his interest in the relation between the new Asian cultures and the European traditions. His novels show his capacity to define the general in the particular. He says that Forster, Malraux and Camus tend to impose their philosophical doctrines on their novels whereas Anand draws all his lessons from his exploration of life. Lindsay says that the strength of Anand as a novelist lies in his intimate concern with domesticities.

There are two doctoral dissertations which need a special mention: *The Theme of Social Justice in the Novels of Mulk Raj Anand and Bhabani Battacharya* by V.H. Bhaskaran and *The Novels of Mulk Raj Anand and Thakazhi Sivasankaran Pillai: A Thematic Study* by Girija G.R. Priyadersini. Bhaskaran points out Anand's passion for social justice as a prominent theme. He says that the two novelists gain their significance in their protest against misery, ugliness, inequality and social injustice. Anand's concern for the human underdog is deep. Girija Priyadersini makes a thematic study of Anand and issues such as Untouchability, downtrodden women, class struggle, ill-set education and religious superstition are discussed clearly. This work projects Anand and Thakazhi as two great social reformers who want to improve social life.

The significance of Jayakanthan can be easily perceived in the light of the prefaces he has written to his novels. Some themes of the novels like *Pirammōpatēcam* (Initiation into Brahman) and *Vilutukal* (Aerial Roots) become intelligible to the reader through his prefaces. S. Chellappan, the editor of his prefaces in a separate book points out that many readers have been attracted by the seminal ideas discussed by Jayakanthan in the prefaces.

The next great work of importance is the collection of research articles on Jayakanthan by M. Arivalakan. He has taken great pains to collect articles from many sources and arrange them in a particular order. He has not abridged or simplified any of the articles. His compilation covers many translations of the novels anti interviews with Jayakanthan. T.V. Veerasamy's forward to this work contains an objective estimate of Jayakanthan's achievement as a novelist. He says that Jayakanthan is a revolutionary novelist in that he critically analyses the place of the past.

T.V. Veerasamy has contributed a special article in which he says that the earlier phase of the novelist has a Marxian background which gives prominence to the lives of labourers, workers, agriculturists and poor men. He condemns the forces which favour exploitation and suppression. The author says that Jayakanthan's novel, *Vãlkkai Alaikkiratu* (Life Invites) speaks of the boundless love he has for the human beings. The value of human love is seen in *Unnaippol Oruvan* (One Like You). He points out that life becomes a matter of joy only when it is lived for others. His novels show the basic conflict between tradition and modernity.

The critic says that Henry's character is a kind of vision. The best human nature lives in him. He admires his appreciation of nature as a mark of goodness. Idayan says that Jayakanthan's novels contain the character of a philosophical debate. *Pärisukku Pö* (Go to Paris) is a supreme example of this type. K. Kailasapathy speaks of the relationship between individual beliefs and novel as a form of literature.[2] Jayakanthan becomes a representative spokesman for Kokila in *Kokila Enna Ceytuvittal*? (What has Kokila Done?) and Muthu Velar in *Camükam Enpatu Nalu Per* (Four People Represent Society). His description of Sarangan according to the critic is an example of his enterprise as a novelist who portrays the tragedy of imitation of an intellectual without roots.[9]

According to S. Jesudasan, Jayakanthan's business is not to write emotion-stirring sexual novels but to discuss genuine sexual problems.[10] Dr. Mohan brings out the special psychological motive of the novelist. He says that every novel is a test for his trial as a novelist and that there is also the subsequent experience of triumph in this task. The critic sees the presence of many points of view and finds fault with the novelist for not having conformed to one particular line of thinking. This criticism[11] is not fair because Jayakanthan's main purpose is to see the complexity of human life and so the portrayal of many points of view is inevitable. Jayakanthan believes that every point of view has some limited significance and so he believes in debate and discussion as a form of his novel. The novels *Pirammōpatēcam* and *Pärisukku Po* are examples of this type. They expose the mind to different points of view indicating their unlimited viability. M. Subramanian, another critic, is closer in spirit to Jayakanthan. He says that the novelist has some basic convictions and beliefs about life. According to him life is not in accordance with one's own expectations.[12] This view is acceptable because Jayakanthan believes in the importance of life but is not prepared to jump to conclusions. The main reason is the complexity of life.

N. Sivaraman says that Jayakanthan's novels are interesting as they indicate the clash between tradition and the practical realities of life. Ranga is an 'unrooted intellectual' who fails to relate his knowledge to the practical reality of life.[13] R. Periyalvar makes a reference to the widespread use of the Brahmin dialect in the novels of Jayakanthan, many of which draw even their titles from the Brahmin dialect. The themes of these novels also relate to the social problems of the Brahmins. *Pirammōpatēcam* and *Rishi Mulam* (The Past of Rishi) are novels which embody the complicated social issues of the Brahmins. The critic also points out that Jayakanthan's long association with the Communist party has inspired him to make use of the Marxian dialectics, the strong social outlook, creative method of research and also incorporate all other ideas into his novels along with their special style.

S. Thothathri speaks of Jayakanthan and social change. Like Gorky, he does not portray a newly transformed society. He says that Jayakanthan's *Cila Nērankalil Cila Manitarkal* (Some Times Some People) is a failure.[14] This complaint has no basis because Jayakanthan succeeds in depicting the conflict in the life of Ganga. Siddharthan points out Jayakanthan's Marxist bent of mind in paying attention to the dark side of life.[15] Starvation, prostitution, and other social problems are his themes. He follows in the footsteps of Pudumaipithan but his social outlook is completely different from the latter's. He has the positive confidence which indicates that everyone can shape his own future in a good way.

Thothathri finds fault with Jayakanthan for his failure to conform to the Communist ideology in his creation of a character like Seshadri. The novelist is a Marxist with an open mind. The critic is a Marxist with a strong Marxist bias and hence he fails to appreciate the philosophical disputation between Sharma and Seshadri. Moreover Jayakanthan's new vision of life treats religion and atheism as two companions that must work in close co-operation with each other. His preface explains this view. Moreover Thothathri has no sympathy for the novelist's later outlook which indicates his interest in spirituality. T. Pakkia Muthu speaks of the salvation of man in the Tamil novels.[16] He cites *Oru Manitan Oru Vitu Oru Ulakam* (One Man, One House and One World) as an example. He appreciates Henry's freedom from attachment to any religious dogma. Henry is noble and unoffending in his nature. The novelist wants everyone to be like Henry as he works without any mean motive. His love of human beings is unique to him.

Vallikannan says that the novelist is in the tradition of Subramanya Bharathi who performed the revolutionary act of converting a non-Brahmin into a Brahmin. N. Arumugam sees untouchability as an expression of the degenerate middle phase of the Hindu religion. Kalpanadasan appreciates the novelist's aim of creating a Vedic society while S. Narmada thinks that the novel *Jaya Jaya Sankara* (Hail Sankara) is untrue to life. Vimarsagan and Jothirlatha Girija describe the novel as an unsuitable venture which is not true to the spirit of the times. Some of the negative critics have failed to respond to the new idea of Jayakanthan. It implies that modern life cannot he renewed without reviving the springs of spirituality. The friendship that he shows between Āti and Sankaran is a symbolic dream of his vision of human unity. The ideal of the Vedic dharma lies in the welfare of all human beings.

The study of Anand and Jayakanthan comes under the sphere of analogy in the field of Comparative Literature. As there are no internal and external concrete evidences to show that Anand has influenced Jayakanthan, there is no scope for an influence study. In his letter to the present researcher, Anand says, "I have read a few of Jayakanthan stories in English translation, but none of his novels. But he himself told me during our visit to Leningrad that he had a similar attitude about the human condition."[17] This letter indicates the choice of these two writers for a comparative study.

A broad parallel study is possible as their outlook is identical in many ways. There are many social issues which bring them together for the purpose of a comparative study. Anand writes, "I suggest that you do a general introduction on the human condition as the obsessive theme in novels of both writers."[18] Anand's letter to the present writer throws light on his profound concern with the human conditions or predicament which brings him close to Jayakanthan. Their novels focus their attention on two main themes: Why does man suffer in society? What is the reason for this? These two questions lead them to make a detailed survey of the entire gamut of life.

The relevance of this study lies in the fact that life is complex and the same issues appear again and again. These two novelists engage themselves in the examination of a common question: why does society remain in a backward state? Their answers to the question are similar. According to them, the main defect lies in the practice of religion and tradition. They state that caste and class are the creation of religion and capitalism. The suffering of Munoo and Bakha has a close relation to class and caste while the suffering of Citti and Raja comes from economic impoverishment. Social analysis of life leads them to reject religion and place faith in humanism.

The need and justification for this comparative study is closely connected with the different kinds of crisis in human life. For example, the conflict between tradition and modernity is still crucial. Anand justifies the need for modernity in the light of his perception of the social backwardness. His belief in the creative use of science justifies his faith in modernity. The transformation of life is impossible without the help of scientific device. According to Anand human suffering has its roots in capitalism.

Jayakanthan is an avid believer in promoting the merit of science. His insight into human nature is very relevant today. He sees before him a huge world of diversity. His perception of irreconcilable contradictions in life does not lead him to evolve an easy rational solution. A believer in the Marxian dogma is a believer n social change. Anand and Jayakanthan conform to this dictum. But Jayakanthan sees in life a certain complexity which cannot be reduced to a simple phenomenon according to him. Anand is different in this respect. The Marxian dogma of economic justice remains with him to be a source of permanent inspiration. He believes that poverty and human suffering spring from wealth and ownership. Jayakanthan does not negate this preoccupation but is ready to see life from different angles.

Anand was born in Peshawar in the year 1905. He obtained the B.A. (Hons.) degree of Punjab University and continued his study of

Philosophy in English under Professor G. Dawes Hicks. His meeting Irene, daughter of a scientific philosopher, was a significant event in London. He received his Ph.D. Degree in Philosophy in 1936 from London University. He stayed with Mahatma Gandhi in Sabarmati Ashram and there completed the first draft of *Untouchable*. In 1936 he joined the International Brigade in Spain. His visit to Berlin to attend the world peace council session was a feather in his cap. In 1952 he secured the International peace prize of the World Peace Council as his works promoted human unity and aimed at a creative encounter between East and West. In 1956 he organized the first Asian Writers' Conference in New Delhi. He went to USSR as a joint leader of Indian Delegation to participate in the Afro-Asian Writers' Conference. He visited Australia for a lecture tour and in 1962 became the Tagore Professor of Art and Literature in Punjab University. In 1972 he won the Sahitya Akademi Award for *Morning Face*. He passed away in September 2004.

Unlike Anand, Jayakanthan comes from a poor family, which could not give him much formal education. He had to stop it at the fifth class. At a very early age, he took up manual labour in the printing press of the newspaper *Jana Sakthi*. This gave him a chance to stay in the office of the Communist Party. He came to know about Marxism and met many great Communist leaders. He went to Cuddalore when the Communist party was banned in 1948 in Tamil Nadu. He performed several odd jobs in Cuddalore and led his life as a porter and seller of film songbooks. He went to Madras in 1950 where he became an exponent of Communist ideology. His study of Marxism made him a fighter for human justice and he evinced keen interest in the lives of the poor people. He took up work in *Jana Sakthi*, *Manitan* and *Tamil Mulakkam* and became a sub-editor of *Samaram*. After sometime the regular work of editorship came to him from *Jeyaberikai*, *Jayakkodi* and *Gnanaratham*. Jayakanthan's life was a great struggle and his first source book for writing.

The main philosophical outlook of Anand and Jayakanthan lies in humanism. For them all concerns of life gain their merit only in relation to human issues. Their humanism is a fundamental denial of belief of God. There are four factors which go into the making of their critical tenet of humanism. All human affairs have no relation to God. Human life is valuable only in terms of how it is found on earth. Love of human beings is a mark of joy. Life is a struggle and the real value and charm of it is found in poor people.

In accordance with these principles, five novels are chosen for a comparative critical discussion. Anand reflects the problem of human injustice and arrogance of class-consciousness in *Coolie* and *Two Leaves and a Bud.* Similarly Jayakanthan portrays the helplessness of the poor people in *Yarukkaka Alutan?* (For Whom Did he Weep?), *Valkkai Alaikkiratu* and *Unnaippol Oruvan.* Their predominant artistic motive is to express their love and sympathy for the poor in the pathetic plight of their life.

There are some problems which engage the minds of the two novelists in their diagnosis of Munoo in *Coolie* and Citti in *Unnaippol Oruvan.* What merits attention in these two characters is the painful predicament in which they are found. For these two characters, society is the greatest enemy. Their happiness is marred by the wretched conditions of the society. Munoo is a coolie while Citti is an ice-cream seller. These two heroes do the job of a menial servant. Such a kind of work carries no dignity in the eye of the society. Munoo's major problem is concerned with the question of human dignity. Wherever he goes, he is ill-treated. Munoo's life is in a kind of direct conflict with the expectations of the society.

Anand's *Two Leaves and a Bud* and Jayakanthan's *Yarukkaka Alutan?* lend themselves to certain terms of comparison and contrast. It is evident that human suffering reaches its height in Gangu and Joseph. Gangu's search for livelihood and his subsequent experience of humiliation in all his attempts forms the theme of the novel The problem of Gangu is connected with the life of the coworkers in the Tea plantation and it represents the state of group suffering. The personal tragedy of Gangu is deeply connected with his loss of wife and a certain anxiety about the future of his daughter Leila. Jayakanthan's Joseph embodies his own intense individual suffering with his enormous capacity for patience.

Some protagonists are chosen from the novels of Anand and Jayakanthan in order to examine their importance and their relationship to society. Āti in *Jaya Jaya Sankara* and Bakha in *Untouchable* deserve a critical study. Anand shows the fate of the Untouchable in

Bakha. The novelist is pained to note that Bakha's misery is related to his lowborn nature. The dignity of Bakha as a human being is questioned by a caste-conscious society. The solution lies in the adoption of Gandhism, conversion and modernization. Āti, unlike Sakha, is a self-confident individual who never bothers about the opinion of the society. His intellectual background has freed him from the limitations of the caste-oriented society. Āti never sinks into despair because of his lowborn nature and is conscious of his independent power of judgement.

Ananta in *The Big Heart* and Henry in *Oru Manitan Oru Vitu Oru Ulakam* form an interesting pair for comparative scrutiny. Ananta is an atheist and a believer in the value of human effort and he is an advocate of modernization through machines. Like Ananta, Henry is an idealist who loves everyone. Ananta has a specific commitment which lies in introducing the use of machines. Henry's only mission is to love all people. Ananta does not believe in God and he has no religion. Similarly Henry is not a conventionalist: nor is he attached to any religion. Ananta thinks of building up an ideal social order with the help of human effort alone. Henry respects human effort and does not dismiss other people's views. Ananta's goodness is comparable to Henry's capacity for flexibility.

Anand and Jayakanthan examine critically the question of untouchability in some of their novels. *Anand's Untouchable* and *The Road* and Jayakanthan's *Jaya Jaya Saṇkara, Piralayam* (The Deluge) and *Munkil Kattu Nila* (Nila of the Forest of Bamboos) deserve to be studied from this point of view. Anand as a humanist and an advocate of the creed of modernity believes that it is the Hindu religion which is responsible for the problem of untouchability. Bakha suffers humiliation on account of caste conservatism which indicates his lowborn nature. His misery as a lowborn human being forces him to search for a remedy which according to him lies in adoption of Gandhism or Christianity or modernization.

Bhikhu is an extension of Bakha. The novelist looks at work as a form of liberation and lays emphasis upon collective mass action as a remedy for the evil of untouchability. The building up of a bridge is an industrial venture involving the use of machines. The industrialized venture makes no scope for dung and latrine cleaning.

An organized social action gives meaning to work and takes away the stigma of untouchability. Bhikhu preaches the theory that there is no salvation without work. Bakha's suffering issues from the traditional work of latrine cleaning. But Bhikhu means by work an organized industrial venture which brings all people to a common purpose. Bhikhu suggests that the only way to remove untouchability is to strengthen the idea of human unity.

Unlike Anand, Jayakanthan re-examines the issue of untouchability and locates the reason for such an evil in the confused practice of the Hindu religion. The novel *Jaya Jaya Sankara* is an attempt at retracing the value of the real Vedic religion. Such a careful probing throws new light on the Hindu religion. He suggests that the union between the temple and the ashram is symbolic of an indirect alliance between religion and spirituality. Āti never bends his head low in the society. Similarly Ammasi Kilavari in *Piralayam* thinks of his self-respect. He says that the realization of one's own dignity through learning proves to be a source of strength to his existence. His great insight is that there must be progress in the growth of one's own awareness of things and without it there is no real reform.

Anand and Jayakanthan explicitly manifest their belief in the emergence of the New Woman. Both of them believe that the concept of a New Woman is the result of the modern need and reaction to the male chauvinism of the society. The law of the Manu Dharma grants greater privileges to men and this special concession keeps women at the mercy of men. Anand has a strong conviction that religion makes room for this kind of male domination. He suggests that the only way for the emancipated woman is to break away from all ties of religion and tradition.

Maya and Janki are created by Anand in his novels, in keeping with this new canon. These two women deviate from tradition and their deeds have no rational sanction of any system. They are symbols of human liberty and their motive is to freely express their choice of life without any inhibition. Their love of life makes them independent in their approach to anything. They advocate the plea that woman must have a say in everything. Without the real sense of freedom, life does not express its charm. Maya and Janki strive towards this principle of freedom. The traditional view of marriage is an arrangement but the new woman says that marriage must be an expression of the spontaneous choice of the individual. Anand as an advocate of modernity allows women to enjoy their right of autonomy.

Jayakanthan resembles Anand in his plea for giving greater freedom to woman. He has a specific tendency to make his women characters highly knowledgeable and talented individuals. The now woman, according to Anand, is one who resists the pressures of tradition and religion. Jayakanthan accepts this view and adds one more point to make his idea clear. Unlike Anand, he lays special emphasis upon education as an important instrument to promote woman's emancipation. Their learning will give them a new awareness and they will draw a limit to the tolerance of anything. Gauri is not an educated woman but her exposure to life teaches her what she should do with Panchi Maya and Janki are militant in their reaction.

Similarly Jayakanthan's women characters like Kalyani, Kokila, Ganga and Sita are uncompromising intellectual individuals. He says that women must have a right to raise a voice of protest wherever injustice prevails. Kalyani thinks that the very charm of life lies in the virtue of individuality. Kokila raises a plea for human equality. Ganga's individuality lies in her preference to remain unmarried. Sita argues that marriage is impossible without the choice of individual liberty. Maya, Janki and Gauri are activists in their outlook without living on an intellectual plane whereas Kalyani, Kokila, Ganga and Sita show their power of thinking without being involved in any emotional action. In the case of Maya, Janki and Gauri, there is a spirited move towards demolishing tradition and religion. In Jayakanthan's women, there is an attempt at reorganizing everything.

Anand and Jayakanthan deal with the crucial question of the relationship between tradition and modernity. The three novels, *The Village, Across the Black Waters* and *The Sword and the Sickle* project the life of the hero Lal Singh who is found at war with everything that is found in society. He sees with his painful perception three important factors which impede the progress of the society. The conservative mentality, lack of scientific awareness and a certain unwillingness to change one's attitude and accept new things lead to stagnation. The hero's experience of the Western way of life after his escape from the village gives him a basis for changing the old habits.

While the novel *Across the Black Waters* gives him a rational and scientific knowledge of the European civilization, *The Sword and the Sickle* brings out his plea for human justice and his spirited protest against the society of feudal aristocracy. In the same way, Jayakanthan in his novel *Pirammōpatēcam* presents Seshadri who is very much like Lal Singh in his spirit and mental outlook. Anand is an uncompromising advocate of modernity. Jayakanthan's *Pirammōpatēcam* and *Pärisukku Po* conduct a dialectical debate between the nature of the relationship between tradition and modernity. Both Anand and Jayakanthan believe in keen intellectual perception as a tool for critical review.

Anand's idea of modernity has to be interpreted in the light of his interest in the European Enlightenment. This leads him to accept science. But Jayakanthan's conception of modernity implies critical review of everything from the standpoint of reason and truth. Jayakanthan in the novels discussed does not explicitly share Anand's interest in science. But this habit of objectively questioning everything is what makes him modern. While Anand treats tradition and religion as roadblocks to human progress, Jayakanthan believes that the importance of anything lies in how it changes the perception of the people. Anand's exposure to the philosophy of the European Enlightenment is what distinguishes him from Jayakanthan who wants to soften the contrast between tradition and modernity.

Anand and Jayakanthan evolve a new vision of life which expresses its preference for their own preoccupations. With Anand, religion is the major target of attack. His exposure to the European Enlightenment has given him a scientific outlook and imbued him with a passion for objectivity. His strong love of life and his poetic preference for the concrete things prevent him from accepting religion with its interest in extra-terrestrial things. The degenerate behaviour of priests like Pandit Kalinath, Pandit Bhola Nath, Pandit Suraj Mani creates in him a revulsion towards religion. Anand's novels, *The Village*, *Lament on the Death of a Master of Arts*, *The Big Heart* and *Death of a Hero* expound his concept of atheism.

Jayakanthan like Anand has started as a denouncer of religion. For him the reality of the external world is fundamental to the perception of anything. He develops a theory which is stated by him in his prefaces to some novels that everything lies outside him. The concept of God and religion involves a subjective form of consciousness. His early novels *Yarukkaka Alutan?, Valkkai Alaikkiratu* and *Unnaippol Oruvan* are written in this agnostic spirit. Later on Jayakanthan experiences a change. One advantage with him is that his mind is not fixed in any dogma as he happens to be a critical realist. He learns to make a distinction between religion and spirituality under the influence and inspiration of Swami Vivekananda.

His novel *Vilutukal* is an attempt at an appreciation of the life of Sanyasis. The novel *Piralayam* is a description of the objective mind of the hero who stands as a bridge between tradition and modernity, In the novel *Pirammōpatēcam*, he expounds the view that real religion and atheism are companions. His more revolutionary novel *Jaya Jaya Sankara* is a careful venture of the novelist in distinguishing the truth of the Hindu religion from its prevailing false and degenerate form. Though he has rejected in the earlier phase of his career traditional ethics and morality, he argues that people must live life in a more meaningful way. He prefers to be unorthodox in his approach to life. He says that love, marriage, sex, morality and chastity gain their meaning in relation to the human context and like Anand he is not interested in premature judgement of anything.

All the major novels of Anand and Jayakanthan have been discussed in this study. Only those which may not serve any purpose in a comparative study of this type have been ignored. The titles of the novels of Jayakanthan have been transliterated, with their English equivalents given in brackets. All the English renderings of passages from Tamil works quoted here are mine.

## NOTES

1. C.D. Narasimhaiah, *The Swan and the Eagle* (Shimla: The Indian Institute of Advanced Study, 1969), pp. 109-10
2. M.K. Naik, *Mulk Raj Anand* (Delhi: Arnold-Heinemann India, 1973), p. 86.

3. K.R. Srinivasa Iyengar, 'Foreword,' G.S. Balarama Gupta, *Mulk Raj Anand: A Study of His Fiction in Humanistic Perspective* (Bareilly: Prakash, 1974), p. vi.
4. G.S. Balarama Gupta, p. 29.
5. Saros Cowasjee, *So Many Freedoms* (Delhi: Oxford University Press, 1977), p.99.
6. A.V. Krishna Rao, *The Indo-Anglian Novel and the Changing Tradition* (Mysore: Rao and Raghavan, 1972), p. 28.
7. Idayan, Qtd. N. Arivalakan, *Jayakanthan Ayvatankal* (Cuddalore: Amaravathy Press, 1978), p. 255.
8. K. Kailasapathy, *Ibid.*, p. 261.
9. Loc. Cit.
10. S. Jesudasan, *Ibid.*, p.271.
11. Mohan, *Ibid.*, pp. 273-74.
12. M. Subramanian, *Ibid.*, p. 274.
13. N. Sivaraman, *Ibid.*, p.276.
14. S. Thothadri, *Ibid.*, p. 287.
15. Siddharthan, *Ibid.*, p. 287.
16. T. Pakkiyamuthu, *Ibid.*, p. 291.
17. Mulk Raj Anand, Personal letter to the author dated 18.6.93.
18. *Ibid.*

# Mulk Raj Anand and Jayakanthan as Romantic Humanists

Man is the measure of all things.

The word 'humanism' represented in the beginning of the fifteenth century a movement for an extensive change in art, literature and thought. An increased interest in the Greek and Latin classics and the pursuit of classic eloquence was for a time the most conspicuous element in humanism; the freedom of the spirit of humanism became a declaration of independence of thought from the restrictions imposed by ecclesiastical authority. Education was considered an important element in the field of humanism, and by the end of the sixteenth century humanism became an interest and an impulse and drive towards knowledge and has formed one of the main threads in the web of modern life.

In the main, humanism has been antagonistic to authoritative religious belief and opposes the other-worldly spirit. It is marked with absence of all enthusiasm in religion and a devotion to culture on intellectual grounds. In men like John Stuart Mill and Matthew Arnold, humanism is seen as a refined but non-religious outlook on life. The humanism which was considered to represent an enthusiasm for the classics at the beginning enlarged its canvas to imply a revolt against injustice, cruelty and suffering.

It would be seen that the Western philosophy of humanism arose as a kind of revolt against the established value of Christianity. A refined belief in the supernatural revelation seemed to be the basis of the Judaic Christian faith. Humanism is an expression of an intellectual reaction to this type of supernatural revelation. The Biblical theory that God is the author of the world and creation is His product came to be viewed with suspicion. The theocentric view of the Christian universe was replaced by the anthropocentric view of humanism. The chief cause of the dissatisfaction of the humanists emerged from the perception that many problems of life remained unsolved. The grand belief in divine revelation and the widespread social injustice carry no relation at all. There were two broad types of humanism. The first type accepted the ethical values of Christianity rejecting its supernatural system while the second category went into Buddhism and Confucianism. All the classical humanism believed in the value of tradition; but they did not place faith in the resources of man. Unlike them the romantic humanists argued that man is naturally good and tradition and convention only corrupt him and his unlimited potentialities can grow only in an atmosphere of freedom.

Humanism thus has several layers of meaning. It may be reasonable balance of life that the early humanists discovered in the Greeks; it may be merely the study of the humanities: it may be the freedom from religiosity; it may be the responsiveness to all human passions or it could be a philosophy of which man is the centre and action. It is in this last sense that humanism[2] has had its greatest impact since the sixteenth century.

This brief survey would reveal that what Anand and Jayakanthan believe cannot be totally identified with any one of the well-known tenets of humanism. They are one with the Renaissance humanists in their celebration of the dignity of man and the importance of the present life, as against medieval thinkers to whom the present life is only a gateway to a new life after death. Like the New Humanists, they also believe in the essential goodness of man, but do not subscribe to their distrust of science. Through their works, Anand and Jayakanthan sing of simple common people about the common experiences of man. While doing so, their hearts cry on witnessing the pain of the poor and the downtrodden. Giving allegiance to the underprivileged and the disadvantageous sections of the society, who are despised and abandoned, they take up cudgels against this cruel society, in defence of the weaklings.

Anand's main concern in his writings is humanism as he considers "literature and art as the instruments of humanism."[3] With a firm conviction he writes about the suppressed humanity. In his *Apology for Heroism*, he defines his humanism: "I believe, first and foremost in human beings, in Man, in the whole man. . . . The humanism which I prefer does not rest on a Divine Sanction . . . but puts its faith in the creative imagination of man, in his capacity to transfer himself, in the tireless mental and physical energy with which he can, often in the face of great odds, raise himself to tremendous heights of dignity and redeem the world from its misery and pain."[4]

Anand's boundless compassion for the lowly and the lost-Daridra-Narayana can be seen in his essay, "Why I write?":

> I immersed myself in the sub world of the poor, and the insulted and the injured through continuous pilgrimages to the villages, the small towns and big town bastis of our country.
>
> As a writer I have tried to drink from the sources of love in our people, specially poor people, and to give them my own exuberant passion by joining in the 'burning and molting' that goes on in life at its intensest.[6]

Hailing from the North-Western frontier of India to a traditional Coppersmith father who later turned to the army for a living and to a pious mother who came from a peasant family, Anand inherited from his father a craftsman's industry and a sense of adventure and from his mother a sense of ache at the heart of the Indian humanity and his compassion for the downtrodden and the underprivileged.[7]

During his childhood and youth, Anand has been moving and mixing freely with the children of coolies and untouchables and poor peasants. It is natural, therefore, for Anand to develop a feeling of love, tenderness and compassion for the pariahs and the bottom dogs of the society. This humanism was the compulsion and urge in him to write books. He gradually grasped it under the impact of Marx, Leo Tolstoy, Martin Luther King and Guru Nanak, Gandhi and Nehru. His intellectual well-being was very much influenced by the European literary tradition; similarly his emotional life was the outcome of the richness of the Indian past.

Gradually he identified himself with the core of humanity; while doing so he discovers his own self:

> I was not only a member of a family risen into the well-to-do middle class, but that was one of the millions of human beings, a member of

> the human race who had inherited this terrible and beautiful world of the twentieth century.[8]

This identification with the humanity, this love for the entire mankind cutting across all the possible man-made boundaries of caste, creed, economic and social status and nations is the base of Anand's philosophy. By expressing his love for the mankind, Anand strives to find out solutions to the problems of misery, poverty and inequality. He desires to find a new society free from exploitation and social marginalisation.

Anand presents in his novels the problems, conflicts and aspirations of the poor and the downtrodden with compassion. As Leo Tagore rightly puts it, "Anand is a searcher, a seeker with an open mind and a large heart . . . through pity, compassion or sympathy."[9] As one reads his novels his commitment to the millions of our poor people and his concern for their lives, problems and issues will be seen.

To Anand a writer is essentially "a crusader in the cause of humanity." In his works one does not find Vedantic strains or mystical elements: but he finds expressions of Anand's supreme faith in man. This gets abundantly concretized in his writings.

Anand's novels celebrate the dignity of man. While doing so, he never loses sight of man's lapses and weaknesses. In the process he expresses his deep concern for the suffering mankind. While showing his boundless love for man, he wages a war against inhumanity in his novels. G.S. Balarama Gupta rightly points out that "Tenderness or Karuna is the very essence of Anand's humanism."[11] Anand's letter to Gupta reiterates his philosophy: "The Chinese philosopher, Merscius, once said, 'A sage is the instructor of a hundred ages.'. . . I hope I can teach even a few people of my generation that tenderness is our only asset."[12]

Anand's philosophy of humanism, though not strikingly original, emphasizes "the Human Centrality"[13] in his fiction. One is reminded of Anand's observations in his "Prolegomena to a New Humanism": "By humanism I do not mean anything more or less than what it has always meant, illumination or enlightenment in the interest of man, true to his highest nature and his noblest vision."[14]

So the essence of Anand's humanism lies in his obvious allegiance to the cause of suffering humanity. Anand himself is very much aware of his "constant struggle over the past thirty years to give expression to my [his] passion or compassion to my [his] people--the victims of so many wrongs and of so much misunderstanding."[15]

Like Anand, Jayakanthan's greatest allegiance has been to the cause of the downtrodden and the underprivileged. Participating in a 'Meet the Author' programme sponsored by Sahitya Akademi at Madras in 1989, Jayakanthan declared,

> The world remains divided—between the cheats and the cheated, the exploiters and the exploited, the mighty and the meek, the rich and the poor, the bad and the good . . . at writings, I felt that in this divided world I was with the underprivileged, the cheated, the exploited and the meek. I thought I should raise my voice against injustice and that was my dharma, sudharma.[16]

Raising his voice against all forms of exploitation and injustice, Jayakanthan has shown a stern consistency of purpose in his writings:

> When you are aware that writing is your duty you don't feel it a waste or burden. The spontaneous cry out that comes with fervour becomes creation. An artist's 'Cry Out' is his creation. It has a purpose.[17]

In his foreword to *Oru Piti Coru* (*A Handful of Rice*), a collection of Jayakanthan's short stories, Ti Janakiram[18] is of the view that in Jayakanthan's novels the characters are the dwellers of the street, huts, platform and the bank of cooum river. His characters are indeed the downtrodden. So the essence of Jayakanthan's humanist philosophy lies in his vision of the goodness of the poor emerging everywhere, be it in a slum or in a palace. In his preface to *Unnaippol Oruvan*, he shares similar sentiments:

> The 'Bharat' that boasts of its temples of pristine beauty also bears the dirtiest slums which are permanent residences of the goddess of misfortune.
> So what is India?
> Is it Taj or Tharavi?
> Is it Meenakshi temple in Madurai?

> Or is it Puliamthoppu of Madras?
> Which is India? Where does then India live?
> Is it on the tattered mat of a prostitute?
> Yes, even there India lives,
> Its soul struggles hard to breath, and to survive there . . .
> The sanctity of a temple resides even in a slum.[19]

Jayakanthan has a robust optimism about the inherent goodness in human beings; he has an ardent faith in human potentialities. The basis of his philosophy of humanism is his profound compassion for man and mankind. In his preface to *Piralayam*, his short novel, he observes: "However base and lovely is the subject I have undertaken to describe, I always sing the glory of life with my strong accent on the nobility, meaning and loftiness of man."[20]

Jayakanthan is the only son of a rich but ruined family. In his childhood and youth he had to witness double tragedy, the death of the issues after him and the squandering away of the family property by an individualistic but irresponsible father. Having failed twice in his fifth class and without completing his elementary school education, he left home only to learn more about rickshaw pullers, tonga-wallahs, porters, sweepers, newspaper boys and all other types of coolies and working people. While discerning the dignity of human soul from them, he developed compassion towards the underdog.

Like Anand, Jayakanthan had lived in his early days as one among the meek and the poor. Among his close friends were rowdies, rickshaw pullers, prostitutes and pickpockets and scavengers. He happily recollects his cherished experiences with them:

> For years together I had made it my aim to identify myself with humble people. I had been with them and enjoyed their benevolent and loving care. With them, I could feel my life 'alive'. These people were highly sentimental and emotional with the hearts of children. . . . I had been with these humble folk, enjoying their company in the streets and pavements of Madras. I had conversed with them throughout the nights, being with them in their haunts . . . spending sleepless nights. . . . Seeing them and being with them often is life. I can forever enjoy their company.[21]

Jayakanthan's humanism also emphasizes the human centrality in his fiction. For him, the external world with all its defects and imperfections forms the province of his humanism. He engages in an active study of human beings and his focus is on life followed by a true desire and instinct to know it from a first hand experience of everything. In his writings, there is an intense search for the discovery of real human beings. The starting point for him lies in coming into contact with all types of human beings and to know and examine their life with compassion and love seems to be his main endeavour, his ethics as a humanist. One is here reminded of Jayakanthan's own statement which again emphasizes his philosophy of humanism: "Even when I select meanest matters to be portrayed in a broad canvas, I stress the best that is found in it; which gives meaning to life—the glorious human nature—I sing the grandeur of life."[22]

As a champion of the poor and the downtrodden, most of the heroes and heroines of Anand are born to suffer and die. The hero Munoo in *Coolie* is a patient sufferer. Anand here raises a low class boy to the position of a hero and insists on his belief in the dignity of man, irrespective of his place in the society. True to Anand's intention to write about the poor, Munoo is a representative of millions of unfortunate souls like himself. He depicts in *Coolie* the evils of class structure, an awful consequence of social revolution, which is a product of the twin forces of industrialization and the flow of wealth arising from it.

The three classes of society and the evils enveloping them are highlighted by Anand in *Coolie*. Munoo is treated as an individual in the first three chapters, loses his identity among the masses of other coolies in the fifth chapter. Munoo is a typical example of the homeless and moneyless coolies in factories.

The sympathy for the poor and the downtrodden retains its hold on Jayakanthan's social novels. His early novel, *Unnaippol Oruvan* is a class novel and it celebrates the loftiness of Citti, Thankam, Annamma and Manickam. Like Anand, Jayakanthan raises here a low class poor boy to the level of hero and insists on his conviction in the dignity of man, no matter what his position in society is. Citti is a burning symbol of millions of unfortunate souls like himself—lost and bereft, abused and downtrodden. He is a creation through whom the misery of the whole India speaks.

*Coolie* depicts with compassion the pathetic downward journey of a poor orphan who suffers for his poverty. Munoo, the protagonist, is presented as living in three classes of society—the low class, the middle class and the upper class. He travels from village to town to find his livelihood. His journey is that of a pilgrim's progress only in reverse. His life-journey is a downward journey into damnation.

Anand takes up five specimens of evil[23]—a village (Bilaspur), a town (Sham Nagar), a feudal city (Daultapur), a metropolitan city (Bombay) and India's imperial summer capital (Simla) as five grades of hell on earth. In quest for happiness, Munoo travels through the five centres only to meet the inevitable end. As K.R. Srinivasa Iyengar rightly points out, "*Coolie* is verily a cross-section of India, the visible India, that mixture of the horrible and the holy, the inhuman and the human, sordid and the beautiful." (337)

In *Unnaippol Oruvan* the poor people are pictured neglecting the ill-treatment that they undergo in different classes. Annamma, Thankam, Manickam, Mannaru and Duraikannu are the admirable characters. For Thankam, Annamma is the sole companion. As in *Coolie*, we find that silent and lovable companionship exists only among the low class people. Thankam wants to marry Manickam for she has developed an emotional relationship with him. She gives him shelter, in spite of the lack of enthusiasm about it from his son Citti. He is timid and loving to Citti, though the later hates him. He considers him as his own son. Citti who has been selling ice-lollies during daytime and supporting his mother has once again fallen on evil days by renewing the intimacy with Kanniappan, Elumalai and Kabali. He takes recourse to this extreme step as he sees for himself his mother's affairs with Manickam. He rebels against her and his love for her suddenly becomes an emotion of the past. He stays away from home and leads an uncontrolled life, as he cannot withstand the sight of Manickam at his home. Only after his fleeing away from his home Citti returns home, and this too, when his mother is at the death-bed. Thankam dies at the end, leaving the new-born baby to the care and concern of Citti. Citti now becomes a father as well as a brother to Sornam, the new-born baby.

Munoo in *Coolie* has no control over the series of situations he finds himself in during the short course of his life leading to his untimely death. This does not mean that Anand believes in God or fate which controls man's actions. As we have seen already, Anand believes that man makes himself. Munoo tries to make himself and attempts to grow into a respectable man, but he fails in his pursuit. His failure is not due to an inherent tragic flaw in him but due to the circumstances and the greed, selfishness and cruelty of his fellow human beings. One feels that Munoo deserves a better life. By showing the spirited ambitions of his protagonist frustrated in all his endeavours, Anand suggests that "a little more tenderness on the part of the society could have turned Munoo into a happy individual." (41)

Like Anand, Jayakanthan showers his affection on children. He sympathizes with the children of the poor because they do not have security and future in life. He expresses such sentiments in his preface to *Tevan Varuvara?* (Will God Come?), a collection of short stories.

> The children of the have-nots do not have any future. They become orphans of the society . . . when I see these flowers get trampled down and crushed down by the society, there is a sensation of burning in me. I feel like shedding tears.[24]

Citti in *Unnaippol Oruvan* is not in a position to attend school because he sells ice creams during daytime and adds a bit more money to the meagre wages of his mother. "See here! I have brought money. Here is the money I've earned for you. Don't worry mother." (17) He also tells his mother not to go to work as a helper to masons later when he would earn more:

> Just wait for a few more days. Yes, just wait mother. Then you should not go out for work. . . . We don't want such relations [referring to supervisors and other co-labourers]. I am here for you. You should not go out to work if I start earning more. (19)

Referring to the plight of his hero, Jayakanthan observes,

> If Citti, who has completed only twelfth year, was born in a palace, he would have remained a child who lisps. He is born neither in a palace

> nor in a middle-class family which is fond of aping the upper class. Yes, it is his heinous crime. (34)

Jayakanthan is keen on depicting the joys and sorrows of his twelve-year old protagonist; he views the misery of the poor hero with sympathy. Perhaps it is his compassion for the children who have no future that brings back Citti to his home and makes him the brother of Sornam, the newborn infant, who otherwise would have become an orphan in the society. Here also Citti has no control over the happenings in his home; against his wishes, his mother brings Manickam to her home, gives him shelter and company and lives with him. Instead of confronting the problem he is faced with, he takes recourse to the escapist route, fleeing away from home and befriending the evil company of former friends. His sufferings are more of a psychological nature, unlike the physical torments of Munoo, than due to the circumstances and cruelty of his fellow human beings. One feels that Citti also deserves a better life, with a little more concern and a little more sympathy and tenderness on the part of his mother.

Anand in his next novel, *Two Leaves and a Bud*, a grim tragedy, establishes his life-time conviction that human suffering has an appalling character. Here also, as in *Coolie* and *Unnaippol Oruvan* one finds an artistic portrayal of "the yawning hiatus between the haves and the have-nots and the exploiters and the exploited."[25] While "*Coolie* portrays the tribulations of an individual coolie in a class-ridden society, *Two Leaves and a Bud* portrays the same problem as a group experience in the framework of a vast capitalistic organization." (32)

The complicating problem in this novel is that he brings a few Indians and places them in direct confrontation with a few Englishmen. The novelist takes these two civilizations not for the purpose of any deliberate comparison. The immediate aim of Anand is not to propound the concept of an East-West synthesis. For example, E.M. Forster's *A Passage to India* contains such a theme which tends to liberalize the relation between East and West. Anand as a liberal humanist believes in the sameness of human nature which is found in all places. His interpretation of suffering does not spring from a narrow range of human experience found in a particular culture and continent. He is able to rise above the limiting barriers of time, nation and race by his powerful humanist sympathy. It is this motive which impels Anand to portray certain English personages, both noble and ignoble, in relation to Indian characters.

Gangu, the hero of the novel, gives expression to the axiom of Anand that life is a trial for struggling poor man. He is middle-aged native of Punjab who has lost his ancestral property of land and hut owing to debt of the greedy moneylender, Seth Badri Das. This peasant of Punjab is now left with no chance of earning his livelihood. Carried away by the flowery words of Buta, the coolie--catcher, Gangu leaves his native place in despair and goes to Assam. Macpherson Tea Estate gives him employment and Gangu becomes a hard worker. But the promised land of fortunes turns out to be a jungle of miseries. Assam and especially the tea estate is rightly described by Narain: "This prison has no bars, but it is nevertheless an unbreakable jail."[26]

The real tragedy for Gangu, "an older version of Munoo,"[27] begins when a malarial fever attacks him. He is relieved of this peculiar disease. The great irony is that Gangu's malarial fever seems to be contagious and it consumes the life of his dear wife, Sajani. Death is a sorrowful phenomenon. The passing away of a life-partner is a serious one and it brings before the novelist's mind the scene of human bereavement. Anand shows a different dimension when Gangu has no money to arrange for the funeral of his wife. To pay respect to the departed person by way of making preparation for a proper funeral is certainly an instance of nobler human sentiment. Gangu is not able to fulfil this need for want of money. So he appeals to the Chief Planter, Charles Croft-Cooke, for financial assistance. He has wounded dreadfully Gangu's feeling for human dignity by turning him out of his office. For Anand the English manager is only a human being and he is not interested in clubbing goodness or badness with any nationality. He is simply interested in the behaviour of human beings. The novelist's concern is with the element of insolence found in human nature.

The English manager, Croft-Cooke, is not sensitive to the sorrow of Gangu. Lack of interest in alleviating the misery of human beings is what pains Anand as a humanist. Gangu is not treated as a human being. The reason, according to the novelist, lies in class-consciousness. The division between the rich and the poor paves way for upper class sensibility. As Balarama Gupta says, "The sharp contrast between the docile Coolies and the crude capitalists is obvious. In this sad and mad world of the estate, the affluent eat and drink and play polo, while the poor underpaid and overworked slaves who are endlessly suppressed and scoffed at, starve and suffer." (47)

Anand maintains the view that class consciousness is found to be a permanent part of the human psyche. Gangu is not received with any human warmth or respect. The English manager fails to react to the crisis of Gangu on account of his insensibility to human misery which is born of class consciousness. One major aspect of Anand's liberal humanism lies in laying emphasis upon the sameness of human behaviour and the sameness of human nature. Human beings are essentially the same everywhere according to Anand and it is on this ground that he treats the English manager as a human being who behaves in an uncharitable manner. The novelist also highlights the brutal behaviour of Reggie Hunt, the assistant manager. When Gangu is involved in a personal clash, Reggie Hunt who is an arrogant person takes revenge on the poor labourer by employing men to beat him mercilessly. This is certainly a highhanded action which provokes the feelings of workers and leads them to show their protest against the injustice through a demonstration before the manager's house. The violent situation is brought under control and the workers are shocked into a terrible submission by a powerful military regiment. Anand seems to agree with the Marxist saying that any rebellion can be easily controlled by power and wealth. The free society comes when it becomes classless and the workers receive their freedom only in an overthrow of classes through an organized revolt. With humanistic sympathy, the novelist shows the sad state of Gangu who is treated as a fly. The English physician De La Harve shares his sympathy and tenderness with the workers and so he is asked to leave the place forthwith. He is a man of charitable disposition and he is also shown to be out of place in a class-conscious society. Here, in the words of Premila Paul, "the world of Assam plantations is too dense a jungle for the ray of love to penetrate." (33)

Anand treats class-consciousness as the greatest social evil. He has a humanist's pity and tenderness in taking sides with the poor and glorifying their suffering which indicates to him their good nature and their capacity for calmness and endurance. When a poor person appeals to the rich for help, if the rich person, instead of being generous, shows his haughtiness, it indicates rottenness in human nature and also proves the truth that mere wealth and rank do not endow a person with nobility. So in the fictional world of *Two Leaves and a Bud*, says Balarama Gupta, "[The two classes of society]—the leisure-loving and the leisure-seeking affluent on the one hand and the sweating and toiling poor on the other . . . are unmistakably demarcated and the gulf between the two is too enormous to be easily bridged." (46)

For Anand, the behaviour of the rich man is always an enigma. This is brought out clearly when Reggie tries to molest Gangu's daughter Leila. Luckily Gangu enters his house and discovers the outrageous act of Reggie Hunt. But he is shot dead. A trial is held to judge this incident. The novelist does not spare his artistic energy to bring out the nature of the existing corrupt world and how it fails to adhere to any notion of justice. He who really commits the mistake is allowed to escape from ignominy and the man who intervenes to set things right is branded a criminal. The innocent is charged with guilt and the culprit is exonerated from the charge of seduction. Anand as a humanist with painful awareness portrays the world in which values have been turned topsy-turvy. There seems to be no poetic justice in this world where evil is not punished and good remains unrewarded. Gangu is a very calm and innocent being. When he is perplexed by injustice, he becomes a creature of extremes like Othello in Shakespeare. Gangu is portrayed as an expression of man's struggle for existence, where he being denied of all rights and pleasures in this world is born to suffer, starve and die. There are signs of existential humanism in Anand here. Gangu becomes a toy in the hands of rich people's tyranny. The novelist does certainly some kind of moralizing. For example, he points out the unholy alliance between money and happiness:

> Money is everything. . . . It is the crux of the world. . . . Gold is the living soul of man, the colour of rajahs, and gazelle-eyed courtesans, beautiful to the sight. Every absurdity appears agreeable in a man on whom gold has smiled. . . . Yes. . . . Money is everything. It is the root of happiness. (195)

The main artistic motive of Anand is to interpret truth from the realities of life. His moral seriousness comes out in his capacity to reflect on the issues of life profoundly. When he shows the evil of capitalism which leads to the death of Gangu, the novel certainly carries a moral strain. The hero is not able to fight against the forces of the society and he perishes in the struggle. This really is a tragic fact. This 'dramatic novel'[28] has the character of a great epic poem. According to Aristotle, tragedy is the outcome of the limitations of a character. For Anand, tragedy is the result of the limitations of the society. It is a corrupt society which makes heroes like Munoo and Gangu tragic. What is significant for the novelist is that their suffering is intense and is manifested in multifarious dimensions. Therefore, Anand considers intense suffering to be tragic and a novelist who portrays such agony has a moral preoccupation. Refusal to listen to the plea of Gangu for his wife's funeral expenses, merciless attack on him by Reggie Hunt's men, his mad frenzy at the attempt at the seduction of Gangu's own daughter, and Gangu's intervention to preserve her modesty and his consequent death in a brutal manner carry a vast tragic spectrum which is comparable to any dimension of tragedy. Anand's humanist conclusion is that the hero is not responsible for his suffering but the society is responsible for his agony. This analysis of Anand constitutes a new framework in the conception of his tragedy.

Two early novels of Jayakanthan, *Yarukkaka Alutan?* (For Whom Did he Weep?) *and Valkkai Alaikkiratu*[29] in terms of his humanistic perspectives can be taken up now for a critical examination. He sees life nakedly and openly and he thinks that his perception is so real and authentic that religion does not go into the complicated roots of life. In the early phase of his career as a novelist, Jayakanthan feels that religion has failed to judge life properly and he lays emphasis upon the need for a new way of looking at life. What happens in life must be seen and studied without any preconception. According to Jayakanthan, humanism takes its new role as a judge and inspector of life in the place of religion. The predominant motive of the novelist is to establish a new angle that strong humanist overtones are found in an implicit manner in *Yarukkaka Alutan?*

The novelist's understanding of life is different from the perception and judgement of the world. What goes straight is correct and what appears in a crooked form is wrong and defective. This is the usual religious judgement of the world. Religion adopts intellect as an instrument in assessing the values of life. Jayakanthan says that religion starts with a wrong yardstick and so it produces inevitably a mangled view of things.[30] Human relations are so complex that they cannot be judged simply by logic and intellect.

The novel *Yarukkaka Alutan?* is so new in its nature that there is no use bringing it under a religious purview. Jayakanthan says that intuition is much better than intellect. (6) So he presses the need for a new evaluative criterion to judge his novel. The hero of the novel is Murugesan who assumes a Christian name Joseph on the occasion of his mother's death under the benign guidance of a kindly priest. Joseph's conversion indicates to the novelist the view that heart is more important than head. Intuition and imagination seek heart as a channel for their expression. Joseph was originally a gardener working under the supervision of the Christian priest. His marriage with Parvathy mainly took place on the inducement of his mother who thought that without such a proposal she would be forced to live in this world without any relation. Her motive for this marriage draws its strength from compassion and mercy. But later on Joseph sees a contradiction in his marriage. He thinks inwardly that a black figure like him is not a match for his beautiful and elegant looking Parvathy. Moreover his conversion to Christianity is a source of irritation to her. These two facts, namely, his physical appearance and his newly assumed Christian name make him critical and reflective in his marital relation with Parvathi.

Jayakanthan thinks that Joseph's marriage is a failure as there is no mental harmony between the two partners. The novelist perhaps feels that an arranged marriage takes care of only technical things and it overlooks the necessity for emotional harmony. Joseph becomes the mouthpiece of Jayakanthan in echoing this view. When the hero sees his wife Parvathy in bed with his handsome friend Marimuthu, he does not lose his temper as normally people do. It only confirms his already concealed view that he is a poor match for her and his marriage is a contradiction and the only course left is to solemnize their new relation and give it a marital status. This giving away of his wife in marriage to his friend seems to be the supreme sacrifice that a person is capable of, and only such poor and innocent men like Joseph are prepared for such sacrifices.

The yardstick of the world is the yardstick of religion. But the novelist is not at home with the world and the religion. Joseph does not care for the world's opinion which is derived from religion. To allow ones's own wife to live with someone else on the ground of mental incompatibility is a sin according to the religious standards of the world. Joseph's desire to offer gifts in the form of dress and saree to Parvathy and Marimuthu implies an open acceptance of their relation and elevates it to a new marital status. In the process he is also elevated as an ideal figure. Govinda Samy Naidu, a cook in a hotel treats this attitude of Joseph as an example of real Christian charity and love. In the eyes of the world, Joseph's acceptance of the new marriage is a mistake. But in the eye of the novelist the hero is right and his admission of this new venture is based upon the demand for emotional readjustment.

Jayakanthan shows a new dimension in the character of Joseph. The perennial cry of the novelist is that he should not be judged by the normal standards of the world.[31] The hero takes a new position as a server in a hotel. A person who works according to the rule-governed routine is said to be a man of prudence. Joseph works more than what he is expected to do. This shows that his inner heart is not in harmony with the existing expectations of the world. When a man works more than the expected schedule he is described by the rational world as nothing less than a fool and simpleton. An incident occurs in the hotel when Gopinath Seth stays there leaving his purse containing Rupees Three Thousand under the custody of Ratnavelu Mudaliar. Gopinath Seth who is a man of drunkenness and forgetfulness cries in the morning over the loss of his purse. The owner of the hotel knows the fact and the truth that the money is with him.

His intention is to make capital out of the oblivious nature of the Seth and so he remains silent. Therefore the blame is easily shifted to Joseph who is a poor server. It is generally believed that poor people have a natural propensity for stealing. It is this kind of customary judgement which easily convicts Joseph of theft. This charge is false if one goes according to the real facts but it is forced on him by the world. This incident of theft offers an opportunity to the novelist to bring out the different reactions of the characters. These characters like the gambler and the friend and the prostitute reveal their inner motive and nature. Joseph's innocence is not discovered by the shallow standards of the world. In the eyes of God, Joseph is a Mahatma while he is a thief in the eyes of the world. The prostitute comes to the rescue of Joseph but the world does not listen to her verdict. A woman of loose morals cannot be a good judge of men and matters. This is how the world invalidates the real estimates of the immoral woman. The falsity in the gambler who thrashes Joseph is not discovered by the world. The truthful nature found even in a character like a prostitute escapes the notice of the world. Govindasamy Naidu, the cook, brings the truth of the matter to limelight and exposes the deceitful nature of the hotel-owner who is the actual culprit. The innocent person is treated as a thief while the real culprit is extolled and depicted as the very image of honesty and nobility. Ratnavel Mudaliar with all his rank and wealth is a thief at heart while the cook Govindasamy Naidu is a noble man at heart although he possesses a cultured learning without the benefit and advantage of wealth. The humanist norm of Jayakanthan proves the truth that goodness and wealth do not travel as amicable companions. The Marxist tone of the novelist becomes evident when he says that it is wealth which gives support to the existence of false values. The really good person is bad and the really bad person is good. The worldly standards supported by wealth and religion accept this perverted and topsy-turvy formula. The novelist is a humanist and so he praises the prostitute, the clerk and the convicted hero and takes sides with them in upholding their real honesty and dignity. It is proved in this novel that the voice of a poor man never gets its due legal hearing.

It is in the creation of the character of Joseph that Jayakanthan succeeds in producing some bright hints which should be taken as stating his clearly pronounced philosophy of humanism. The Christian view of the non-resistance of evil seems to be fully embodied in the figure of Joseph. For the novelist, he represents a new phenomenon which is strange to the usual expectations of the world. His silent submission to the evil forces is just an indication of his large and benign heart which remains silent even when its very integrity is challenged by the gambler. 'For whom does Joseph weep?' is a question which engages the mind of the novelist. Had Joseph wanted to extricate himself from the charge of theft, he could have done it. But he remains unresisting even though he is endowed with a tough physical frame to tackle all odds. This shows that Joseph deliberately chooses the line of non-resistance in order to demonstrate the truth that good in a corrupt society cannot flourish and evil easily gains undue patronage. Therefore Joseph is made to represent a liberal humanist perspective of Jayakanthan who believes in the Gandhian philosophy of Non-violence.

There seems to be some point of resemblance between Joseph and Gangu in *Two Leaves and a Bud*. But there is a more fundamental difference than this apparent resemblance. Gangu resists evil and he is shot dead whereas Joseph does not even show this amount of resistance. In this respect, Joseph is an apostle of the philosophy of Ahimsa.[32] The only comparable point is that both Joseph and Gangu are tragic figures. The distinguishing feature in the character of Joseph is that he does not even plead his innocence. He calmly endures the charge of theft foisted on him. He does cry but the symbolic meaning of his cry is comparable to the agony of Christ on the cross.[33] His anguish is only an expression of his silent protest against the cunning ways of the world. When in the end he shows his warmth towards Mudaliar and Seth, it brings out his forgiving nature. The capacity to forget his disgrace and forgive his offenders elevates him to the status of a Mahatma.[34]

The novel *Valkkai Alaikkiratu* promotes the humanist thesis of Jayakanthan that in this society good people stand condemned while bad remain elevated. He who is really good must be applauded and he who is really bad must be found fault with. This novel is therefore a dialectical debate between the false values of the world and the true humanist perspectives of Jayakanthan. When a rich man commits a mistake, his wealth frees him from the consequences of what he does. When the same mistake is committed by a poor man, the same world takes him to task and describes him as a thief. Chidambaram Filial and Joseph are two examples of these sayings. The capitalist world does not give a breathing space to Raja who is the hero of this novel. He takes different jobs but his truth-speaking nature does not promote his business. In spite of his poverty, he refuses to obey the orders of his masters, "The shop-owner tried to make him a cheat, a liar and a thief. But he firmly refused to be the one."[35]

The business world thrives on dubious means and make-believe strategies. Raja comes to know that a man of honesty has no place in the world. Only a cheat under the garb of a good man can thrive in this world. The humanist conclusion of the novelist is that the world requires only impostors and not honest men. Raja's plain-speaking nature brings in fame and dishonour on him and so he is forced to leave his place. The next episode in his life is his meeting of Thangam and Geetha. Raja is a poor man and so the world does not respect him. This proves the peculiar truth that social status is determined by wealth and not by goodness.

Jayakanthan takes delight in showing the relationship between wealth and its capacity to promote rank and honour. Geetha, the daughter of Vedachalam Pillai is in love with a pauper Raja, while Thangam another rich girl is in love with a server Sankara Narayanan. The server is after the jewels of Thangam while Geetha is fascinated by the innate goodness of Raja. Vedachalam Pillai's class consciousness stands in the way of floating a marriage proposal between Geetha and Raja. Chidambaram Pillai is a notorious visitor of a brothel house, Sithanaloor Chatram, and his son is the notorious son of a notorious father. Vedachalam Pillai accepts wholeheartedly and even unreservedly Chidambaram Pillai's son as the bridegroom for his daughter Geetha. This choice pushes his daughter into fire. But his wealth and attachment to it blinds him to see the defect in this choice. Jayakanthan says that honour and dignity for Vedachalam Pillai come from wealth. The failure of Vedachalam

Pillai to see the good quality in Raja is a failure to see life itself in the right way. All rich people according to the novelist have jaundiced perceptions. They live in the shell of class-consciousness and refuse to come out of it. There is no realization in them that real moral cleanliness comes from the goodness of the heart. Mere external polish based on wealth and rank hide the inner bad nature. A good man without wealth is a bad man in the estimate of the world while a bad man with the aid of his wealth becomes ironically a good man in the erroneous estimate of the world.

.Jayakanthan is an unorthodox spiritualist and he does not conform to the judgements of the world. He establishes his finding in this novel that mere wealth does not generate goodness. Vedachalam Pillai's choice of wealth as the only criterion for promoting the marriage of his daughter Geetha kills her. Similarly Sankara Narayanan's passion for wealth does not enable him to see anything worthwhile in Thangam and he abandons her after he procures what he needed. For him, jewels are more important than the precious life of Thangam. Jayakanthan as a humanist says that wealth and class-consciousness stand in the way of furthering true human relations. Geetha's proposed marriage with an immoral fellow and Sankara Narayanan's discarding of Thangam after gaining the jewels demonstrate the awful truth that for them, life is inferior in preference to external goods. Lifeless materials like wealth and property are more important than lifelike beings like Geetha and Thangam. What is owned by a person becomes more important than what he is really. Vedachalam Pillai in his excessive interest in wealth and rank prefers a scoundrel to a good man. Sankara Narayanan's passion for gold makes him ignore a good and virtuous woman like Thangam. His abandoning of Thangam makes her helpless and she is retained in the chatram by force, by Razac. She is caught in the evil clutches of the society with no possibility of escape. Raja appears there and shows his love for Thangam ignoring her present life.

Jayakanthan's next aim is to show that people who are really ruffians are not without good qualities. Sarangan is a good example of this truth. It is he who brings Thangam to the chatram for the purpose of pleasing Chidambaram Pillai. When Raja saves Thangam from this infamy, Sarangan who comes to know of their love affair spares them. There is a stronger motive than this because Sarangan sees in Raja the figure of his dead brother, Pasupathy. Sarangan is a ruffian but he is shown as having a good heart which can respond to things. The entire nefarious trade in the chatram is sponsored and assisted by his physical bravery. He is good by nature but his good nature takes sides with villainy for some time. His bullying trait obscures his innate goodness. Sarangan's meeting with Raja brings to prominence his innate good and it starts fertilizing it further. So long as he is caught in the clutches of wealth, power and evil company, his innate goodness has no chance to manifest itself. What the novelist wants to emphasize here is that man is a product of external environment. Sarangan is essentially a good man but he becomes bad by circumstances which bring him into association with wrong people and wrong things. Raja is a good man but he becomes poorer as the circumstance in which he finds himself makes him deplorably miserable. Good circumstances are not produced by the society as it is determined by false factors like wealth and class-consciousness. Circumstances can become productive of goodness in a new order of society.

Jayakanthan's belief in humanism lies in changing the external circumstances in order to create a new social order. A rowdy like Sarangan is supported by evil circumstances while a good character like Raja is let down by the same evil circumstances. For the novelist one important truth emerges from his investigation, that is, all circumstances in the society promote evil and not good. Evil circumstances destroy the innate goodness of Sarangan and the same evil circumstances drive a good man like Raja to depression and despair. The contents of the society are wealth anti class-consciousness All the evil circumstances are determined by the contents of the society. The good characters are judged to be bad by the world and the bad characters are judged to be good by the novelist. A clear contrast is drawn between the standards of the world and the perspectives of the novelist. Vedachalam Pillai and Chidambaram Pillai and Sankara Narayanan represent the world while Raja, Geetha, Thangam, Kamatchi, Sarangan stand in opposition to the false standards of the world. The novel seems to be a debate between the influence of wealth and the possibility of the survival of goodness in such a set-up. Wealth wins and goodness is put under the banner of shame and dishonour. A legitimate love affair between Raja and Geetha is not accepted whereas illegitimate sexual relations are carried on in the chatram by persons who frustrate the prospect of true love.

The death of Sarangan seems to be a turning point in the judgement of the novelist. When this ruffian is in the grip of truth, he has the will to defy Chidambaram Pillai and challenge the police. When he is caught in the evil grip of power and wealth, he can lend support to injustice. This kind of divided sensibility in him makes him incapable of attaining a higher stature. His death is a fitting verdict. He is like an imperfectly blossomed flower and so its fate is to rush to a natural process of decay. His life in the world partly degrades him and partly elevates him but his death fully absolves him of his sins because he loses his life in his attempt at reuniting Raja with Thangam. It is this noble enterprise which redeems him from his past imperfections. The greatest consolation of the novelist is that he at least dies a reformed man. In contrast with Sarangan, Vedachalam Pillai pays lip homage to Vedic ideas. His religion is an external embellishment and it does not show his spiritual sensibility. Geetha is a victim of his wealth and class-consciousness. When Kamatchi, who starts loving Sarangan after the demise of his brother Fasupathy, shouts at Chidambaram Pillai, she shows the real colour of her character without any shadow of doubt. She knows she is wrong in what she does. At the same time, she is alive to her conscience and so she does not spare any pains in exposing the lustful nature of Chidambaram Pillai. She is a good character who becomes bad when she is caught in the network of the society.

The solution offered by the novelist is in accordance with the spirit of the times. The question arises as to whether the evil forces of the society can be resisted by the physical powers of a man. Jayakanthan takes immense care in showing a very important fact. The remedy for social suffering has to come through a change of circumstances. That is one reason why a character like Sarangan has to meet with his death. He has the physical power to resist but according to the novelist he is not an ideal character and he falls short of required expectations. Raja is helpless and although he is in true love with Geetha, he never takes any steps to defy Vedachalam Pillai and elope with her. His consciousness of social inferiority in life pricks his self-respect when he knows that non-possession of wealth and rank is the reason for the rejection of their marriage. Much to the dismay of readers, Thangam elopes with Sankara Narayanan but it becomes an abortive affair. In the case of Geetha, true love does not run a smooth course. On the other hand, it has a tragic end. In the initial stage false love of Sankara Narayanan for Thangam takes on the appearance of true love. But the novelist comes out with his verdict when he says that false love makes its way to some extent but it flounders in the middle.

Raja, Geetha and Thangam want to live and experience joy and bliss. But the structure of society is such that it does not permit them to taste life fully. It is evident from the portrayal of the novelist that premature death of Geetha and abortive love affair of Thangam are their fate. Even Sarangan's attempt to set things right does not promote the flowering of good; it only prevents evil from further breaking out. His rescue of Thangam and his willingness to allow her to go with Raja are some redeeming features and saving graces. Sarangan is a thoughtless partner to evil and it is this which displeases the readers. When he resolves to put an end to the evil, he is not able to do it fully and successfully and the tragedy is that he has to offer his life as a price for his heroic effort to put an end to evil.

There is a marked non-religious attitude to life in the novels of Anand and Jayakanthan. It should be borne in mind that the novels of Jayakanthan that have been examined are his early novels, during which time there were perceptible Marxian sympathies in him and his attitude to religion was agnostic. There has been an attempt in the early pages in the discussion of *Yarukkaka Alutan?* to probe into his non-religious outlook on life. It is very obvious that Anand has no faith in the existence of God. On the other hand he has an abundant faith in man who makes himself. Munoo tries to make himself but fails mainly because of the cruelty of the society and the circumstances. His rejection of God is also evident in *Two Leaves and a Bud*. He does not share the fatalistic attitude of Gangu who goes to the extent of believing that the death of his wife caused by Malaria is due to the blow struck by God. As Balarama Gupta rightly says:

"Anand shows that the Indian peasant's ignorant belief in fatalism and God are to be rejected, and it is for his own betterment that he should see that the cruelty of a few men in position around him is the cause of his troubles, and not God or fate." (47)

In the old traditions it is the central belief in God which inspired the formation of all values of life. This tendency of judging every thing with the help of religion is discarded by them. A new way of reviewing life results in the growth of a new non-religious consciousness. Their profound interest in the reality of the world is something that clearly distinguishes them from the life-negating preoccupations of religions.

In the traditional set-up it is assumed that life prevails only in rich classes of society. Consequently, one of the canons of classical aesthetics is to make a leader of the state or a rich member of the aristocratic family the hero of a literary work. These two novelists are not in agreement with this view which states that high born human nature alone deserves artistic attention. Their novels develop a clear thesis that real dignity does not reside in highborn human nature. The classical view is that the suffering of a rich man, duke, king or a leader arouses sympathy, pity and fear whereas the suffering of a poor man fails to awaken pity and real compassion.

Anand and Jayakanthan steadily oppose this classical view of art which refuses to treat the common man's suffering with respect and dignity. Their philosophy of humanism implies the love of the poor and an attempt at exalting their innate goodness. They project humanism as a special worldview in order to restore the common man to his real dignified stature. Many of the novels deal with the life of very average and ordinary people. Many characters of their novels come from very low levels which indicate their poverty and lack of affluence. There are four principles which attract these two writers. They believe in the basic goodness of the human beings. There is an active desire to exalt the life of the poor people. This instinct for the glorification of the low persons comes from their perception of their innate dignity and good nature. They argue in their novels that poor people are good but they are subjected to untold torture. It is this fact which mainly engages the minds of these two novelists. They perceive the truth that life is made tragic by virtue of class distinction between the rich and the poor. As Marxist sympathizers, they discover that human suffering is a product of class-consciousness.

Anand and Jayakanthan proceed on common lines in their analysis of human suffering. Though they are broadly known as humanists there are some subordinate divisions which are found in the way they function and operate. The humanism of Anand has an ideal basis. The main evidence in support of this argument is that Anand has an abiding zeal to see only the good and noble side in the human nature of poor people. Munoo and Gangu are characters who are drawn from the low ranks of life. Munoo is a coolie and Gangu is a plantation worker. Although they perform wretched jobs according to the notions of class-consciousness, they show warmth and energy and reveal their undeceiving nature even in great moments of crisis. Anand's idealist portrayal of life shows his fundamental tenet that poor characters are poor by circumstances but they are noble in their nature and behaviour. The tendency to see only the good side in the poor human beings makes him a kind of ideal humanist. The life of poor people is a life of struggle but it is certainly not a life of deceit and dishonesty.

Munoo is a character who is an embodiment of patience. Anand takes great delight in presenting a very idealized picture of his human nature. Munoo is a coolie in the house of a Bank clerk at Sham Nagar. He is severely beaten for having kissed his master's daughter Sheila in an unguarded moment. He silently accepts his destiny as a slave, a man who is born to work and suffer. What is very important in Munoo is his unquestioning acceptance of his position as a low slave. His uncomplaining nature makes him an ideal character, who, though suffers, never loses his goodness and nobility under any circumstances. Munoo's saying 'I want to live to work this machinie'[36] brings out frankness and plain truth-speaking nature which puts him above all the so-called virtuous people who are wealthy.

The description of Anand as an ideal humanist does not rule out certain other dimensions. Munoo's stay in Bombay brings him face-to-face with the incident of a violent communal clash. He discovers that their pompous rhetoric shows their shallow sentiments. He also thinks that mass action is unruly and it carries no genuine motive.

Moreover he feels that the struggle at bottom is a fundamental conflict between the rich and the poor. These three observations of Anand bring out his sense of realism and existential understanding of life and situation. For example, his character Gangu is a simple worker without any inordinate ambition. But unlike Munoo, Gangu is capable of showing his heroic power of resistance. He is not a silent witness to any form of injustice. In the workers's strike in the Macpherson Estate, he makes his protest in a more refined manner. He is one who has the necessary courage to challenge anyone. He loses his life in his attempt to save his own daughter Leila from the clutches of the lust motivated Reggie Hunt. While Munoo calmly endures suffering and injustice, Gangu shows his strength to resist it. In the eyes of Anand, Gangu is a hard fighter who wages a war against injustice. There is therefore a combination of both idealism and realism in the character of Gangu.

Jayakanthan in his portrayal of Joseph and Citti resembles Anand very strongly. The element of idealism is found in the nobility of human nature in Joseph and total change of heart in Citti. It is worth recalling Chellappan's view that in the early novels of Jayakanthan he either idealizes or romanticizes his heroes. Joseph is a Mahatma according to the novelist. He who never tells a lie is a great person. He who does not tell the truth is a greater person as Joseph knows that telling truth in this case brings the owner of the hotel Ratnavelu Mudaliar to infamy and shame. Joseph is pained to think that any frank and bold exposure would offend the dignity of Ratnavelu Mudaliar and put him in a bad and depressed mood. Such an act of exposure is considered by Joseph to be a kind of character-assassination and betrayal of human trust. Man is born to love others and this is a noble maxim of Joseph and so, for him, to offend or wound any one, for that matter, on any ground is an instance of human betrayal of trust. Even when others accuse Joseph and convict him of his guilt and theft, he remains without being perturbed. He reflects on the nature of human beings in broad universal terms and makes a pathetic cry not as a result of his own humiliation but as an outcome of his silent passion for making philosophical enquiry about the sad and depressing state of life. Joseph in his idealized stature is like Hamlet who poses the question, "Why should people be wicked and behave cunningly?"

There is a fine blend of idealism and realism in different proportions in the novels of these two writers. The philosophical creed of existentialism comes under the category of realism and it does not appear under the purview of idealism. When existentialism is interpreted as realism, the novels of these two writers produce different conclusions. Man's destiny is to suffer and endure humiliation. This is one aspect of existentialism which is found in their outlook. Joseph, Munoo, Raja and Citti are all examples of this special stance. The suffering of Thangam in *Unnaippol Oruvan* is an intense expression of human agony. To undergo suffering without getting a remedy or securing a solution is what makes Thangam a tragic character. The treatment of such a tragic character carries an existentialist perspective. In a sense, Citti becomes a very idealized character, For him, his mother Thangam is everything and when Kuruvikaran Manickam intervenes in their happily formed mother-son relationship, the young son resorts to extremes. Thondar Durai Kannu is an ideal character who reforms Citti and he strengthens Citti's love for his mother. At one stage, Citti becomes a man of contradictions. He loves his mother intensely but hates her with equal intensity when he finds her guilty. When he learns from Alamelu that he was an unwanted child, he rises to supreme anger. Alamelu is like any other ordinary character in the world who assumes the role of a tale-bearer. Ayya Annamma is an incarnation of overflowing love, goodness and compassion.

It is in the characterization of Citti that the novelist achieves a supreme mark of idealization. Citti is a character of contradictions because he happens to be a character of extremes, despising his mother, loving her, hating himself and in the process losing interest in life. Jayakanthan wants to resolve this problem of character contradiction. The novelist's method of reconciling the contradiction becomes a kind of a new psycho-social-spiritual vision. Here one must recall the findings of N. Arivalakan in his essay, "*Unnaippol Oruvan*: Social and Spiritual Outlook." He observes, "Jayakanthan is of the opinion that for a man's desire to progress in life he needs some kind of attachment. So Jayakanthan creates a responsibility and an attachment for these humans; a reference mainly to Citti and his friend Kanniappan who is converted into a regenerated man by Citti, thereby converting him to fit into the society he lives in. Citti who hated his life before lives for his sister now. He thereby becomes one among the society. They were social outcasts. They have found a hold in their life. . . . Jayakanthan makes them accepted members of the society. This is his social and spiritual outlook."[38]

This humanistic outlook of Jayakanthan incidentally invalidates the view of Karu Muthiah that the ending of the novel, *Unnaippol Oruvan*, is unbelievable and therefore unacceptable.[39] But from the point of social and spiritual outlook of the novelist, the end of the novel is not only tenable and justifiable but also a lofty one.

'Kuruvikaran' Manickam cannot be a father for Citti. For Citti, his mother loses her motherly stature when she is found in the company of Manickam. Thangam did not have happily married life and so she wanted some kind of psychic consolation through physical contact with Manickam. Citti is too young and highly emotional to know the psychic discomfort of his mother. This failure to understand his mother takes the form of negation and he condemns her and starts hating himself. A man who cannot love himself cannot love others. This is the verdict of Jayakanthan put in the mouth of Duraikannu.[40] His decision to be out of the sight of his mother arises out of his expectation of an ideal mother. The novel reaches the climax when Thangam is in deathbed. The novelist seizes this occasion to make Citti an ideal character. Duraikannu advises Citti to visit his dying mother who has given birth to a female baby. The last scene of the novel presents a moving dialogue between Thangam and Citti. The novelist produces a new vision of life in this section.

Jayakanthan captures a new vision of life in the act of reconciliation of Citti with his mother in deathbed. The point of Thangam is that there was no one to shower affection on her. This loss of human affection is a blow to her life. Human life without mutual exchange of love and affection is like a dry desert without a fountain. Thangam requests Citti to be an ideal brother to his newborn sister. She forcefully visualizes what her life would have been if she had a brother like Citti. Much of her tragedy would have possibly disappeared if such a thing had happened according to her. Her dying request to Citti is that at least this newborn child must not be bereft of this chance of having a good brother. This special plea of Thangam redeems her from any kind of moral dishonour and stigma and elevates her character to a new status of noble idealism. This is an expression of the novelist's existentialist perspective. Citti's total change of heart and his willingness and preparedness to be a brother to the newborn sister makes Citti an ideal character. This last scene may be taken as a powerful description of Jayakanthan's longing for a new psycho-social-spiritual vision where idealism and realism are married on the basis of a revolutionary hypothesis. A new scheme of life is necessary to justify Jayakanthan's unorthodox (practical-realist-idealist-humanist) account of life. Citti is an illegitimate son of an illegitimate father. The irony is that he becomes the focal point of a new vision of life.

Anand never makes a predominant poor character assume the role of a wretched or wicked creature. He is consistent in his representation of poor characters whom he upholds as examples of goodness and dignity. It is this particular habit of representing a poor man as a good man which makes Anand an idealist humanist. Unlike Anand, Jayakanthan wants to be true to the complexity of life. Citti is certainly a man of contradictions and waywardness. He is at once capable of being good and bad. Jayakanthan is aware of this divided sensibility in him. It is only towards the end when Citti's mother is in deathbed that Citti slowly takes the decision to be a character of harmony and idealism. This growth in the character of Citti is what makes the novelist a realist and practical humanist. Anand does not undertake to show such a psychological problem of growth in the character of a person, because his hypothesis is that poor characters are invariably good characters. Joseph, Gangu and Munoo are characters of harmony. In Jayakanthan's novels, characters like Citti and Sarangan appear as characters of contradiction but in the end they show their resolve to become characters of harmony. Jayakanthan does not prefer to admire poor people unreservedly. He is critical and realistic enough to perceive certain defects in characters like Sarangan.

In Anand, the Marxian antithesis between the rich and the poor is predominantly found in his consciousness. Therefore he assumes that poor characters are victims of class consciousness and caste discrimination. This Marxian ethics creates certain special duties for Anand and he fittingly endows his poor characters with goodness and dignity in accordance with his chosen ideal. His function and nature of art draws strength from the Marxian ethics which makes him an idealist humanist. Jayakanthan equally endorses his faith in Marx and upholds poor characters like Joseph as apostles of truth, goodness and wisdom. Both accept the Marxian ethics but their art functions slightly under different conditions. Jayakanthan is prepared to take into account the complexity of human character. This is an instance of realistic humanism and Sarangan is an example of this pragmatic realism. He is not an ideal character to start with but later on circumstances force a change on him as a result of his meeting with Raja. Jayakanthan believes in the evolutionary growth of characters and in this respect, he can be described as an evolutionary humanist. He does not accept Sarangan as an ideal character and Raja describes him as a cancer to be inevitably eliminated.[41] Jayakanthan wants to be true to life and so he does not ignore the complexity of the human situation.

To sum up, Anand and Jayakanthan in his early phase as Romantic Humanists oppose religion and uphold life on earth. Their humanism covers the concerns of existentialism in showing the reality of life and its tragic conditions of suffering and misery. Usually existentialism describes the anguish and agony of human life. These two writers develop a thesis that life on earth is suffering and struggle. When they make an analysis of the sources of human suffering, they naturally become Marxist sympathizers. Their study of life reveals the conclusion that poverty, suffering and agony are the result of wealth and class consciousness. Their humanism including the concerns of existentialism endorses its faith in the Marxian ethics. At the same time they are liberal humanists and not radical humanists. They do not believe in any form of aggressively organized mass action as a way of changing the corrupt order of the society. Therefore, for both, art is an instrument for social transformation. These two novelists glorify the life of the poor and praise their innate goodness. Anand is more an idealist humanist in showing the bright side of the protagonists and never describes a poor man as a villain. He is a believer in the essential goodness of the poor people. There is no conflict in his characters in the sense of a fight between good and evil and their subsequent inability to choose the one or the other. Jayakanthan is also an idealist humanist in his portrayal of Joseph and Raja. The difference between Jayakanthan and Anand is that the former perceives the complexity of the human situation. This critical awareness of life makes Jayakanthan a realistic humanist also. The creation of Citti and Sarangan is an example of his critical understanding of life. His idealism does not allow him to ignore certain defects found in poor people also. The main reason for this difference between the two novelists is that while one develops faith in comprehensive historical humanism, the other puts his emphasis upon evolutionary humanism. The idea of comprehensive historical humanism deals with a certain state in human life where religion has taken away all human concerns. Anand's creed of this kind of humanism is a revival of the real roots of life. Jayakanthan has this preoccupation of Anand. His evolutionary humanism indicates his belief that characters grow like Citti and Sarangan and circumstances steadily change. This kind of conflict and growth in character is not found in Anand. But both are believers in change. They long for a new order of life. So this presentation of celebrating the poor and glorifying their innate goodness is the essence of humanism in Anand and Jayakanthan.

## NOTES

1. Protogoras, qtd. G.S. Balarama Gupta, *Mulk Raj Anand: A Study of His Fiction in Humanistic Perspective* (Bareilly: Prakash, 1974), p. 15.
2. For more information on the historical and philosophical aspects of humanism, read *Encyclopaedia of the Social Sciences* (New York: Macmillan, 1949), pp. 537-44.
3. Mulk Raj Anand, "Why I Write?" *Kakatiya Journal of English Studies*, 2, No.1 (Spring 1977), p. 252.
4. Mulk Raj Anand, *Apology for Heroism* (Bombay: Kutub-popular, 1946), p. 93.

5. K.R. Srinivasa Iyengar, *Indian Writing in English* (New Delhi: Sterling, 1985), p. 334.
6. Mulk Raj Anand, "Why I Write?", p. 251.
7. K.R. Srinivasa Iyengar, p. 332.
8. Mulk Raj Anand, *Apology for Heroism*, p. 23.
9. Leo Tagore, "Social Justice in Anand's *Coolie* and Achebe's *Things Fall Apart*," *The Novels of Mulk Raj Anand*, ed. R.K. Dhawan (Delhi: Prestige, 1992), p. 86.
10. Mulk Raj Anand, qtd. G.S. Balarama Gupta, "Towards a closer understanding of Anand," *Perspectives on Mulk Raj Anand*, ed. K.K. Sharma (Ghaziabad: Vimal, 1977), p. 10.
11. G.S. Balarama Gupta, "Towards a closer understanding of Anand," p. 12.
12. Mulk Raj Anand, qtd. G.S. Balarama Gupta, p. 1.
13. C.D. Narasimhaiah, *The Swan and the Eagle*, qtd. G.S. Balarama Gupta, "Towards a closer understanding," p. 9.
14. Mulk Raj Anand, "Prolegomena to a New Humanism," *Lines Written to an Indian Air: Essays* (Bombay: Nalanda, 1949), p. 7.
15. Mulk Raj Anand, Letter to Krishna Nandan Sinha, *Mulk Raj Anand* (New York: Twayne, 1972), p. 30.
16. Jayakanthan, "Jayakanthan tells his story," *Indian Express* (Madurai), 16 December 1989.
17. *Ibid.*
18. T. Jayakanthan, "Mukavurai," *Oru Piti Coru* (Madurai: Meenakshi Puthaka Nilayam, 1974), pp. 6-7.
19. Jayakanthan, *Unnaipol Oruvan* (Madurai: Meenakshi Puthaka Nilayam, 1991), p. 6.
20. Jayakanthan, *Piralayam* (Madurai: Meenakshi Puthaka Nilayam, 1976), p. 9.
21. Jayakanthan, *Avarkal Ulle Irukkirarkal* (Madurai: Meenakshi Puthaka Nilayam, 1972), pp. 114-15.
22. Jayakanthan, *Piralayam*, p. 9.
23. Saros Cowasjee, *So Many Freedoms* (Delhi: O.U.P., 1977), p. 63.
24. Jayakanthan, *Tevan Varuvara?* (Madurai: Meenakshi Puthaka Nilayam, 1961), p. 6
25. Premila Paul, *The Novels of Mulk Raj Anand: A Thematic Study* (New Delhi: Sterling, 1983), p. 32.
26. Mulk Raj Anand, *Two Leaves and a Bud* (Delhi: Orient Paperbacks, n.d.), p. 32.

27. J.M. Williams, *Indo-Anglian Literature 1800-1970: A Survey* (Delhi: Orient Longman, 1976), p. 42.
28. K.R. Srinivasa Iyengar, p. 336.
29. Choice of these novels for discussion is based on M.S. Thothadri, *Jayakanthan: A Study* (Sivagangai: Annam Press, 1976), p. 7.
30. Jayakanthan, *Yarukkaka Alutan* (Madurai: Meenakshi Puthaka Nilayam, 1986), p. 5.
31. *Ibid.*, p. 7.
32. Gnani, *Markciyamum Tamil Ilakkiyamum* (Coimbatore: Parinamam, 1988), p. 210.
33. *Ibid.*, p. 211.
34. *Loc. cit.*
35. Jayakanthan, *Valkkai Alaikkiratu* (Madurai: Meenakshi Puthaka Nilayam, 1957), p. 8.
36. Mulk Raj Anand, *Coolie* (Delhi: Hind Pocket Books, 1972), p. 157.
37. K. Chellappan, "Caste as theme and background in Tamil Fiction," *Indian Express* (Madurai), 30 September, 1989.
38. Arivalakan, *Jayakanthan Ayvatankal* (Cuddalore: Amaravathi Press, 1978), pp. 300-1.
39. Karu Muthiah, *Jayakanthan Navalkalil Pattirappataippu* (Devakottai Muthumeenal Patipakam, 1980), p. 216.
40. Jayakanthan, *Unnaippol Oruvan*, p. 161.
41. Jayakanthan, *Valkkai Alaikkiratu*, p. 220.

# Sufferers, Strangers and Idealists

> I tell you the machine is in our midst already, there! And we have got to decide to go and work it rather than sulk.[1]

Anand and Jayakanthan generally follow an identical view that good novels strike a balance between the formation of characters and creation of incidents. Sir Walter Scott and Jane Austen represent a total contrast. For Scott, incidents assume importance while for Austen, characters are the hearts of the novel. In Henry James and Joyce, there seems to be a change. The theme is centralized in the consciousness of protagonists and incidents are subordinate to them. The flow of consciousness and the unorganized outpouring of human emotions change the very structure of the novel. Aristotle's emphasis upon plot as the soul of the tragedy does not receive much attention.

The complexity of modern life is against presenting any idealized picture of it. To discover the commonness in the emotions of the human race is no longer in vogue. The emphasis upon the individual's psychological predicament is what animates the minds of the modern artists. A greater attention to life with all its complexity and peculiarity engages them. The relationship between character and incident has changed. The complexity of life does not permit characters to exist in subordination to situations. The working of the protagonist's mind is determined by external, life situation. What happens to the protagonist as a result of his interaction with society is much more important than the situation which affects him. The individual withdraws from life and lives in his own closed chamber of the mind. His spirit is no longer in harmony with what is found outside life. Therefore modern art concentrates on the behaviour of the inner self and how it works and expresses itself.

Anand and Jayakanthan endorse a moderate view of art in looking upon novel as a simultaneous combination of characters and situations. Anand has stated that his business is to describe the 'love for suffering humanity' and so he has put in his novels what he has known about life in the world.[2] Similarly, Jayakanthan says in his prefaces that 'loving life and men is his philosophy'. These two statements of the novelists establish an integrated balance between characters and situations. Almost all the novels of Anand are located in some villages in Puṅjab. In the same manner, most of the novels of Jayakanthan are placed in and around Madras. Both concentrate on men and situations in relation to each other.

All the protagonists of Anand and Jayakanthan represent a conflict between tradition and modernity. Anand creates protagonists like Bakha, Ananta and Nur. All these characters throb and bristle with life. These protagonists are compared with some of the protagonists of Jayakanthan—Bakha with Āti, Ananta with Henry, and Nur with Prabu. All these protagonists are life-like without any element of abstraction. They embody several cross-sections of social life.

Bakha in *Untouchable* and Āti in *Jaya Jaya Sankara* fight against untouchability. Bakha being a passive rebel, his physical and mental agony is graphically portrayed while Āti is presented as an idealist. Ananta and Henry are two men of good heart who believe in loving and serving the human race. Nur and Prabu represent the problems of poverty and excess of wealth which cause alienation from life and society and do not put them at home with themselves and others.

**The Two 'Untouchables': Bakha and Āti**

Anand and Jayakanthan deal with the theme of untouchability from different angles although the implications of the issue are the same for both the writers. The general conviction of Anand is based on a severe critical examination of the ancient Indian heritage. M.K. Naik observes that the evil of untouchability is the result of years of suppression of a class on religious grounds: "the caste Hindu is armed with the feeling of six thousand years of social and class superiority—a feeling which refuses to accept the fact that the untouchable is a human being, but insists on treating him like a sub-human creature, to be ignored or bullied or exploited as the occasion demands."[3]

Anand boldly puts the blame on the religion of Hinduism for the practice of untouchability. In his book, *Apology for Heroism*, he indicates that he is a firm and uncompromising denouncer of the Hindu religion.

> It is not very well known that Hinduism has tended for a long time to be more and more the social organism of caste and less and less a unified religion.[4]

The religious consciousness of the Hindus engendered a feeling of superiority and it slowly led to discrimination of one set of people from the other. That religion which called one group of people untouchables is not only a bad but corrupt religion, according to Anand.

Unlike Anand, Jayakanthan is not fully prepared to go to the extreme in condemning the Hindu religion for the practice of untouchability. For a novelist like Anand, there is an unbridgeable opposition between tradition and modernity. Any notion of human progress, according to Anand, has to come from the West only. The degeneration in social life is considered to be the result of a conservative religion. Jayakanthan's way of analyzing all social evils takes a new line. Like Anand, he does not want to use tradition and modernity as terms of opposition. He is for a fresh and critical review of everything. Therefore Jayakanthan is neither a modernist nor a traditionalist. What moves him to examine any issue is his spirit of critical enquiry. Anand is very much rooted in the ideology of the modern spirit and so he is forced to take a hard line in his analysis of the social evil of untouchability. The main approaches of these two novelists are seen in their excellent description of the two protagonists Bakha and Āti who are shown as two 'untouchables'. The physical and mental suffering of Bakha is portrayed realistically whereas Āti is described as a great idealist.

Bakha belongs to a socially depressed class of people whose habits and knowledge of life are deplorably poor. Lakha, the father of Bakha, does not grow critical of the treatment shown to the people of his class. He perhaps believes like a timid man that the traditional doctrine of untouchability is a sacred one and so it should not be spoken of in critical terms. Unlike his father, Bakha wants to be a rebel. At the same time, he is not able to take any concrete action in a moment of crisis. "In his almost physical inability to revolt, his submission, his habitual subservience to superiors who insult him, he is one with the vast majority of the outcasts."[5] He is sensitive and intelligent enough to see that his people are left uncared for in the society on the ground they lack dignity and refinement. Bakha knows that such a pitiable state is generated by religion.

Like Bakha, Āti has come to know about the tragic state of affairs resulting from the practice of untouchability. Both Bakha and Āti are men of hope and self-assurance. Bakha knows that all people are equal before God. But the irony, according to him, is that some people are not equal to some other people. They look detestable with their unclean manners and uncouth habits. Bakha is eager to know the reason for such degradation. He feels that such a plight has been forced on his people by years of continued suppression. Naik makes a reference to the problem of Bakha: "the action closes in golbagh in the town, where Bakha becomes aware of possible modern approaches to his problems, the town indicating an aspect of modernity." (27)

Bakha is a latrine cleaner and he lives near cow dung with moths and flies all around. This kind of life causes mental agony to him. He feels very unhappy about his state. The greatest factor which pains Bakha is that latrine-cleaning job carries no social status and so he is shunned and ignored wherever he is seen. Like Bakha, Āti is not placed in a socially attractive job. Bakha is a sweeper while Āti is a rearer of cattle. Bakha is a realist and a person dissatisfied with his own life but he has a passion for doing the work in an alert manner based on sincerity. While Bakha is not respected anywhere, Āti is a man of self-confidence.

The fact that he belongs to a suppressed class does not put Āti in a state of sorrow, because he is an idealist. The situation in which Bakha finds himself is highly painful and there seems to be no relief from such a tragic state. Unlike Bakha, Āti follows a new technique, that is, the strategy of defeating the opponent with his own weapon. The Hindu religion called men like Āti untouchables. Āti masters

Sanskrit, Vedas and Shastras and yet he does not give up his work of rearing the cattle. It shows that Āti is keenly alive to the reality of the situation. But there is no one to guide Bakha.

The misery of Bakha is derived from the social evil of untouchability. That a latrine cleaner is a detestable person is an unbearable fact for him. Āti has no such feeling as he feels inwardly that he is a man of dignity and respect and he does not want this to be acknowledged by people. In this respect, Āti is different from Bakha. Āti does not care for the judgement of the people as he knows the psychological truth that a particular thing affects a person mentally if he allows himself to be so affected by it. Bakha is a living embodiment of this kind of psychological truth. Āti remains above the popular feelings of the people. One factor worthy of notice is that Āti is a student of Sathasiva Iyer who is a revolutionary Brahmin very much interested in the uplift of such untouchables. Bakha is denied of this privilege of education which gives enlightenment to people. In the novel *Untouchable*, Bakha is represented as a victim of the social evil of untouchability and he is unable to overcome his feeling of depression and appear confident in achieving status. But in the novel *Jaya Jaya Sankara*, Āti is depicted as a man of courage and knowledge who is capable of overcoming this social evil which does not respect certain class of men.

Anand and Jayakanthan agree in their representation of the social problem of untouchability but they differ in their methods of resolving this crisis. This difference is crucial as it influences the mode of characterization. Jayakanthan believes that leaders for reforming the evil of untouchability have come from the Brahmin class. Some of them are forward-looking revolutionaries like Sathasiva Iyer. Jayakanthan shows in his novel that Jagad Guru Sankara is unorthodox in his understanding of life. The novelist points out through this character that the life of a Brahmin is different from that of other men because he has a definite purpose in life and his existence must have some meaning and it must move towards a sense of selfless service. Jayakanthan states in this novel that a Brahmin is a person specially charged with the highest responsibility of helping all people in a spirit of love and self-sacrifice. It is this view of Jayakanthan which distinguishes him from Anand. Jayakanthan is interested in discovering a solution for the prevailing problem while Anand wants to know the history and root cause of the problem. Bakha and Āti differ in accordance with the difference in the perspectives of the novelists.

There are three incidents which show Bakha in a mood of depression and low spirit. Bakha accidentally touches a man in the street and is burdened with the charge of polluting him. Kalinath, the village priest, under the pretext of giving water, encourages Bakha's sister Sohini and tries to molest her in the temple. At that moment, Bakha says fearlessly, "I will go and kill him."[6] But as he goes to the temple, his spirit gets fully choked. The consciousness of his social inferiority overwhelms him. "The instinctive anger gives way, and the slave in him asserts itself."[7] The third instance is where Bakha is driven out of the house when he lifts a boy in his endeavour to rescue him from the confusion which comes from some kind of skirmish. Bakha is pained to see the fact that an untouchable has no right and dignity to touch another man.

Anand shows how Bakha suffers owing to this social evil. His novel, *Untouchable*, therefore presents a picture of realism. He describes the circumstances in which this social evil oppresses a person and makes him unhappily aware of his poor social status. Jayakanthan is not interested in this picture of realism. He is actively engaged in a new revolution of reforming such people, as he is of the view that the degrading social status of a person cannot be improved without acquiring learning. According to him, a really religious man does not hate some people but is endowed with love for all.

The social setting in which Bakha is placed is different from the background in which Āti is placed. The tremendous amount of learning that Āti has acquired with the good will of a Brahmin reformer Sathasiva Iyer has enabled him to surmount all barriers which arise from a phenomenon called the evil of social ostracism. Bakha is a heavily built man with his routine hard work. Cowasjee describes him as "an attractive person [whose] physique is distinctive." (48) About his physical appearance Anand says,

> The toil of the body had built up for him a very fine physique. It seemed to suit him, to give homogeneity, a wonderful wholeness to his body, so that you could turn around and say, 'Here is a man.' (11)

Bakha has physical strength while Āti is known for his strength of mind. Bakha's bodily strength does not give him a strong mental determination. As he belongs to an oppressed class, it is not possible for him to liberate himself from that psychological feeling of social degradation. M.K. Naik explains this point clearly: "six thousand years of suppression have left deep marks upon the untouchable's life and psychology. Weakness corrupts, and absolute weakness corrupts absolutely. He is caught in a vicious circle from which there is no escape." (30) Bakha sees the evil clearly, but is not able to react to it very strongly. He only feels depressed.

Although Bakha and Āti are Harijans by birth, there is a difference in the orientation and upbringing which they receive. Jayakanthan describes Āti in this manner, "He is a first grade student in Sathasiva Iyer's Gandhian school functioning in the slum area."[8] Two facts need to be indicated here. A revolutionary Brahmin imparting education to a Harijan is worthy of attention. The second fact lies in the Gandhian cultural ethos in which the school flourishes and functions. These two facts have conferred on Āti some special benefits and advantages which Bakha awfully lacks. Āti does not experience any feeling of social inferiority. The special mark of merit in him is that he has the necessary resources to form his own independent judgement of things. Jayakanthan brings out this side of Āti clearly:

> Maha Siva Rathiri is fast approaching. . . . Āti expresses his opinion of not entering into the temple as per the Gandhian movement. . . . Āti opines that he won't enter into areas where he is not wanted and he knows that God is everywhere and not only inside the temple. (43-44)

Jayakanthan himself admits the fact that Āti is a unique person among the slumdwellers. His independence of judgement comes from his learning which makes him thoroughly different from Bakha. When Bakha sees injustice done to him, his spirits go up. He is alert enough to show his resistance in mind although he is not able to put forth his courage in action. Bakha is unique like Āti because he is able to register his protest in some manner or other.

Bakha looks at the problem of untouchability without any way of resolving it. Anand writes a novel in which his major motive is to depict the suffering and helplessness of Bakha. Perhaps the novelist thinks that Bakha has to negate the culture which has made him an untouchable. Anand believes that only an adequate knowledge of modern outlook can be a source of strength in removing this social evil. Bakha has a keen sensibility to perceive the social injustice but he does not know the means of removing it. Anand is very careful to point out that education is not imparted to these people like Bakha. The slightest acquisition of knowledge will bring awakening to them and so the novelist treats this act of denying education as the greatest conspiracy of religion to perpetuate the habit of servility. It is the conviction of Anand that a caste-oriented religion can never cast away this social evil. The remedy comes from the assimilation of modern scientific outlook. Bakha's plight is pitiable because he is found struggling without any satisfying solution. Anand has darkened the possibility of any solution in the mind of Bakha as he very well knows that the answer has to come from an external observer who has absorbed the modern scientific outlook. The basis for this rational method of criticism is to be derived from the insights of the European Enlightenment. Bakha is not equal to such a task with his position of latrine cleaning and living amidst cow dung.

Anand's protagonist Bakha is in search of a solution for the purpose of eradicating the evil of untouchability. His life of latrine cleaning imposes limitations upon his mental outlook. Anand does not show a fully emancipated hero but he only takes pains to represent him as a passive rebel. The novelist knows that education is necessary for emancipation of men like Bakha from the social evil of untouchability. Their degradation is due to lack of education and their lack of education is due to the planned conspiracy of a corrupt religion.

Jayakanthan differs from Anand in that he shows Āti as a fully emancipated hero. Therefore Āti does not face many problems. Moreover Āti has married Sutantra Devi, the daughter of Sathasiva Iyer. It is nothing but an inter-caste marriage between a Harijan and a Brahmin woman. Bakha expresses individuality intensely in reacting to situations which put him in a state of humiliation. He realizes helplessness in the light of his social inferiority. Āti, like Bakha, explicitly manifests his individuality. Bakha's individuality is born out of his awareness of the injustice done to him. He is alive to the reality of social injustice unlike his men. Āti's strong sense of individuality is born out of his independence of judgement which is derived from learning. Bakha does not have the mental make-up to realize that he, as an individual, must be a man of dignity and self-respect. Āti fully realizes that he is a man who believes in his own dignity and self-respect.

Ati is described as a liberated individual in a specific situation by the novelist. What is uppermost in the mind of Āti is that there is no need for others to respect untouchables. The greatest strength, according to him, lies in the fact that the 'untouchable' must have faith in his own inherent dignity and must first regard himself as respectable. Whether others respect the so-called mean person or not is quite irrelevant for Āti. He realises that to fully develop faith in himself is the first step in the process of liberation. Jayakanthan excellently brings out Āti's sense of hope and self-confidence in a particular context:

> Swami, just as you feel reluctant to enter into a slum, I feel reluctant to visit your place, a gathering of Vedic pundits. Both my body and soul feel so. But don't consider this feeling as my inferiority complex because of my birth. (82)

What occupies Āti's mind when he speaks like this is that he would not like to be humiliated by others. His consciousness of self-respect acts as a force on his mind and he feels that he should ignore people who are not prepared to respect him. Āti thinks that unless 'the untouchables' behave in a manner of self-assurance there is no hope of emancipation for them. Anand's hero is very much influenced and conditioned by the complex consciousness of the society.

Anand is concerned with a logical exposition of the conditions and situations in which Bakha suffers and feels frustrated and humiliated. He says boldly that a caste-conscious society is fully responsible for his suffering. Bakha sees the hypocrisy of Kalinath as well as the good nature of Havildar Charat Singh, who is free from caste consciousness. When he pours tea from his own tumbler and gives it to Bakha, he simply melts into self-pity and tears and says, "For this man, I wouldn't mind being a sweeper all my life. I would do anything for him." (87) Bakha is not able to forget the consoling words of the woman who gives a chapati to him, "My child, you shouldn't sit on people's doorsteps like this." (57)

Bakha is objective enough to realize the merit of some caste Hindus just as he is pained by the unclean nature of his own brother Rakha. But incidents like Bakha's accidentally touching a person and thereby polluting him and Kalinath shouting "polluted" in order to escape from dishonour are the major focus of the novel in which the protagonist is placed in a state of agony and shame. Āti, like Bakha, experiences the same feeling when he sees Mahalinga Iyer with all his conservative notions about purity and cleanliness.

Like Bakha, Āti is able to appreciate the merit of Sathasiva Iyer and discover the defect of Mahalinga Iyer. Āti is so advanced in his mental outlook that he is able to see the difference between a traditional religious leader like Jagad Guru Sankara and a revolutionary spiritual reformer like Sathasiva Iyer. Even Sankara is shown as a leader endowed with a broad base when he says that helping the entire human race is his sole concern. Jayakanthan shows Sankara and Sathasiva Iyer in their idealized form. Āti retains his capacity for self-respect in his own way and does follow an ideal pattern of life in organizing the ashram.

Bakha comes across three solutions to the evil of untouchability. The act of conversion to Christianity, accepting Gandhi's christening them as Harijans and introductions to a new system of sanitation do not attract Bakha. They do not remove the evil but they only mitigate it. The hope of a satisfying solution is not fully visualized by Bakha. But Āti has the advantage of education and sees the possibility of a solution. The greatest point of merit found in the protagonist Āti is that he feels that any depressed man must feel that he is his own saviour and that an external liberator can only do limited work in deepening the awareness of one's own dignity. Bakha does not reflect along the line of Āti for the simple reason that his situation is different and moreover he feels intensely that he has become a butt of ridicule in a caste-conscious society.

### The Big Hearts: Ananta and Henry

Anand and Jayakanthan have an identical tendency to portray some major characters who are full of revolutionary idealism. Ananta in *The Big Heart* and Henry in *Oru Manitan Oru Vitu Oru Ulakam* are the protagonists who possess nobility of heart and boundless compassion. The foremost trait that brings them together is their love of human beings.

Ananta is a coppersmith by profession. The introduction of modern machinery has taken away the jobs of many coppersmiths. He has before him two major tasks. He has to unite his brethren and secure jobs for them from great factory owners like Lala Murli Dhar and Gokul Chand. Ananta's main enterprise is to remove the ignorance of his people and prepare their minds for accepting the modern machines. "Though Ananta suffers from the introduction of the machine, he can still see their usefulness."[9] Machines, according to him, are not objects of terror but gifts from modern science. It is this spirit which moves him to organize people and make them understand the value and benefit of machines. What induces him to do this is his love for all people. His only wish is that all people must live happily without any problem.

The major philosophy of Ananta is to help people at all costs. Anand makes this clear:

> And I know there will be no more happiness in this darkening world for anyone for long times to come. And I feel I ought to do something good before I die, so that the others who come after can be a little happier.[10]

The love of Ananta is expressed in his spirit of rendering service to all without any motive. He has a broad heart in keeping all people uniformly happy. All his life is only a struggle to attain this ideal. In this respect Henry is comparable to Ananta. Gnani observes, "The way in which Henry celebrates love with regard makes him a Jesus. This Henry is against all possession."[11]

Jayakanthan himself has said in his preface that he is going to concentrate on the brighter side of life in portraying the character of Henry.[12] The novelist shows the good heart of Henry in this passage:

> He loves to admire the village atmosphere, the half-clad people and children, their simple desires and enjoyments in spite of poverty, their speech and behaviour, their animal folk, their habitats and kitchen gardens, the hen with its chicks, and the clarion call of the cock on the thatched roof. (29)

The capacity of Henry to extend love to all creatures is what makes him a Christ-like figure.

Ananta and Henry believe in egalitarian principles and they do not want people to make distinctions which are born of caste hierarchy and class consciousness. Ananta has a first-hand knowledge of how poor and socially downtrodden Thathiars suffer at the hands of rich people:

> Why, indeed are the dealers torturing the Thathiars at all? I know full well that we suffer from the day we are born till the day we die, but this cruelty is unnecessary. A little reason could settle this difficulty between the Kesaras and us. (143)

Ananta believes that all men are after all human beings and he feels that the habit of discriminating one set of people from the other on the basis of wealth or caste is a threat to human dignity. When Mannangatti requests Henry to take his supper, the latter shows his respect and affection by grasping his hands:

> Henry holds out his hand with a formal introduction saying, 'I am Henry'. Mannangatti is shocked. He could not leave Henry as such after he has given that much respect for an ordinary soul like him. (71)

Like Ananta, Henry does not make a distinction between the rich and the poor. They believe that all men are noble creatures and should be loved. Henry believes in the equality of all people. The novelist says that Henry's respect for the menial shepherds makes Devarajan wonder at such a man.

Ananta's mission is to introduce the benefits of modern science and technology to all people. He thinks that the traditional life of the people will be changed through modern machines. His compassion prompts him to feel that all people can live without drudgery and meaningless hard labour. In accordance with Anand's ideology of modernism, the character of Ananta is portrayed. Through the protagonist, the novelist tries to remove the traditional mentality of the people, and to resolve the gap between the rich and the poor and to dislodge the feeling of inequality among the people. Henry is created with the same ideological fervour. His decision to hand over his father's property to Duraikannu once again after obtaining legal clarification shows his great heart and disregard for possession. Like Ananta, Henry is not after wealth. Henry and Ananta love simplicity and dislike sophistication. Henry respects the girl who has no proper dress. He thinks that a good heart is more important than mere external dress. Ananta and Henry are essentially men of self-sacrifice. Commenting on Ananta's sacrifice, Cowasjee rightly points out that "his sacrifice is the sacrifice of the unselfish man for humanity." (131) Their only dharma is to increase the happiness of all people.

*The Big Heart* is a novel of human crisis while *Oru Manitan Oru Vitu Oru Ullakam* is a novel of bright idealism without any tinge of complication. Henry sees human life in an atmosphere of freedom while Ananta sees it in a moment of conflict and crisis. Their approaches to life are the same although their backgrounds are different. Ananta does not express his belief in God openly. The presence of human misery, especially the misery of the unemployed, makes him sceptical. He thinks that religion has not created changes in life or helped or promoted the growth of human life in any way. Ananta sees that the state of man's unprogressive nature is the outcome of his age-long attachment to religion. Much human suffering that exists flows from man's conservative habits. The traditional job of a coppersmith is very hard, according to Ananta. The energies of the coppersmiths are sapped by the drudgery of work. Moreover they have lost their faith in the value of individual effort. Ananta is pained to see that his kinsmen are not men of courage and self-assurance. His function is to instil hope in them and awaken a new kind of awareness.

Ananta and Henry exist on different planes. While the former is imbued with revolutionary idealism to fight against tradition and conservatism, the latter views life with the spirit of a poet filled with wonder and awe at the sight of everything. "Henry who enters the village is thrilled at its beauty and landscape. Like a child he looks at every creature, be it animate or inanimate with awe and wonder and starts showering his love and affection."[13]

Anand's Ananta is uncompromising while Jayakanthan's Henry is flexible. Ananta never gives in, in his effort to improve life and modernize it with the help of machines. Henry has no job or vocation. Ananta has a specific purpose in his life. It is to unite the jobless workers and make them learn the value of machines. This process of popularizing the value of machines and making the workers aware of their merits seems to be the mission of Ananta.

Ananta is a believer in the galvanizing power of the individual. Without human effort, nothing can be achieved: "Ananta knows that revolution will be a far cry unless the coppersmiths learn to unite. He tells them plainly 'Men are the makers of their own deeds, the makers of their own character, good or bad, and they are the shapers of their own destiny'. So come and make your fate."[14] This passage clearly brings out the attitude of Ananta towards religion and God. He believes that religion is a hindrance to the development of social life. Ananta feels that in the process of realizing the infinite powers and energies of the individual, all the past values flowing from religion must be set aside. There can be no improvement in social life without a definite break with the ties of the past. Then only the individual's capacity to reshape life is made possible. Ananta comes very close to the Buddhist view that man is the maker of everything. The onward march of man depends on his power to alter his attitude to religion and God.

There are different purposes which govern and animate the characters of Ananta and Henry. The views of the novelists in regard to tradition and modernity get reflected in the creation of these two protagonists. Anand is an ardent supporter of modernity and a strong denouncer of tradition, while Jayakanthan is of the view that what is good in both must be discovered and cherished. Ananta attacks religion and tradition and so he becomes exclusively an advocate of modernity. Henry remains unorthodox and unconventional in his attitude to religion and God. But he does not dismiss anything unreservedly. What he wants is a sympathetic critical enquiry based on impartial understanding of things. Jayakanthan himself says that Henry has no religion but believes in God. (50) He is a Christian in name but remains unattached to any exclusive religion till the end.

Henry's father, Sabapathy Pillai, trained him to be a liberal man in matters of religion and theology.

Ananta has formed certain strong convictions which are drawn from his criticism of tradition and religion. Henry, on the other hand, would like to respect everything. When Kiliambal, the daughter of the Maniakkarar of the village, gave birth to a male child, Mannangatti did not go to see the child claiming that the childbirth has made the house impure. Devarajan calls such a belief nothing but blind superstition. (127) Henry does not want to easily brush aside the beliefs of the people as he thinks that there may be some reason hidden behind them. Ananta unlike Henry is not a believer in any superstition. But Henry is not for superstitions. He does not like to dismiss anything easily as each belief carries a history of its own.

The mission of modernity makes Ananta a radical fighter. Henry is neither a conservative nor a progressivist. But he is a man for all waters and has such a great love for all people that he wants to advocate a liberal understanding of all things. Commenting on Henry, Karu Muthiah says, "If ever he meets people with contradictory ideas he would not clash with them. He usually avoids such situations." (238) Henry does not want to create disharmony in anything. He is very mild, gentle and highly conciliatory in his reaction to anything.

Ananta is a definite disbeliever in God and religion. When Akkamma, Devarajan's sister, compares Henry to Christ, (66) he is not astonished, because he says God dwells in everyone. He has no conventional idea of an abstract God existing somewhere. His burning zeal is to relate God to the reality of life. For him God is love and so he thinks that all human relationships must be based on love and compassion.

**The Alienated Heroes: Nur and Prabu**

Anand and Jayakanthan deal with the theme of alienation in their novels, *Lament on the Death of a Master of Arts and Cila Nēr-ankalil Cila Manitarkal* respectively. Nur and Prabu are heroes who are not happy with themselves. It is the passion for social honour which drove Nur's father to educate him. Nur says in his tragic mood, "Why did you drag me into the dust by making me an M.A."[15] Nur's education is his peril because it has made him a snob. He has no respect for menial labour and his education has not enabled him to live a noble life. Nur's classmate Gama has a pungent remark to make, "What is there in education, brother! Waste of time." (46)

While Nur's misery comes from a kind of false education, Prabu's trouble comes partly from lack of good education. He tells Ganga that he is an unworthy fellow. He describes his lack of education as a defect: "An uneducated, unworthy fellow to stand beside her. He had his education upto high school in a convent."[16] It is very clear that Nur and Prabu are characters who possess no spiritual orientation. Nur's failure to get a job and Prabu's failure to have a good friend make them feel miserable.

Nur and Prabu have been brought up in different ways. Nur's father is a 'hard-hearted confectioner.[17] "His father, a constant source of terror, beats him and nags him, and imposes on him such rigid discipline that the boy detests him."[18] For Prabu, his own father was his gravedigger. Jayakanthan makes a pointed reference to this, "He loved his son dearly. Indirectly he was responsible for the sorry state of his son." (210)

Nur has a father who has no love for him, while Prabu's father was deeply attached to him. They are both tragic failures in life because of the peculiar qualities of their parents. Too much love did no good to Prabu while total absence of love landed Nur in an atmosphere of emotional dryness characterized by lack of warmth. For Nur, this world is a world of frustration as he feels he is not respected or rewarded with any job. Nur attributes his failure to the world and the surroundings. In the case of Prabu, the world is not responsible for his failure. He is the chief reason for his own failure. Prabu makes wrong use of everything and so gets into complications easily.

The enemy of Nur is his poverty. As he is not able to fulfil any of his wishes on account of poverty, it slowly perverts his being and frustrates any possibility for achieving a good purpose in relation to life. Anand has basically a Marxian attitude to life. The health and fulfilment of a human being depend on a sound economic base. The suffering of Nur is connected with his economic condition. Anand describes this problem clearly:

> But poverty . . . how it had hardened him to life, how it had made him insensitive to the colours, the shades, the forms of things, to the thoughts, the feelings of people, till he had no contact with anyone or anything and went irritably through the world without any perception of even the lumps of human existence, to say nothing of the subtle nuances of experience. (51)

The chief cause of Nur's alienation comes from his poverty which deprives him of all material comforts.[19] Nur loses his capacity for human tenderness. He becomes a stranger to everyone and no one makes an appeal to him. While poverty takes away the mental health of Nur, too much of wealth spoils Prabu. Wealth, a source of life for Prabu leads him along blind alleys. The very wealth which is a source of inspiration for him becomes a source of estrangement from life.

It is poverty which compels Nur to do the job of a clerk in a post office. Nur experiences frustration as he performs a work which is not commensurate with his educational status. Anand feels that Nur's education has not given him any maturity but has only produced a sophisticated outlook. The demand and urge of ego to capture public fame and eminence is what Nur's education has done to him. It is a kind of over-refined intellectual education which cramps the heart and feelings as human dimension is absent in this scheme of instruction. Nur's tragedy arises from over-ambition and lack of opportunity to fulfil it. The reason for Nur's alienated state lies in his over-sophisticated education which dehumanises feelings and lessens the possibility for human warmth and response. Prabu also becomes a tragic character. The main source of Prabu's discomfort lies in his excess of wealth. While poverty kills Nur, wealth degrades Prabu. Prabu accepts this fact in his self-critical mood:

> To show his father his savings he started stealing. . . . Now he feels that excess of money would spoil anyone and an abrupt end of that supply would destroy a man. It is indeed the worst weapon to destroy an enemy. His father used this weapon to spoil his own son. All these thoughts have come now in his mature state of mind. (211-13)

Wealth does not endow Prabu with a balance of judgement. Life is only a game and women are just playthings for sensual pleasure to him. His perception of life does not go beyond the realm of comfort, pleasure and ease. He falls into a pit without being aware of it.

Nur has a longing for a rich human relation. He feels that his life can be nourished only by love and affection. But men and the world around him paralyse this prospect. Nur is not at home with his father's idea of what he should be in life. Moreover his search for a good job ends in futility. His education does not humanise him, and so he seems to be an odd mixture of many things with no proper attachment to his father or his own wife and child. He suffers and lives and his existence is devoid of any meaning or purpose. He is caught in an existentialist predicament which estranges him from people and things. There is no one to guide him in his crisis. Nur has lost his mother. His father chides him. His wife is unequal to deal with his crisis. Prabu echoes similar feelings in his self-confession:

> None of the women loved me including my wife. I am fed up. I have given up searching for true love. Whenever I get acquainted with a woman, I'll say to myself, "this is love." But after some time I will realize that it is not so. (151)

Wealth offers to Prabu a variety of opportunities for different kinds of experiments with his life. None of these attempts satisfies him really and therefore he slowly loses his interest in life. Prabu looks for some kind of abiding contact with life and people. Ganga alone offers him love, comfort and relief. The greatest tragedy is that Prabu is not able to share his sorrow with anyone in his family. Gama is a kind of consolation for Nur. Prabu sees no real human relation based on love and mutual affection. The problem with him is that he never looked for the right thing in his early life. His misery is partly his own. His complaint against people who show no love to him arises from his wrong understanding of life.

Nur's experience of estrangement from life comes from his shallow education and lack of economic support and his failure to get a job of rank and merit. All these subsequently lead him to a cynical attitude. Unlike Nur, Prabu has everything and yet is caught in a state of crisis. Excess of wealth, lack of good education, inordinate interest in women for pleasure, failure to possess conviction and a half-hearted approach to things without a desire for refinement land him in a crisis of alienation. He identifies the whole of life with drinking and womanising. His axiom of life is a perverted one. He admits in a melancholic mood that it is better to die drinking than to live without the drinks.

Health and sanity in living are born of a serious understanding of life. Both Nur and Prabu lack a serious and balanced attitude to life. It is this which makes them roll in a welter of emotional confusion. Prabu developed a habit of looking to superficial things of life and this has not helped him to form a conviction in regard to anything. His interest in pleasure for the moment leads him to a permanent state of sadness. Nur's sorrow comes from a different source. His passion for honour makes him shallow in his attitude to life. His education has destroyed his sensibility while wealth has not improved Prabu's mind. The reason for their frustration stems from a wrong and improper understanding of life which is generated by their respective backgrounds. Nur is with his family without any emotional tie while Prabu wishes to be away from his family as his interest is elsewhere.

Nur is a frustrated intellectual who has not tasted love in any aspect of life. Loss of interest in life leads him to turn a blind eye to everything in life. For him living has become a burden and family responsibility appears ridiculous:

His unhappy childhood and loveless youth leave him a spent force, diseased in body and mind. He is torn between death and instinctive love for life. But his sufferings are too acute to allow him to recover normalcy. Physical exhaustion, apathy, self-pity, and regret for his failures—all join hands to make his disillusionment complete.[20]

Nur lives without any interest in anything and waits for his death. Still he desires to live. But he sees no possibility of a happy expression of life. His love for life and his inability to live satisfactorily on account of some psychological depression caused by society make him a tragic figure.

With Prabu, the case is totally different. He gets all comforts in life and yet he is not happy. Nur thinks that it is society which causes his misery. But for Prabu, his unhappiness is the result of his interest in shallow things of life. The difference between Nur and Prabu is that the former has not lived happily while the latter has lived superficially. Prabu moves from a shallow state of happiness to deep frustration while Nur longs for happiness and moves to a state of depression. Prabu is the agent of his own misery; but for Nur, society is the agent of his agony and despair.

Nur thinks that the enemy of his peace is outside him while Prabu thinks that he is his own enemy. He realises that his deliberate abuse of wealth is the cause of his own undoing. His intense dissatisfaction with life is expressed in a moving way. Prabu tells Ganga who becomes the only source of consolation:

> Life has become a total bore. I think that it has come to an end. I feel that I would go mad. All these years I have lived for my own pleasure. That too has come to an end. Life has lost its charm. Everything now has turned to be a routine, a bore, a stagnation. . . .
>
> That is not the only thing. Ganga. To tell you the truth—If it is not for you, I would have committed suicide by now. Why should I live? I have lost my honour, and prestige. Who is here for me? You are a crack and hanging on to me. . . . I feel one should have a purpose in life, whether we achieve it or not. As a student I was a muff; as a businessman I am a flop: as a husband I am unworthy: as a father I am undeserving. (325-29)

Prabu is different from Nur, in the sense that he is able to identify the reasons for his own shameful degradation. He is aware of his own flaws. This is the context which prepares his way for a future reformation. For Prabu it becomes clear that his own unwise pattern of life does not sustain him in that mood of self-complacency and self-satisfaction.

There seems to be no hope for Nur's prolonged state of distress. He dies a tragic man with no sense of relief. But Prabu develops a mood of penitence at one stage to analyse his own state of mind and the reason for his failure. His self-critical spirit is what moves him to a close exploration of his own weakness and unsound pattern of life. With Nur, certain factors responsible for his degradation remain unchanged and fixed. For example, shallow education, economic distress and inhuman treatment of the society create the conditions for the suffering of Nur. According to the novelist, the misery of Nur is caused by the society. Unless these conditions change, there is no redemption for Nur. Till such change of social climate comes, Nur will be inevitably in the predicament of alienation. The condition of Nur is hopeless because the change has to come from outside. The thesis of Jayakanthan is different, as he believes that character is destiny. Prabu moves to a realisation of his own evil way of life as a cause for his alienated state of mind. The consciousness of his own guilt engenders in Prabu a new tendency which enables him to visualise the necessity for a remedy. Wealth, women and drinks have spoilt him. What was previously a thing of pleasure becomes a matter of pain now. He sees that he cannot continue the old pattern of life any longer. This feeling isolates him from others as he wants to be alone in that mood of penitence. This kind of longing for loneliness makes him an outsider in the society. He thinks that unless he becomes a stranger to the false way of life led by him, there is no redemption for him.

Nur, on the other hand, does not experience any feeling of remorse. For Prabu, there is a state of repentance. His desire is to move from falsehood to truth. He talks about his new vision of life in a strong manner:

> He of late feels that he should leave everything here and fly away to an unknown area. He tells her. "Ganga! I think I feel like leaving everything. I should go away from this life. There should be no communication. I should leave my car, money, liquor, women, wife, daughter, children and friends and settle at some unknown region where none should recognize me. There I must start a fresh life. I should earn my food by hard labour. Struggle there--roam about in streets. I should learn to live in hot sun and snow, to lie in dust and ground. There are people who have just a single clothing. I must mingle with them and become one among them, forgetting the past. . .. There is no meaning in anything. Let us live the life with detachment." (343-47)

Prabu sees the origin and history of his own life with the vision of a Christian apologist. He undergoes a revolution in his consciousness and realises that a moderate involvement in life would not have caused any disaster. Man learns through his own mistakes. His decision to bid farewell to society and the false way of life is an indication of his remorse. He almost becomes a sage when he says that life should be lived with detachment.

Prabu shows his preparedness for the acceptance of a new spiritual orientation which is conceived as the true remedy for his frustration and alienation. In the case of Nur, there is no possibility for such a spiritual transformation. Anand's belief in humanism does not put Nur in the spiritual stage for a change. The novelist's disbelief in God does not permit him to hope for a spiritual remedy. According to him, society is a monster and it has made characters like Nur wretched and less lovable. Balarama Gupta refers to the sceptical mind of Nur, "his education in modern science--Huxley and Darwin, in particular--has taught him that there is no God." (101)

Nur finds no point of integration for his faith in anything is sapped by the conditions of the corrupt society. His intellectual education thwarts his religious belief. Anand refers to this state of Nur, "Call the faithful to prayer, dog! I hate you all. To incur your wrath I spit in the face of your God." (27)

Anand concentrates his attention on the conditions of the society in which Nur is found. He never approves of modern education which produces the feeling of careerism and competition. Poverty is a social phenomenon which depresses the spirit of men. Nur's lack of affluence puts a discount on his life. He is like a caged bird caught in a hostile society and his free expression of anything is made impossible. Nur's enemy is his own society. No relief seems to be forthcoming for him as conditions remain unchanged. Nur is a tragic character in an existentialist dimension. Prabu is equally a tragic character because his new way of life involves estrangement from family, society and loss of Ganga in the river Ganges and his search for her, but the difference is that Prabu in the end is spiritually oriented. Nur lives unhappily with his consumption and only death brings final relief to him.

# NOTES

1. Mulk Raj Anand, *The Big Heart* (Bombay: Kutub-Popular, n.d.), p. 81.
2. Krishna Nandan Sinha, *Mulk Raj Anand* (New York: Twayne, 1972), p. 12.
3. M.K. Naik, *Mulk Raj Anand* (Delhi: Arnold-Heinemann India, 1973), p. 29.
4. Mulk Raj Anand, *Apology for Heroism* (New Delhi: Arnold-Heinemann, 1975), p. 1.
5. Saros Cowasjee, *So Many Freedo*ms, (Delhi: Oxford University Press, 1977), p. 51.
6. Mulk Raj Anand, *Untouchable* (New Delhi: Arnold Heinemann, 1981), p. 49.
7. Saros Cowasjee, p. 52.
8. Jayakanthan, *Jaya Jaya Sankara* (Madurai: Meenakshi Puthaka Nilayam, 1992), p. 34.
9. Saros Cowasjee, p. 129.
10. Mulk Raj Anand, *The Big Heart*, p. 154.
11. Gnani, *Markclyamum Tamail Ilakkiyamum* (Coimbatore: Parinamam, 1988), p. 154.
12. Jayakanthan, *Oru Manitan Oru Vitu Oru Ulakam*, (Madurai: Meenakshi Puthaka Nilayam, 1983), p. 11.
13. Veerasamy, Qtd. *Arivalagan, Jayakanthan Ayvatakal* (Cuddalore: Amaravathi Press, 1978), p. 253.
14. Krishna Nandan Sinha, p. 55.
15. Mulk Raj Anand, *Lament on the Death of a Master of Arts* (Delhi: Hind Pocket Books, 1967), p. 2.
16. Jayakanthan, *Cila Nērankalil Cila Manitarkal* (Madurai: Meenakshi Puthaka Nilayam, 1993), p. 141.
17. Krishna Nandan Sinha, p. 39.
18. G.S. Balarama Gupta, *Mulk Raj Anand: A Study of His Fiction in Humanist Perspective* (Bareilly: Prakash, 1974), p. 100.
19. *Ibid.*
20. *Ibid.*

# The Curse of Untouchability

> His Indian day is over and the next day will be like it but on the earth if not in the depths of the sky, a change is at hand.[1]

Anand and Jayakanthan handle the problem of untouchability from different angles in keeping with their preoccupations and dispositions. There are two novels in which Anand mainly deals with the question of untouchability and they are *Untouchable* and *The Road*. Like Anand, Jayakanthan has explored the question of untouchability in three novels which suggest remedies which are somewhat different in their methods and they are *Jaya Jaya Sankara, Piralayam* and *Munkil Kattu Nila* (Nila of the Forest of Bamboos).

The critical faith of Anand as an artist is drawn from the tenets of humanism. One of the basic doctrines of humanism is to give a second place to the role of religion as it always blocks the work of human progress. A society which is deeply sunk in religion becomes insensitive to human issues. This leads to stagnation of life and consequently a great evil comes into existence. Such a monstrous evil is the problem of untouchability. This is the stand of Anand. Jayakanthan's way of studying the Indian history and society and the place of Hindu religion in it is different from Anand's. His main mission is to study the Hindu religion as an integrated whole.

But he does not deny the fact that it is certain peculiar development in the Hindu religion which led to the conglomeration of caste. According to Jayakanthan, this kind of caste conservation occurred in the middle phase of the religion.

The Hindu religion in the course of its historical transition gave birth to the concept of Varnashram Dharma. It divides the human race into four forms: Brahmins—priests. Kshatriyas—Warriors, Vaishyas—merchants and Shudras—menial workers. Originally this concept was flexible and its principle was to represent human occupations quite in accordance with human disposition. Later on it became rigid and unfortunately the external form of the concept became more important than the inner spirit.

The middle phase of the Hindu religion led to a good deal of ossification. It is in this context of a peculiar historical movement of the religion that the four-fold classification generated watertight division. This concept of Varnashram Dharma was conceived as a kind of strategy to facilitate performance of work. This religious doctrine, instead of being a source of help, became a hindrance to human progress.

Moreover, in the course of the movement of the Hindu religion in its historical transition, a way of regarding ritualism as a genuine expression of religion came into vogue. But the original root of the Hindu religion is viewed as an expression of spiritualism. Anyway spiritualism and ritualism are regarded as complementary to each other. But the peculiar nature of the human mind disturbed the right relation between the two tenets and distorted their very function. When religion was projected more and more as a manifestation of ritualism, the notion of human purity acquired greater significance. The religious axiom went like this: the purer you are, the nearer to God you are. From this axiom it was conferred that human impurity blocks the way to God.

The intermediary phase of the Hindu religion has projected religion as ritualism and it has also led to the growth of the doctrine of human purity as the only avenue to gain entry into God's residence. This led to distinctions among human beings. All those people who were clean and those who were unclean were treated differently. A large group of people plunged in poverty and ignorance was placed in a degraded state. These people became the target of attack. They were treated by religious people as low and sub-human, as they contacted unclean habits and ate all kinds of animal flesh. The religious argument was that these people, who kept themselves away from good things by way of their habits, were kept away from the premises of the temples.

The shadow of these low persons should not fall on the high born people. Their sight and touch pollute the sacredness of things according to this doctrine of religious purity. They were kept away as outcasts in a separate colony far from the limits of the village or the city. Their predominant professions were disposal of sewage and dung, gutter and latrine cleaning. The peculiar nature of these jobs did not impart dignity to their life. They were scavengers cleaning dirt and so they were treated as dirt. They lived on the leftovers of the rich people. A dark gloom enveloped their lives and no one enjoyed the status of a human being. This is how Hinduism, which was essentially spiritual in its original form and ideal, has become ritualistic in its middle and later phase and as a result caste-consciousness has assumed an integral part of the Hindu society.

Anand's handling of the theme of untouchability can be traced back to his association with Mahatma Gandhi and his stay at Sabarmati Ashram. Saros Cowasjee provides the background for Anand's novel *Untouchable*: "In 1932, while perusing the pages of Gandhiji's magazine *Young India*, he was impressed by Gandhi's narrative about a sweeper called Uka, and decided to meet the Mahatma and to read him his novel."[2]

Anand's experience of being ill-treated by the Britishers in the ship on his return to India made him feel the problem of the untouchables much more keenly. With the help of Gandhi, Anand saw a new dimension to the problem. Like the Mahatma, Anand believes that untouchability is a hydra-headed monster[3] and it is the greatest blot on Hinduism. Marlene Fisher refers to the change in Anand: "The entire experience of Sabarmati Ashram changed Mulk and therefore changed his book."[4] Moreover the novel is based upon the memory of his childhood experience of the tenderness shown to him as a child by a sweeper boy.

The history of the Hindu religion, as already seen, bears a close reference to the concept of Varnashram Dharma. The nature of human psychology is revealed here. Men divide themselves into different groups in accordance with their inner dispositions which determine their outer vocation. The Brahmins, Kshatriyas, Vaishyas and Shudras are the four-fold classes and they are known as the priests, the warriors, the traders and the menial workers. Balarama Gupta analyses this problem very carefully: "The Hindu caste system intended originally, perhaps, as an organization to facilitate mutual cooperation among different sections of society—eventually degenerated and petrified into an utterly divisive force with destructive effects particularly on untouchables, people who are considered too low and dirty to merit subsumption under any of the four castes."[5]

These untouchables are outcasts whose family occupations constitute sweeping, scavenging and shoe-making. Their life, which involves disposal of sewage and cleaning of dirt, generates complexes in the high caste Hindus. Such people should not be touched but should be kept out in an outcast colony at a respectable distance. These untouchables do not enjoy the normal status of human beings, as they are treated as lepers to be shunned and hated.

The hero of the novel, *Untouchable*, is Bakha who is an eighteen-year-old lad doing the work of a latrine cleaner. His misery goes beyond all powers of description, as he happens to be an untouchable. Lakha, Bakha's father, is in search of a doctor and wants his dying son to be saved. No doctor comes and sees him because of his being an untouchable. He learns the bitter lesson that an untouchable has no place at all in the scheme of social life. Bakha passes through all possible types of frustration and despair. There are about four major incidents in which Bakha is put to shame.

Bakha stops at the shop of a betel-leaf seller, in order to buy a packet of 'Red Lamp' cigarettes. When he puts an anna on the board, the shopkeeper sprinkles water on the coin and throws it into the counter. Then he throws the packet of cigarettes at the untouchable "as a butcher might throw a bone to an insistent dog sniffing around the corner of his shop."[6] The sensitive Bakha realises his position and subsequent humiliation created by this episode. The coin of an untouchable can carry the seed of cancer disease; this seems to be the belief of the high-caste society. In the main street Bakha proceeds and he desires to purchase jilebis from a Bengali sweetmeat stall. There also, his coin is washed in water and the packet is simply thrown to him without any respect.

Bakha's over-enthusiasm in eating the jilebis makes him forget himself, and he in an unguarded moment hits against a Lalaji inadvertently. For an untouchable like Bakha to touch a Lalaji is a sign of deadly sin. All the holy waters of the river Ganges cannot purify this sin of pollution by touch. What is to be noticed is the reaction of the crowd. A group of caste-Hindus who gather there shower the most abusive epithets on him calling him a dirty dog and son of a bitch. Bakha realises his unintentional mistake and begs Lalaji's pardon. Lalaji gives him a slap on his cheek and disappears in the crowd. Bakha has a dual instinct to show in this incident. Had he wanted he could have easily thrashed him. But centuries of submission to the caste-Hindus paralyses his feelings. One may refer to the passage where Anand explains Bakha's hesitation which springs from a moral ground:

> But then he realized that he was surrounded by a barrier, not a physical barrier, because one push from his hefty shoulder would have been enough to unbalance the skeleton-like bodies of the Hindu merchants, but a moral one. (35)

Bakha reviews his own life and realises that a person who touches dung and cleans latrines has no right to touch others.

Another incident occurs in the temple where Pandit Kalinath tries to seduce Bakha's beautiful sister Sohni, after pretending to be considerate to her, by offering her water from the well. The priest cunningly averts the crisis by throwing the blame on her. Bakha wants to kill him when he knows the real story. Lakha appeases his anger by telling him, "No, no, my son, no," said Lakha, "We can't do that. They are our superiors. One word of theirs is sufficient against all that we might say before the police." (88) Bakha knows well that a low caste man can never have justice on his side. As Girija Priyadersini observes, high-class people have low class morality.[7]

When Bakha proceeds to Silversmith's lane to bring food, he is abused by a traditional woman who accuses him of having defiled her house by his contact. The greatest irony is that some chapatis are hurled down. They fall on the place where the old woman's son was relieving himself. Actually the place is defiled by her son relieving himself there and not by Bakha. In the hockey match, a small boy is injured. Bakha out of love and compassion carries the child to his house. This action of Bakha does not elicit appreciation from Babu's wife. She scolds Bakha for having touched and polluted her son. Bakha is insulted and sees his tragedy clearly. He can never enjoy the status of a human being so long as he is an untouchable and an outcast. He goes in search of some solution for eradicating untouchability. Here one may recall Lindsay's observation, Anand "has never lost his direct and concrete sense of the suffering and aspiring individual—the Indian individual who, fully realized, becomes of universal significance."[8]

Bakha's hope for a solution brings him face-to-face with three possibilities for change. The three alternatives he is confronted with are Christianity, Gandhism and modernization. He meets Colonel George Hutchinson who belongs to the Salvation army. He believes in conversion and Bakha is initially attracted towards him. The main reason is that in Bakha's scale of values, a White Sahib like the colonel is superior to a caste-Hindu. Hutchinson grows highly emotional and impresses upon Bakha the need for accepting Christ. When Bakha wants to know the merit of Christ, Hutchinson is not able to offer a satisfying explanation to him. His answer that Christ sacrificed and died for both the rich and the poor does not carry weight. Hutchinson's proselytizing zeal does not allow him to go to the core of Bakha's grief. As M.K. Naik says, "the colonel's proselytizing zeal and blundering humanitarianism only confuse and repel Bakha, who runs away from him."[9] Bakha's failure to understand the Holy Trinity and the concept of Original Sin throws light on his rejection of Christianity as a solution for the removal of untouchability. As R.T. Robertson observes, "the whole basis of Western culture is wholly rejected in Bakha's comic encounter with the Christian missionary, Mr. Hutchinson."[10]

Bakha's good fortune brings him into contact with the meeting of Mahatma Gandhi who spoke separately on the theme of untouchability. It is a source of big emotional consolation for Bakha to hear that the condemned people are conferred, by the Mahatma the highest title, 'Harijans'. He feels that it was a big revolution on the part of Gandhi to have called them the children of God. It came as a kind of relief for him to know that even Bakha was a Harijan, a child of God. Gandhi regarded untouchability as the greatest disgrace to Hinduism.

Gandhi laid emphasis upon the dignity of manual labour. He adopted two clear approaches for the purpose of eradicating untouchability. He himself undertook the work of sewage disposal. The notion that no one is superior or inferior by the nature of his work is inculcated in the minds of all people. The second line of the approach is brought out by him in a powerful way. "In order to emancipate themselves they should purify themselves. They have to rid themselves of evil habits like drinking liquor and carrion eating." (163) Gandhi's approach makes an appeal to Bakha and he becomes thoughtful about it. He was happy to see that Gandhi at least attempted to remove the age-old stigma attached to scavenging and dung and dirt cleaning. Moreover Gandhi struck at the false idea of the superiority of caste by advocating the dignity and sacredness of all work. No work is mean and so no worker is mean.

Bakha is pleased to listen to the voice of the poet Iqbal Singh Sarshar who advocates the installation of modern sanitary system as a way of removing untouchability. It is like returning to "the modified culture in which one is born—a purified Hinduism which can incorporate aspects of Western Culture, such as the flush system." The poet says,

> And they can do that soon, for the first thing we will do when we accept the machine will be to introduce the machine which clears dung without anyone having to handle it—the flush system. Then the sweepers can be free from the stigma of untouchability and assume the dignity of status that is their right as useful members of a casteless and classless society. (171)

Bakha feels that the poet is closer to the heart of the problem because dung-cleaning which brings indignity to the man is performed by a machine. The hero knows that Gandhi gave a new psychological and spiritual status to the untouchables by glorifying them as harijans. The poet's plea for modernization based on the water closet and flush system does not keep out the Gandhian remedy. As P.K. Rajan says, "What the poet envisages is modernization through industrialization within the framework of Gandhism."[12]

The problem of Bakha involves an essential question of recognition of his social status. This is what R.T. Robertson calls 'the central paradox of the novel'. Bakha is craving for an identity with his culture. But he "is both isolated from and bound to his culture: it will not allow him fully to participate in the society and it cannot release him from it because of the essential service he performs for it."[13] The infamy and dishonour associated with his dung-cleaning profession is no longer tolerable. He is least interested in conversion to Christianity, as it does not directly deal with his problem. But he saw in Mahatma a new dimension. The change of name from the untouchable to the Harijan is something that satisfies him as it confers dignity on him. The poet's suggestion of the flush system pleases him very much. Saros Cowasjee observes: "But the mention of a 'machine' which clears dung and which would enable a sweeper to change his profession so that he would no longer be thought of as an untouchable grips his attention." (59)

P.K. Rajan says that Anand displays the reformist fervour of a bourgeois humanist and he wonders whether externally introduced solutions can work a fundamental change. He rightly points out that the property relations are at the heart of caste discrimination. He further points out that the mere introduction of flush system does not change the caste-class structure. (22-23) But there is no doubt that the water closet does lessen the evil of untouchability in some way or other. It is an indispensable step in the reformer's scheme of mitigating the evil of untouchability. Julian Simons points out that it was Anand's firm belief that plumbing plus good will can destroy caste-distinctions. A close reading of *Untouchable* will make it clear that Anand's "commitment to the dehumanizing situation of the teeming millions of our country's poor is absolutely unmistakable."[15] His commitment is revealed in the form of "a message for his culture in *Untouchable*."[16] An internal change in the heart and an external change in the form of a machine will remove the evil of untouchability in slow degrees; this is the message Anand offers through his novel, *Untouchable*.

Jayakanthan suggests the framework of an imaginary story in *Jaya Jaya Sankara* in order to indicate his way of analyzing the problem of untouchability. There are two places, namely Sankarapuram and Moongilkudi which are associated with specific attitudes. Sankarapuram has Sankaralingeswarar Temple which indicates a place of religion while Moongilkudi shows the establishment of an ashram. The novelist brings these two places together in order to make an alliance between these two units. The temple represents devotion, piety and ritualism while the Ashram embodies the actual spiritual life, simplicity and a passion for ethical perfection. The fullness of life is perceived on the basis of a cooperation between the temple and Ashram in terms of their work and function. Mahalinga Iyer and Satasiva Iyer are two brothers, one reposing faith in tradition and orthodoxy and the other believing in revolutionary spiritual reforms. Mahalinga Iyer's attachment to the temple is so great that he does not appreciate his brother Satasiva Iyer's idea of the ashram and his belief in the Gandhian doctrine of removing untouchability. Mahalinga Iyer's lack of sympathy for his brother's spiritual ideal of an ashram indicates the crux of Jayakanthan's analysis of the history of the Hindu religion and its decline.

The existence of mere temple will breed bigotry and narrow-mindedness. The temple representing orthodoxy, devotionalism and ritualism will be balanced and liberalized only by the real establishment of an ashram. According to the novelist, the problem of untouchability is the result of a rift between the temple and the ashram. Mahalinga Iyer and Satasiva Iyer cannot come to a common compromise on the issue of untouchability. Mahalinga Iyer's traditional religion of devotionalism and ritualism is only one aspect of religion. His son Sankaran represents the other aspect of religion which is based on the free enquiry of the Gnana tradition. Satasiva Iyer goes one step beyond and he stands for vigorous revolutionary spiritual reform. There is no possibility for a compromise between Mahalinga Iyer and Satasiva Iyer as the notion of orthodoxy opposes liberal views which pave the way for reform. The author visualizes a new technique. Sankaran, the inhabitant of Sankarapuram, and Āti, the dweller of Moongilkudi, see each other face-to-face and they develop an abiding and ideal friendship. The loss of partnership between the temple and the ashram is what generates social evils like untouchability. The novelist's deliberate attempt at establishing the friendship between Sankaran and Āti is conceived as a worthwhile way of solving the problem of untouchability. If the pariah and the Brahmin behave properly, there is no necessity for any enmity between the two.

The slumdwellers of Moongilkudi will enter the temple of Sankaralingeswarar on the Maha Sivaratri Day according to Satasiva Iyer's plan. Mahalinga Iyer is mentally confused on hearing this plan and he wants to see the Jagad Guru to know what he should do and how he feels about the entry of the untouchables into the temple. Jagad Guru wants to appease him and so he says:

> The action of your brother will have their limits and nothing will happen to "Sanatana Dharma.". . . (do your duty devoting each and every action to Lord Eswaran). A yogi is one who should have the mentality of a child to laugh at the world and he should possess the mind of a lunatic who never cares for the society.[17]

The advice of Jagad Guru to Mahalinga Iyer is that he must remain indifferent to what happens around him. He must be untouched by the happenings at Sankarapuram. The truth of the matter is that Mahalinga Iyer does not want the untouchables to enter the temple. To remain indifferent to all the events of the world including the entry of the untouchables into the temple is suggested by Jagad Guru as a solution for Mahalinga Iyer's problem. This remedy does not face the problem; it sidetracks the crucial issue. When Jagad Guru says that nothing will happen to Sanatana Dharma, it means that the entry of the untouchables into the temple will not affect the purity of the religion.

Jayakanthan is not in agreement with the teachings of Jagad Guru for the simple reason that he represents the headship of an orthodox traditional mutt with no spiritual flexibility. The entry of Acharya Sankaran Swamikal makes the way for a new approach. The author indicates that the clue for the new attitude comes through the passage of time by referring to the many changes that have taken place at Sankarapuram. (56)

This shows that Acharya Sankara Swamikal who heads the mutt is liberal in his perspective and opens his eyes to the change of the times. His interpretation of the Vedic teaching is based on a new line. He says that the original spirit of the Vedas is to promote the real significance of life. All people must really understand life and follow truth. There is no reference to any section of people and no mention of caste is made. Acharya Sankara Swamikal, unlike Jagad

Guru, attaches himself firmly to the original teachings of the Vedas. The welfare of the whole world is what the Vedas want. This Vedic demand for the welfare of the whole world includes the well being of all people. Jayakanthan views that this mission of the Vedas deserves admiration and its lack of application in fulfillment of the ideal and mission is what vitiates the real truth of the Hindu religion. How does a religion, which places its belief in the welfare of all, come to degenerate engages the mind of the novelist in his investigation of the problem of untouchability.

Acharya Sankara Swamikal represents the true and the original spring of the Hindu religion, according to the novelist. A careful historical investigation of the Hindu religion reveals that caste conservatism is a later phenomenon. There is no point in clubbing caste conservation with the fresh spring of the Hindu religion. Such an identification of the one with the other is illogical. It is quite rewarding to examine the preaching of the Acharya when Krishnaswamy, his assistant is unwilling to bring Āti to his presence on the ground that the invitation is extended to a Harijan. The immediate reaction of Swamikal is highly rhetorical, "Swamikal taunts him by commenting that if Āti is a Harijan what about others? Are they Sivajans?" (76) If Āti is a Harijan, are others really men of God (Sivajans)? What Swamikal implies is that to a man of God, such a question is irrelevant. Krishnaswamy's description of Āti as a Harijan is only a pointer to the degraded condition of a person. His indirect indication of his low birth or caste irritates Swamikal. Therefore he starts exploring the reason for the misery and degeneration of the world. He thinks that men and the world have forgotten the ideals by which all people must live. The reason for the decline in the conduct of life lies in the deviation of men from their ideals.

The problem of a social evil like untouchability is the result of the failure of people to follow the true ideal of religion, according to Swamikal. Jayakanthan admits the fact that the true pursuit of the noble ideal of a religion will not land a person in making obnoxious reference to caste. The actual problem arises when the Brahminical religion of priesthood and ritualism is identified with the original spirit of the Hindu religion which includes spiritualism as its main mission and regards ceremonies only as means to an end. Acharya

Swamikal says very meaningfully, "I don't worry about abolishing castes. I am worried about the welfare of the world." (77)

His primary emphasis is laid upon people's welfare. The abolition of caste is no problem for him if all people follow the true ideal. Jayakanthan feels along with Swamikal that a religion which lays stress on the welfare of the world and all people could not have made references to caste. For him, the Vedic belief in the welfare of the world and references to caste are contradictions. Caste conversation lessens human dimensions. The Vedic ideal is to enlarge human dimensions of love and kindness. A deep understanding of the origin of the Hindu religion clears up this confusion.

Acharya Swamikal comes very hard upon the Brahmin community for having failed to live up to the expectations of the Vedic ideals. A Brahmin voluntarily suffers and he takes upon himself the sins of the world to ward off the very source of human corruption. The tone of righteous indignation of the Swamikal is seen in this passage:

> If we gradually lose these Vedic chantings and Vedic knowledge among this people we can never recreate this generation. All these untoward happenings and miseries are the result of Brahmins' negligence of the Vedas. If a man lives a life as depicted by the Vedas, then does it matter to which caste he belongs? (77)

The simple explanation of the Swamikal is that a Brahmin does not live for himself whereas he lives for others. To identify caste conservatism with brahminism is unwarranted. The function of a true Brahmin is to lead a life of renunciation and self-sacrifice. For him no one is born low and no one is born superior. His primary belief in the welfare of the entire world does not strictly permit him to make references to caste. But when the brahminical ideal of renunciation and self-sacrifice disappeared, all problems like untouchability reared their ugly heads.

Jayakanthan clearly points out that there was nothing wrong in the original scheme of the Hindu religion which could have generated a social evil called untouchability. Moreover it is evident from the passage quoted, when a man leads a life in accordance with the Vedic conviction, the question of his caste is highly immaterial. The choice is between a Brahmin who fails in his duty and a harijan who follows a noble path, and in such a case Sankara Swamikal says that the Vedic ethics will prefer a noble Harijan to a Brahmin who does not live upto anything that is worthwhile. If all the people, especially the Brahmins had followed all the ideals, many miseries could have been avoided. Jayakanthan as a shrewd sociologist points out, where there is a failure to follow the true ideal it has tremendous social repercussions.

Acharya Sankara Swamikal generates a new type of spiritual leadership. Jayakanthan believes that people of all castes and distinctions can be brought together more and more on the basis of such a dynamic and all-embracing spiritual leadership. Many evils like untouchability prevail due to lack of leadership and vision. Jayakanthan admits that the original nature of the Vedic ideal is to promote the uplift of all people including untouchables. Sankara Swamikal in his second round of preaching says that all the sins of the world are to be borne and endured by him. He realises that his spiritual responsibility is greater in guiding the conduct of the people. His spiritual leadership must have the capacity to remove the misconduct of all people or else his presence carries no meaning. There is a false opinion which prevails that Sankara Swamikal has greater affinity with the Brahmin community. He says that the Brahmins are charged with the heaviest responsibility in these words:

> For the Jagad Guru everyone is the same. Actually he is all the more dissatisfied with the Brahmins who have stopped chanting Vedas. Brahminism does not arise to chide others or to elevate the Brahmin community. . . . Brahmins should have a purpose in life. If they are not going to be fruitful to the society, what is their purpose in their existence? (93-94)

Jayakanthan examines in this passage the ideological base of the religion and the spiritual ethics of Brahminism.

In these two passages in which Sankaran Swamikal speaks and preaches, Jayakanthan provides a background for exploring the real cause for the prevalence of untouchability. The simple answer that he gives is that real religion is spiritualism and ritualism. It is only the wrongly oriented ritualistic religion which speaks of the purity and the impurity of things. In this context, an argument arose that the Brahmins are a divinely blessed race and all other castes are cursed ones as their food habits and incapacity to keep things clean show their Karma which keeps them in a low position. It is very clear that Sankara Swamikal's description of Brahminism is not in harmony with the ritualistic. oriented Brahmins. The Vedic religion believed in enlarging the human concerns but ritualism seems to be the narrowing of human interest. Jayakanthan says that a religion gathers many encrustations while it passes through the passage of the times.

Ati feels that their ancestors had lost in their battle against untouchability. Though this is not the ultimate end, how did this happen as a slip in the mid way?

N. Arumugam pays attention to this passage and admits that people could not abolish untouchability.[18] But this defeat is not ultimate. Therefore the phenomenon of untouchability came in a historical transition and the defeated attempt to eradicate it is equally representing an intermediary phase. Caste-conservatism is a period of transition. To estimate the Hindu religion in the light of this degenerated transitional phase is a wrong way of reading it.

M.K. Naik maintains the view that Anand's second novel on untouchability *The Road* written after Independence does not indicate a return to the sources of creativity. (35) What he implies is that the same theme handled by him in *Untouchable* is repeated in *The Road.* But a careful reading reveals that Anand has a specific preoccupation in *The Road.* His main mission as a social reformer is to lay emphasis upon mass action and collective transformation. Anand's *Untouchable* portrays the sufferings of a low caste person who is put to shame and humiliation in many situations on grounds of low birth. Anand suggests three possible remedies, Christianity, Gandhism and modernisation. In the novel, *The Road*, the novelist suggests a fourth remedy which he considers to be more worthwhile for removing untouchability.

Anand feels that the depressed class remains divided and they must organise themselves into a powerful group working towards a common programme of social action. The novelist thinks of a coordinated social programme involving work and activity. He projects a new ideal whereby people can work together for their emancipation from social stigma. The gospel of work seems to Anand a major source for liberating the depressed class from indignity and wretchedness:

> Strong and sincere but calm, he was spiritually too pure to hate and had learnt through long submission, to endure evil and violence from upper castes, without protest, only hoping that, through work and more work, he would be liberated, somehow, he did now know how.[19]

Bhikhu, the protagonist in *The Road*, feels that it is difficult to change the mentality of the caste-Hindus. He thinks of a mass scale of work which symbolizes concerted and organized action on the part of the depressed class. He feels that work is a means of deliverance and that cooperative enterprise provides a new dimension to an old problem. M.K. Naik is of the view that though the novel *The Road* was written twenty-six years after Anand wrote *Untouchable*, people's minds had not changed and the old caste taboos exercised their despotic authority and influence. (36) But Bhikhu possesses a formidable forward-looking disposition. He gathers his people and puts them on a new path. His plan is to build an approach road which will link the village with the town. "Thus, he is engaged in a meaningful social action."[20]

While Bhikhu is busily concerned with the construction of the road, he comes across two factors. The project of the common construction of the road is conceived by Bhiku. He and his people are enough to put forth the new ideal into actual practice. A powerful opposition is made from the platform of the higher castes. They have no objection to the construction of the road but their objection is that such a road should not be constructed by low born people. They will not join low caste people in constructing the road though they know that it will be equally useful to them. The high caste Hindus think that the construction of the road confers economic freedom on the depressed classes by bringing them better wages and substantial job opportunities. But the rapid social changes brought about by the new industrialization keep their evil thought under pressure.

It is wise to say that communities should not be condemned in a general manner and so individuals who harbour evil thoughts should be censured. All the caste-Hindus are not bad according to Anand. For instance, Havildar Charat Singh brings out this aspect clearly: "They have, however, a powerful ally in Dhooli Singh, who helps them continually, at the cost of alienation from his caste and even from his family."[21]

Dhooli Singh is projected as a great crusader for the cause of the depressed class. In the perspective of the novelist, both Bhikhu and Dhooli Singh are important and indispensable. What the novelist implies here is that the caste-Hindus and the depressed classes must come together and understand each other. The depressed classes cannot achieve what they want by remaining isolated. The caste-Hindus need their help and they should not look down upon the depressed classes on account of their low birth.

Anand believes that the coming together of Bhikhu and Dhooli Singh is an indication of the dream becoming a reality. What brings these two together is their philosophical belief in the concept of work.

Both Dhooli Singh and Bhikhu strongly believe in this precept and they also put it into practice. Unmindful of all threats and obstacles, they successfully build the road. Understandably Bhikhu loves to sing that song of Kabir, the weaver saint; "work, work devoted ones, for through work all sins are washed away, by the earth and sweat."[22]

Unmindful of all caste barriers, people must place their faith in work. A new social dynamism through work based on human cooperation is what Anand has in his vision. The depressed classes are caught in the cobweb of poverty and social degradation. They can secure social status and gain economic freedom only through the gospel of work. Anand is interested in a collective social action and he thinks that the salvation of human beings lies through work. It is in this respect that the novelist raises the question of the future of the depressed classes. He feels that their social life must be actively involved in an ongoing programme of work. The impact of industrialization is felt in the construction of work.

Thakur Singh, the landlord, devises a strategy to frustrate the plan and project of laying the road. He even tries to excommunicate Dhooli Singh with the help of the local priest, Pandit Suraj Mani. These conflicts affect the prospect of the proposed marriage between the children of Thakur Singh and Dhooli Singh. Pandit Suraj Mani and Thakur Singh invoke the theory of Karma to keep the people in a state of perennial subservience to them. Balarama Gupta rightly observes that caste and Karma are two weapons invented by mankind to keep the people in a state of perennial subservience. An important passage wherein the message of the novel is delivered may now be investigated:

> "Son, we are at fault," Lakshmi said, "Join hands to them. Don't fight. . . ." And she turned to the superior ones saying, "Have pity on Bhikhu. He is a hot-headed boy! And we will not get to the temple if you think he will pollute it."
>
> "Ma . . . what are you saying?" Bhikhu protested.
>
> "Son, we are Chamars," she tried to persuade him, "and they are twice-born."
>
> "One is a leather worker by profession and not by birth!" Bhikhu shouted. (6)

Lakshmi, Bhikhu's mother, submits a two-fold plea. She tells Bhikhu that he should be moderate and requests the caste-Hindus to be kind to her son. Lakshmi is a staunch believer in non-resistance. Later on also, in keeping with her belief, the burning of the huts of the poor people is looked upon by her as a divine punishment for her lapse in worshipping the goddess.

Anand thinks that the liberation of the depressed classes depends on their attitude to life. The salvation of the depressed classes is connected with their mental power to emancipate themselves from the cleverly advocated beliefs of Karma and fatalism by the caste-Hindus. If there is no critical growth of awareness in the depressed class, it will not pave way for their bright future. The passage in which Lakshmi refers to the superiority of the caste-Hindus shows that she is under the strong control of the age-old Hindu beliefs of Karma and predestination. She is too weak to resist this theory of human destiny and so she becomes an uncompromising rebel.

Lakshmi's devotion forces her to enter the temple and Sajnu's conservation based on his hatred towards the lowborn woman does not permit her entry. Sajnu is the son of Thakur Singh who is the "highest of the village by caste and rank and ownership of twenty acres of land" (2) His wealth and high caste status add arrogance to his words. Sajnu has no sign of good culture to appreciate her devotion to God and respect for religion.

Lakshmi represents the belief that every existing thing is an expression of God's will. She wants to work out a policy of compromise in saying that 'Chamars' (leather-workers) do not have the good destiny to enjoy while at the same time the high caste should be more considerate in their attitude towards them. She even retains the view that continuous good deeds will elevate the lowborn to the status of a higher caste. This echoes the words of Mahatma Gandhiji who said that the untouchables must give up their dirty habits and evolve themselves steadily into a new race of men of perfection. Although Lakshmi is a believer in Karma, she is dynamic enough to suggest a plan of reformation for the depressed classes. Her view that virtuous deeds can erase their low status (6) deserves notice in the way of removing the stigma of untouchability.

Bhikhu represents the humanist tenet of Anand. While Lakshmi believes in religion and God, her son Bhikhu dispenses with them. Karma and fatalism do not provide sufficient motivation for action. Bhikhu as a humanist relies on human effort and not on blind dependence on God. Lakshmi's entry into the temple is not very much relished by him. His question is why should a person keep entry into the temple as a great preoccupation in the scheme of life. One is here reminded of Āti who also holds a similar view and declines to join the harijans' movement of temple entry on the eve of Maha Sivaratri in *Jaya Jaya Sankara*. But unlike Āti, Bhikhu thinks that God has no relevance to human problems. When the caste-Hindus like Thakur Singh and Pandit Suraj Mani invoke the theory of Karma and fatalism, Bhikhu's policy is to remain indifferent to these questions and ignore them as having no value.

The greatest crisis in the life of Bhikhu arises when he visits the house of Thakur Singh at his instance. He announces his entry into the house with a word of request for water, "I am Bhikhu-harijan! I would like a drink of water." (94) Sajnu expresses his irritation with Rukmani's act of giving water in a brass vessel. A blatant indication of caste conservation comes out in Sajnu's fiery words, "Bhikhu Chamar! . . . How can you touch the brass cup and soil it forever! Have you no thought of your status?" (95)

Bhikhu is infuriated. He has the strength like Bakha to pulverize him. His realisation of his low status keeps him calm. The words of the novelist are significant, "But instantly he remembered he was a Chamar, untouchable and controlled himself." (95)

Bhikhu shrinks from any violent attack because he sees no hope of change in the mentality of the caste-Hindus. His act of self-restraint raises the question of the future prospects of the depressed classes. Bakha in *Untouchable* wanders in the plains hoping that a sea change is at hand. Bhikhu's act of control and self-restraint indirectly provoke the vital question, "When will the caste-Hindus change their hearts and stop being harsh and inhospitable?" Bhikhu's question is like asking when will the leopard shed its spots or is it possible to build the kingdom of God on earth? The novelist knows that only an answer in the form of speculation is possible.

Bhikhu moves on the road to Delhi where the question of caste and outcast never arises. His exit only shows his speculative wish for a perfect coming together of the caste-Hindus and the Harijans on a basis of mutual trust and understanding. He leaves the place in a state of frustration because his longing for a mutual cooperation between the two classes remains unrealized. The harsh attitude of the caste-Hindus puts him on the road for a departure from the village. This need not be construed as failing to face the issue or escaping from the problem. The immediately unrealisable nature of his idea of human cooperation unsettles his mind. Anand knows that six thousand years of caste-Hindu superiority cannot be wiped out in a day. It requires a long passage of time and transition and Bhikhu's departure looks for a time gap for the needed change in the minds of all people. The title of the novel, *The Road*, therefore becomes a symbol. One may refer to the brilliant interpretation of the symbol by K.N. Sinha: "It is evident that Bhikhu works out his own salvation with diligence. The road thus stands for the way out of hell one has built for himself. Bhikhu visualizes a heaven which may not yet be attainable, for custom, superstition, and habit hang like a dead weight, clouding one's vision. The golden dream of a classless society may remain in the realm of possibility." (75)

A close reading of *The Road* along with Anand's disposition will yield the following interpretations of the symbol, the road:

1. The road is a symbolic protest against the concepts of Karma and fatalism.
2. The road initiates men's faith in the glory and efficacy of human effort.
3. The road is symbolic of the use of machine which lessens the drudgery of Harijans.
4. The Buddhist notion of salvation through ethical perfection with the help of work is symbolized by the road.
5. The road implies the Buddhist canon that purity of good deeds presupposes the purity of good thoughts.
6. The road represents a period of transition where the old order of the Hindu beliefs in untouchability will change yielding place to a new vision of human unity and cooperation.
7. The road looks to the time-gap needed for the change in human mind for the vision of the coming together of the Harijans and the caste-Hindus.
8. The road shows the place of leaving but the proposed place of arrival is yet to appear in sight. The impossible must become possible.
9. The road is a journey to the unknown place. It is striving towards an ideal which is yet to become attainable.
10. The road is symbolic of a speculative state to wish for the disappearance of custom, habit and superstition.
11. The road symbolizes the golden dream of unity between the harijans and the caste-Hindus which will become a reality one day.

Jayakanthan's *Piralayam* gets its inspiration from the book *The Pariah* written by Alcot who is a renowned theosophist deeply interested in removing the evil of untouchability.[3] He ran a school in his name for the purpose of helping the downtrodden destitute children. The hero of *Piralayam*, Ammasi Kilavan, was sold to a farmer when he was young for an amount of three and a quarter rupees. The life of the slumdwellers below the bottom of a bridge amidst dirt, waste and gutter water engages the mind of the novelist. Their life has no charm because poverty and utter lack of education has kept them in a state of ignorance and degradation.

The main flow of the story is concerned with the marriage that Ammasi Kilavan performs between his foster-daughter Pappatti and Thenan, a private rickshaw driver in the house of Alagappar. Pappatti belongs to a high caste and Thenan is a low caste Harijan. The hero reflects over the nature of the marriage and its future prospects. Ammasi Kilavan remains unmarried because he thought that in the event of his marriage, children born of him would bear the mark of low caste indignity. The emancipation of his people from their low caste status is what occupies his mind. The novelist describes a particular trait in him: "Although Ammasi Kilavan was born in the most undeveloped, ignorant community, he behaved like a man of justice and discrimination on all occasions in his life." (13) Among the slumdwellers, he is unique and distinguished by his power of intelligence and his capacity for judgement.

Jayakanthan describes Ammasi Kilavan as an ideal Harijan. Like Āti he is a man who has realized his own dignity and respect. Moreover he is a formidable and unyielding type of man. He has got the capacity to discuss the two sides of the issue and arrive at a conclusion. The novelist feels that if the Harijans depend on external agencies alone for their uplift, it will not bring complete freedom to them. He is of the view that a Harijan at the level of mind and soul is free. Ammasi Kilavan has resisted the dirty habits of the Harijans by leading a soul-fulfilling life. In *Jaya Jaya Śankara*, Āti is a vegetarian. Jayakanthan thinks like Mahatma Gandhi that Harijans have to give up dirty habits, cleanse themselves in order to become fit for noble living. The hero according to the novelist is not an ordinary man: "He has always developed the habit of discussing the pros and cons of the issue in all matters. He does not hesitate to challenge anyone for the sake of a true Idea or true feeling." (14)

Ammasi Kilavan is carefully examining his idea of conducting a marriage between a high caste woman and a low caste man. The novelist says that the hero who could not lift any of his people perhaps invented a short route for fulfilling his ideal of establishing a marriage between a high caste woman and a low caste man. He thinks of the propriety of this marriage. At least he has the satisfaction of doing it as a sign of new revolution.

Ammasi Kilavan believes that human life and especially marriage should be beyond caste considerations. The novelist shows the mind of the hero: "He was troubled and confused as to whether it was an act of discrimination or a mark of justice when he brought about a marriage between a high caste woman and a low caste man. He who never believes in caste-divisions felt ashamed of having experienced this quiet consciousness." (15-16)

Jayakanthan says that discrimination in terms of caste is an unhealthy state and that the character of human nature is to long for fulfillment. Therefore caste is an external factor and it has no relation to the nature of human warmth and fulfillment. Ammasi Kilavan's attitude to the marriage he conducts reflects the hope of the novelist. An inter-caste marriage shows that there is no caste and its purpose is to go beyond it. The novelist brings out the feeling of the hero, "This marriage proves that caste rules and divisions are false and that they have no foundation in nature." (16) To judge human beings on the basis of caste is an unnatural way of looking at life. It will be a sign of psychological depression if the low caste people think low of themselves. This is one reason why the novelist represents Ammasi Kilavan and Āti as thoughtful human beings. They are men of courage possessing immense capacity for self-determination. All slumdwellers have developed peculiar habits and Ammasi Kilavan feels pained to see that these people are in an irredeemable state. There is neither self-knowledge in them nor do the external agencies really help them.

Jayakanthan is also concerned with the peculiar sexual behaviour of the slumdwellers. It is worthwhile to look at the three pairs of people engaged in promiscuous sexual relation. Pappatti-Selvam-Thenan; Kokila-Manickam-Pachiammal; Chinnan-Rangamma-Muthu. In addition to these people Thaili and Chinnaponnu are openly leading the life of prostitutes. Ammasi Kilavan's reflections on these people are very useful. He does not know anything about Pappatti's previous relation with Selvam and their plan. Kokila, his sister's daughter, is abandoned by Manickam who keeps Pachiammal. Ammasi Kilavan thinks that Pachiammal is a noble woman as he takes care of Kokila, the blind woman, and gives food to her. He does not discover any oddness in Pachiammal even though she is not the true wife of Manickam. He consoles Chinnan because he is fooled and betrayed by Rangamma who lives boldly with Muthu.

Jayakanthan knows that there is no law which can bind them into a state of harmony. But these slumdwellers are people who live at the level of feelings. But the hero has a law to judge them and it is in this spirit that he rejects Thaili and Chinnaponnu and does not approve of their life as prostitutes. Ammasi Kilavan is very flexible where he thinks that life requires him to be so. Jayakanthan looks for men like Ammasi Kilavan and Āti to appear on the scene and guide the destiny of low caste people.

Jayakanthan portrays in *Piralayam* a hellish rain which disturbs the normal life of slumdwellers as water gets heavily collected in the bottom of the bridge. Many people who are not really interested in raising their life-status come out in the open to help these people under the garb of philanthropy and public welfare for the purpose of their name and self-advertisement. Jayakanthan as a very keen sociologist observes that it is these rich people who pushed them to this state. The following passage makes this point clear: "The slum which has been isolated and pushed to this state by the cruel hands of the society which has grown, now finds it difficult to tackle this fury and onslaught of nature." (44)

The slum is found in a wretched state and the reason for this condition lies in the cruel hands of society. Jayakanthan strikes here a Marxian note. The society which grows historically with the ownership of wealth and capital tends to exploit the poor people and keeps them in a slavish state forever. The novelist says that those slumdwellers lie like worms in the sands. They have lost their capacity to raise their life to a higher state by their individual endeavour. A cruel society is responsible for their degeneration. They do not possess the mental power to take the right initiative to improve their state. Jayakanthan suggests a two-fold solution. These Harijans must awaken themselves and society must change its policy and help them.

Ammasi Kilavan witnesses many rich men who come and distribute food packets. For the hero, people eating food in a frenzied manner look like a lion making a meal of its prey. He says that hunger has made them less human and robbed their soul. The novelist describes aptly, "These people struggle like men in the desert everyday hoping to get something. The soul of a man can be easily purchased for a handful of rice." (65) Ammasi Kilavan is worried about this state of people who have lost their self-respect and dignity in the face of starvation and hunger. Unless these people cautiously examine their life and the reason for their wretched state, there is no hope for a new life. Therefore the hero thinks that ignorance can be removed only by knowledge.

The removal of ignorance through knowledge indicates an internal condition of an alert mind. The slumdwellers must not be satisfied with piecemeal remedies. No one seems to think of a total change of their life-status. They help them and appease their hunger temporarily without bothering to alter their degraded life. The slumdwellers were taken from the bridge and temporarily accommodated in school premises. Jayakanthan makes a powerful observation: "This incident is a good example to prove that mere change of place will not generate a sea change so long as the general character of society and the individual disposition of people do not change." (67)

A real change involves a different way of looking at the life of the slumdwellers. Ammasi Kilavan is more concerned with the tendencies and attitudes of the slumdwellers who have forgotten their belief in hard work. To earn one's livelihood by one's labour and not to depend on philanthropy for appeasing hunger is what endears him. He speaks of his philosophy of work in an ethical way: "What does it matter if a person is a rich man or a poor man; he who gets slogged in sloth and he who never labours is a sinner; he is his own enemy." (69) He feels that they should actively develop belief in hard work. To live at the mercy of rich people is a sign of failure to improve themselves. There is no salvation for them without a revolutionary change appearing in their mind and attitude. Manickam simply admires the philanthropy of rich men without having the knowledge to know and distinguish true charity from the false one.

Jayakanthan's portrait of Ammasi Kilavan is the picture of an ideal Harijan who has a greater exposure to life. One gathers a very important clue from him in regard to the question of the life of the untouchables. To depend on an external agency for their uplift is a sure sign of falling into a pit. Real freedom comes to them from a realization of what they are and how they must improve themselves. It is this internal awakening which can make them independent and search for a remedy. The average nature of the slumdweller is bad as he is lazy and satisfied with what he gets from outside. As long as he remains like a dependent creature his slum life will be a permanent feature. He must take a decision to be an independent creature and he must have a strong determination to cast himself into the mould of a new man.

The slumdwellers face a wretched situation according to Ammasi Kilavan's estimate: "If they get the house, they don't get food; if they get food they don't get the house. It is done out of pity. Why should there be pity for us? It makes us permanent beggars. He shouted, "hereafter let us starve with honour and dignity." (91) The hero says that those who are responsible for their low state must raise themselves by their constant efforts with knowledge. He believes that laziness and self-complacency are their enemies which perpetuate their low life. Instead of receiving food from others, if they starve, It will open a way for their new life according to him. Jayakanthan advocates through the hero that these people must develop their Inner resources to shape their destiny. Until they realize that they are their own helpers, there is no relief from low life.

Jayakanthan's *Munkil Kattu* Nila is concerned with a conflict between the landlord and slumdwellers. The protagonist develops deep emotional affinity with Nila, a beautiful pariah girl from the slum. She has four brothers of which two died prematurely. The eldest brother called Periavar is a man of evil design. The youngest brother is a man who wants to lead a life of inwardness. He is not interested in worldly things and so often visits his residence in Munkil Kattu. Nila's father could not pay off his debts to Marudhaiyan and so she was offered as a compensation for the loan. The marriage between a ten-year-old girl and a fifty-year-old man is odd. She later serves as a teacher in a primary school and the hero's mission is to educate a pariah girl. The novelist says about her, "By birth she is an intelligent girl and her face has been ever bright in her intellectual warmth."[24]

Nila has the spirit of a social worker and her only intention is to be of some service to the people, "Sometimes she grumbles over the people's sufferings—existing for years in the village and also in general matters. . . . She keeps herself like fire." (19) She and her friends and co-teachers move towards the formation of a new social order. The spirit to fight against injustice is evident in her.

Nila holds party membership for the purpose of deepening her action. Two prominent incidents take place which bring Nila to limelight. The School Management Board terminates her service. The poor people undergo immense suffering at the hands of the rich people, Periavar and his family. The plan of Periavar is to build a cement factory by annexing the lands of the slumdwellers. Their lands lie adjacent to the water canal. His attempt at confiscation of lands with the help of ministers in the name of scientific progress and the scheme to build the cement factory and thereby divert the flow of water canal and deprive the slumdwellers of the benefit of water supply prove to be a source of irritation for Nila.

Jayakanthan points out here that the high caste man like Periavar has no regard for the welfare of the poor people who are looked upon by him as contemptible creatures. Nila gathers the people and puts them on a warpath. Periavar is agitated and reacts angrily by showing his contempt for Nila, "His brother is shouting whether a pariah girl could stop the multi-crore project of the government." (22) But Nila speaks to the people explaining the bad intention of Periavar. Slowly the diversion of the water canal creates a strong resistance movement headed by Nila. The hero, the younger brother pleads with him to give up his idea of the diversion of the water canal and he also indicates the possibility of getting water from the river.

The argument of the younger brother is rejected as his proposal involves exorbitant expenditure. Moreover Periavar comes to know of his younger brother's link with Nila. So he takes stern steps, shuts him in a room and treats him as a mad man with the help of a doctor. The ensuing election prevents Periavar from carrying out his proposal. Meanwhile the death of Marudhaiyan creates a ground for the hero to receive the hand of Nila. But her attitude is different. She tells him that a realistic appraisal of the situation reveals that their marriage will entail death and tragedy. The hero makes an appeal to her, "Why not leave this place and live elsewhere as man and wife?" (43)

She points out the existing caste-fanaticism as an important impediment to their proposal. Moreover she is wedded to a particular ideology and a strong radical movement. Nila is a bold girl who does not even bother about caste-fanaticism. Her interest in social service and commitment to a particular movement for this purpose give no room for her private pleasures. The option of the high caste man for a low woman speaks well of his noble stature. But it is the pariah girl who rejects the option because she has a different kind of mission in her life. At the same time, her attitude to life is revolutionary. She says that there is no necessity for marriage, "Do they need such a social recognition for their friendship? . . . They spend their night in the hut sharing their bed." (62-63)

Nila's ideology involves the attitude of anti-establishment and in her scheme of life social recognition carries least weight. Marriage involves the performance of external ceremony for the purpose of social recognition. But for Nila the inner spirit of harmony and oneness is more important than external ceremony. Soon a crisis arises and the reason lies in the renewed attempt on the part of Periavar to fulfil his plan. There is a quarrel and a conflict between the outside labourers and the slumdwellers. Nila inspires courage and idealism in her people and she leads the group. She knows from her party ideology that it is difficult to resist the treachery of the rich people without organized opposition. She kindles enthusiasm in women for the purpose of making a march and forming a strong protest procession. The police take charge of the scene and they resort to shooting. Nila is one among the three who die. The death of Nila is a loss for the hero. The novelist says that she has won the battle, "She has faced her death in a noble struggle. If at all he should cry, he has to cry for his useless, fruitless life." (73)

Nila's life is filled with a purpose and mission. Her struggle, protest and the spirit of defiance are more important than her death. Jayakanthan proves that a pariah woman can also have the courage, intelligence and the other necessary resources for unifying her people and putting them on the path of rebellion for the purpose of securing social justice. It is not wise to sit with heads bent and legs crossed. One must rise like a whirlwind and act in order to shape a new destiny and future. This is the philosophy of a pariah woman like Nila which is visualized by Jayakanthan in an artistic way.

From the discussion it would be seen that Anand's *Untouchable* and *The Road*, survey the scenes of the social life of this depressed class. The dog and the donkey are respected because these animals are allowed to wander freely. But these untouchables are isolated from decent human habitation. The hero of *Untouchable*, Bakha is treated as a sub-human creature. He accidentally touches a high-caste man and he is thought to be polluted and Bakha receives a slap. Pandit Kalinath attempts to molest Bakha's sister Sohni in the temple but his high caste status saves him from ignominy. Bakha on seeing an injured boy during the hockey match carries him home, only to be hounded out of the house on grounds of his low caste status. Anand leaves Bakha on the plains and Bakha comes across three possible solutions for the removal of the evil of untouchability. While coming down heavily on the Hindu religion, Saros Cowasjee says: "orthodox Hindus who worship a stinking bull but will not touch a human being; Hindu temples whose doors are closed to those who keep its grounds clean." (55)

It is true that untouchability as an evil was generated by the Hindu religion which looked upon human purity as a mark of sacredness at one stage of its evolution. So Anand is of the view that change of religion is no solution at all. The Gandhian method of glorifying untouchables as Harijans is a humanly acceptable solution as it brings dignity and respect to them. The introduction of flush system and water closet appears much more acceptable because their scavenging life of latrine cleaning is replaced by the machine. Their so-called indignity is derived from their wretched occupation and the job is no longer done by them. It is done by the machine. The concept of industrialization involving machine humanizes untouchables, according to Anand.

*The Road* suggests a different type of remedy for the removal of untouchability. Bhikhu, the hero of this novel, wants to work out his salvation with the concept of work and diligence. Anand's belief in the gospel of work acts as a source and channel of liberation of these people from their wretchedness. Work is conceived as a creative activity and it arouses human energy and releases it in expressing and determining man's being and existence. The construction of an approach road creates transport facility and it also expands business possibilities.

Anand's insight in *The Road* is that it is lack of economic freedom which keeps these people in a permanent state of degradation and the laying of the road will bring economic freedom to them. The laying of the road is opposed by Thakur Singh, the high caste landlord, not only because untouchables are involved in the work but also because it pains him to see the slow and gradual process of the people gaining economic freedom by earning good wages. The doctrine of collective action and human cooperation is suggested as another solution. The cooperation between Bhikhu and Dhooli Singh, a caste Hindu is symbolic of the future unity of these people. The concept of organized work in a spirit of unity and on the basis of human cooperation is what solves the problem. Bhikhu's frustration with Sajnu puts him on the road and his journey is a striving towards the attainment of the future ideal of unity between caste-Hindus and untouchables. One may find that Anand's solutions for the removal of untouchability act as external agencies in removing this evil. There is no reference to the development in the inner consciousness of all people.

While Anand argues that untouchability is a phenomenon which arises from the cunning exploitation of the Hindu religion, Jayakanthan attempts at explaining the real position of the Hindu religion in his novel, *Jaya Jaya Sankara.* When the temple entry of slumdwellers of Moongilkudi into Lingeswarar premises is represented to the first Jagad Guru, he says that Sanatana Dharma will survive the onslaught of anything and the best way is to remain indifferent to it. It is not a very straight answer to the question. Jayakanthan takes this advice of Jagad Guru as an expression of the response of the Hindu religion in the middle phase. After some years when some changes have taken place, he shows the coming of Acharya Sankara Swamigal. A perfect friendship exists between the pariah Āti and the Brahmin Sankaran. What is important for observation is that in the ancient times there was no conflict between the pariah and the Brahmin. All quarrels and conflicts are later degenerations.

Sankara Swamikal says that he is not interested in abolishing caste. He is only interested in the welfare of the entire world. Jayakanthan points out that the original teaching of the Hindu religion lies in paying attention to the welfare of the whole world, and in this process no section of the society is kept out. When any mention of the evil of untouchability is made, Swamikal speaks of restoring human dimension of life and indirectly points out that aspect as something which will lessen the evil effect of untouchability. So Jayakanthan represents the original truth of the Hindu religion and he looks upon the evil of untouchability as a wrong interpretation of life which is generated in the middle phase. To distinguish the right state of the Hindu religion from its wrong state seems to be the major preoccupation of the novelist.

There are two ways in which Jayakanthan differs from Anand in his handling of the theme of untouchability. He looks upon caste and its growth as a peculiar historical development in the evolution of the Hindu religion. Therefore he pleads for a right understanding of the Hindu religion. Moreover Anand places his emphasis upon external agencies and solution for the removal of untouchability. For example, conversion to Christianity, endorsement of Gandhism and adoption of machine are only externally induced measures. Jayakanthan suggests different lines. When the temple entry of the Harijans is contemplated, Āti withdraws from such a scheme.

Jayakanthan explains through Āti that a Harijan must be a self-realized individual with courage and power of determination. Moreover Āti never feels that he is an untouchable in spirit and even when others regard him so, he does not care about it. In Anand's *Untouchable*, for example, Bakha is very much influenced and affected by the external atmosphere of the society. But in Jayakanthan's *Jaya Jaya Sankara*, Āti resists the psychological currents of the high caste men and he never gives up his self-respect and dignity. When he shows Āti as a vegetarian, it means that Harijans must purify their food habits. Apart from external agencies, there is a profound necessity for inner change, according to Jayakanthan and it indicates as an imperative on the part of the Harijans that they must realize their imperfections and reform themselves through high intellectual education and spiritual development and transformation.

Jayakanthan maintains the view that great leaders and thinkers can emerge from untouchables, provided they know how to make use of their precious energies and shape them in accordance with the demands of the external environment. Ammasi Kilavan in *Piralayam* is a man of wide experience and mature judgement. When his people beg for food and base their life on the philanthropy of rich man, he rebukes them. His high ideal is that man must work and earn his livelihood. He says that the degraded condition of the untouchable is of his own making.

Unlike Jayakanthan, Anand is of the view that the Hindu religion is responsible for his wretchedness. To some extent the Hindu religion with its emphasis upon purity and ritualism created the background for isolating the untouchables. But at the same time it must be accepted that they are equally responsible for their low state. To look into the external agencies alone for their freedom is to enslave them further. They must make a thorough analysis of their own life. It is not only religion which pulls them down. They have created their own vicious life circle. Gandhi's appeal to change their habits is a way which makes their life worthy.

Jayakanthan therefore shows Ammasi Kilavan as a man of independent judgement and he portrays Nila as a revolutionary leader. Jayakanthan in his vision of their life imagines an ideal situation in which Nila, the pariah woman, has the courage and intellectual brilliance to resist and challenge the false supremacy of the rich people. A life in which one perishes in the struggle is preferable to a life of begging, sloth and degradation. Unless there is a substantial awakening in them, more external solutions are only halfway-house remedies.

Along with Āti, Ammasi Kilavan and Nila, who belong to the community of untouchables, are persons endowed with determination of mind. While Bakha feels hurt by the ill treatment of the caste-Hindus, Āti and other protagonists remain unaffected by such psychological sentiments. Āti is a man of learning and Ammasi Kilavan happens to be a man of wide experience with his passion for original thinking. Bakha is not able to attack Kalinath but Nila is able to challenge and resist the evil plan of Periavar. Jayakanthan shows these three characters as great revolutionaries whereas Bakha and Bhikhu are shown as affected victims of caste tyranny.

Ati objects to the plan of the temple entry of the slumdwellers on the ground that God is everywhere. His originality of thinking and his capacity to retain his individual power in reviewing anything critically differentiate him from Bakha. Ammasi Kilavan comes severely upon his men for their failure to develop their life. He is capable of going beyond the surface reality. It is this extraordinary power of critical perception which enables him to interpret philanthropy as the craving of the rich people for their popularity and self-advertisement.[60] His narration of the story of the Mongoose and Dharmaputra in *Piralayam* is an example of his insight into the true meaning of Dharma. Nila is a character of tremendous mental power. She is a party member capable of breaking away from the normal character-traits of the untouchables. Jayakanthan feels that the uplift of the untouchables depends on how he develops his capacity to think. He says that individual self-awakening is important in the solution of the untouchables's problems. Without the critical process of individual self-awakening, no amount of external help is of any use. Āti, Ammasi Kilavan and Nila fulfil this ideal demand of Jayakanthan. Anand is interested in the initial problem and in an immediate solution while Jayakanthan takes into account the ultimate solution for an ultimate issue. So Anand and Jayakanthan reach the heart of the problem of untouchability by different means. All their methods of approach are equally important. Their difference in the treatment of the evil of untouchability is equally interesting. Their solutions have different backgrounds which need to be respected.

## NOTES

1. E.M. Forster, Preface to *Untouchable* (New Delhi: Arnold-Heinemann, 1984), p. 10.

2. Saros Cowasjee, *So Many Freedoms* (Delhi: Oxford University Press, 1977), p. 42.
3. Girija Priyadersini, *The Novels of Mulk Raj Anand and Thakazhi Sivasankara Pillai: A Thematic Study*, Doctoral Thesis, Madurai Kamaraj University, 1990, p. 28.
4. Marlene Fisher, *The Wisdom of the Heart: A Study of the Works of Mulk Raj Anand* (New Delhi: Sterling, 1985), p. 25.
5. G.S. Balarama Gupta, *Mulk Raj Anand: A Study of His Fiction in Humanistic Perspective* (Bareilly: Prakash) p. 25.
6. Mulk Raj Anand, *Untouchable* (Delhi: Orient Paperback, 1970). p. 46.
7. Girija Priyadersini, p .34.
8. Jack Lindsay, "Mulk Raj Anand," *Kakatiya Journal of English Studies*, Mulk Raj Anand Special Number, 2, No.1 (Spring 1977), p. 4.
9. M.K. Naik, *Mulk Raj Anand* (Delhi: Arnold-Heinemann India; 1973), p. 34.
10. R.T. Robertson, "*Untouchable* as an Archetypal Novel," *Kakatiya Journal of English Studies*, p. 13.
11. *Ibid.*, p. 13.
12. P.K. Rajan, *Studies in Mulk Raj Anand* (New Delhi: Abhinav, 1986), p. 21.
13. R.T. Robertson, p. 9.
14. Qtd. Saros Cowasjee, p. 56.
15. Leo Tagore, "Social Justice in Anand's *Coolie* and Achebe's *Things Fall Apart*," *The Novels of Mulk Raj Anand*, ed. R.K. Dhawan (Delhi: Prestige, 1992), p. 95.
16. R.T. Robertson, p. 10.
17. Jayakanthan, *Jaya Jaya Sankara* (Madurai: Meenakshi Nilayam, 1992), pp. 52-53.
18. Qtd. N. Arivalakari, *Jayakanthan Ayvatankal* (Cuddalore: Amaravathy Press, 1978), p. 293.
19. Mulk Raj Anand, *The Road* (New Delhi: Sterling, 1987), p. 45.
20. Krishna Nandan Sinha, *Mulk Raj Anand* (New York: Twayne, 1972), p. 73.
21. *Ibid.*, p. 74.
22. G.S. Balarama Gupta, p. 34.
23. Jayakanthan, *Piralayam* (Madurai: Meenakshi Puthaka Nilayam, 1985), p. 7.
24. Jayakanthan, *Munkil Kattu Nila* (Madurai: Meenakshi Puthaka Nilayam, 1986), p. 16.

# The New Woman

> Rama and Sita are the ideals of the Indian nation. All children, especially girls worship Sita. The height of a woman's ambition is to be like Sita, the pure, the devoted, the all suffering.[1]

Emancipation of woman is one of the central issues raised by Anand and Jayakanthan in their novels. It is the tragic plight of women which has induced them to reflect on their state and project a new path for them. Anand lays the blame on the Hindu religion for the degenerate state of women. It is the law of Manu which has given a wrong handle to men to exploit women and ill-treat them. Manu's law is made in the interest of social cohesion and its main motive is to safeguard the institution of marriage.

Man has the right to do anything and woman has the only choice to bear it. This in essence is the recommendation of Manu. The idea of woman's obedience to man arises out of the necessity for respect for family and society. This is an extreme law which needs to be adopted as an inevitable necessity in the interest of family harmony. But there are other laws also which describe man as the most responsible person for the well-being of woman. A man whose real intention is bad can quote the extreme law of Manu in his favour for leading a wretched life and forcing his woman to bear with it. This is only a perverted use of the law and man is responsible for what he is. Man is supposed to be a saviour of woman according to another law, but it is not quoted as it fixes man's responsibility.

Anand is concerned with the degenerate state of the Hindu religion and he is right in his perspective as it has determined the general atmosphere of the society. No religion has ever advocated women as slaves to men. The suggestion of the subordinate status of woman to man is made only for the purpose of endowing him with higher responsibility of saving her. The right way of understanding the religious text is what is important. The Biblical description, "He for God only, she for God in him"[2] actually takes care of the superior role and duty of man. The saying that woman is a part of man does not mean that woman is a slave. It refers to the togetherness of man and woman and their oneness is what is important in the saying. But the changing conditions of the world have given a twist to these texts and sayings.

Naturally Anand sees that the general trend of society is soaked in a degenerate form of religion. His plea for humanism, which considers the emancipation of woman as its integral part, is only a way of replacing the corrupt religion. Jayakanthan in his *Suntara Kāntam* has given a clue for the emancipation of woman. (3) All concepts must become facts. The reality is that men are terrible representatives of evils and so they are Ravanas. The birth of Rama in man is the solution for the real freedom of woman. One cannot chase Ravana out but one must subdue Ravana and make him a Rama. He seems to be of the view that women leaving the husband, seeking divorce and opting for remarriage, are only palliatives and they are not real solutions. So long as man does not reform himself, woman's independence is false and fruitless. This is due to the fact that as man cannot live without woman, woman also cannot live without man. Man must mend his ways and woman must become alert. So the reciprocal harmony between man and woman is what appears to give liberation to woman in the real sense.

Anand presents Maya as a revolutionary woman in *The Village* trilogy. She is the daughter of a rich landlord and her life is bound by many restrictions: "A couple of stalwart servants, guard the gate like 'watchdogs' and she is always chaperoned by her mother."[3] The courage of Maya lies in her capacity to cross the traditional boundaries like wealth and class status and embrace the love of Lal Singh. She knows that her relation with Lal Singh is a source of mental discomfort for her father and yet this flirtation goes on against all odds. Her life in the initial stage is unimpressive but it becomes eventful when she boldly expresses her love for Lal Singh.

Maya's father is a total approver of tradition and orthodoxy whereas Lal Singh is a thorough-going radical. Maya's approval of

Lal Singh as a lover is an indirect indication of disapproval of her father's love of tradition and class-based relation. A rich woman cannot court a poor man. The difference in the class must be maintained in terms of distance. Maya's anti-class temperament makes her a new figure. She spreads a new message saying that human love knows no class. Maya becomes a new woman in the initial stage itself. She is a new revolutionary woman in that she does not attach importance to wealth but attributes value to human sentiments.

Maya shows genuine interest in life. For her to judge life in terms of externals is a fallacy. The choice of Maya of a peasant rebel as her lover is a bold expression of her making of a new revolution. Lal Singh's escape from her father's trumped up charge of theft against him and his joining the army and his subsequent flight to foreign land give a brief spell of rest to this love-episode. It is only on Lal Singh's return to Nandpur after his brief stay in France that Maya becomes a gripping force to him.

The second phase of her revolution begins with a conscious recognition of her choice and she realises the bold necessity for a new experiment. Even Lal Singh is stunned to see her capacity for breaking barriers. He knows that marriage is an arrangement of parents and not a choice made by the individual partners. He is fascinated to see her courage in showing her capacity for choice in such a crucial matter. That is the reason why she asks him: "So you thought women only choose their men freely in Vilayat."[4] Lal Singh thinks that the European women are superior to the Indian women in asserting their rights. Maya tells him that the Indian women also exhibit their power of choice. The novelist knows that in Maya one sees her individuality as a sign of an emancipated new woman paving the way for Gauri.

There are two elements which go into the making of Maya. She deeply respects her father who believes in everything which is in agreement with class-based propriety. Maya wants to achieve emancipation from this false notion of class and status. Her elopement with Lal Singh indicates her individual decision. She expresses the concept of an emancipated woman in her act of elopement. The destiny of one's life is to be decided by the individual. As Anand himself has commented, "in the act of running away with [Lalu], . . . [Maya] has surpassed other women. She has made a revolution of her own, liberated herself."[5]

It is to be noted that Maya is a greater radical than Lal Singh because her elopement comes after her previous marriage. She is not only a married woman but is later known as a widowed Maya. She has broken the old grounds. No worthwhile significance is attached by her to her previous marriage. What is more surprising is that she never regards herself as a widow. In the traditional Hindu view, widowhood closes all possibilities of life and puts an end to everything.

Maya is under the impression that she retains womanly qualities of virginal purity and vitality even after her previous marriage. Her widowhood does not diminish complete enthusiasm in life. She remains indifferent to the previous events of her life. The reason is that she loves life, hoping for an opportunity to express it. Her capacity to remain above social consciousness and her deep interest in life make her a very powerful individual. The most formidable revolution she makes is to be seen not only in her act of elopement but in the context in which she embarks upon this bold and radical enterprise.

She contracts a runaway marriage with Lal Singh after being married and widowed, and thereby she breaks all traditional norms. She sets aside her previous marriage and ignores her subsequent phase of widowhood. This means that she still considers that she is a woman filled with joy. Maya perhaps thinks that life need not put anyone in a state of frustration. The diverse possibilities that life offers need not be ignored by the individual. It is this theory of active involvement in life in the right spirit that makes Maya a new woman. So long as men and women survive, life survives. Life never comes to an end while the individual is alive on earth. It may be pointed out here that the Hindu theory of religion brings life to an end after widowhood occurs.

Anand has projected in Maya a new woman whom one can compare with a Renaissance humanist who believes in the fullness of life. It is her belief in the fullness of life which puts her in a state of disharmony with society. Maya feels that life is to be lived in a meaningful manner and she knows that it is only the individual who has to create meaning and live in accordance with it. The boldness with which she sets aside her previous marriage and widowhood is secured from her belief in life. Her runaway marriage with Lal Singh is a sign of revolution which expresses opposition to all established values and views of life. Maya, in this respect, seems to surpass all women in Anand's novels. Her defiance of all established norms is what makes her a rebel.

Maya's runaway marriage has to be estimated in the light of some principles. Marriage by virtue of arrangement with the help of parents is an act glorifying tradition. This mode does not secure freedom for the individual. The next step is to seek marriage independently. It is a sign of emancipation from tradition to seek marriage through the theory of individual choice. Maya conforms to the second phase of marriage through the theory of individual choice with a difference. One has to keep in mind the celebration of her first marriage and the subsequent occurrence of her widowhood. These are two solid facts which create difficulties for Maya. But she has an unhuzzled mind to brush aside these two facts. She is an emancipated woman in the sense that her approach to life remains without social sanction and recognition.

One event which causes perplexity in Maya is her relationship with Lal Singh whose major preoccupation lies in his protest against social injustice. Maya's primary feeling is to gain the status of a wife. Why should the revolutionary Maya demand the recognition of the status of wife is a question which requires to be explored. She knows that it is not a lawfully arranged marriage in which she finds herself. She is a woman and as a woman she feels that it is not enough to live simply as friends and lovers. Many runaway marriages break down as they take place in an atmosphere of high emotional enthusiasm without the support of critical thought. Maya's keen awareness of this fact produces in her an urge to solicit the status of a wife.

What she seeks is marriage through revolutionary arrangement. She is a wife to Lal Singh in her mind and the personal arrangement needs to be stabilized. Maya has abandoned her parents and the society and her claim for the status of a wife springs from her desire to give a certain element of fixity to that runaway relationship. According to Premila Paul, "Maya's demand for status only suggests that marriage is a necessity for woman to appear dignified in the eyes of the society." (114) This view is not fully correct because Maya's longing for the status of a wife does not come from mere feeling of social recognition. One has already seen how her belief in life results in her disharmony with society. To stabilize the runaway relationship and give a firm basis to it is looking for safety in what she has done. Moreover a runaway marriage is still a marriage and the method of achieving it is unorthodox only. It is a marriage by personal choice and inclination. Although the manner of marriage is anti-traditional, Maya wants this personal relationship to be authenticated and this is not to be construed as looking for social recognition.

Anand's Maya is a revolutionary woman while Kalyani in Jayakanthan's *Oru Natikai Nātakam Pārkiṛāl* is presented as a new woman. Ranga, an art-critic, and Kalyani, a stage actress, get married on the ground of intellectual affinity towards each other. Soon a conflict arises over the question of the meaning of true love. The clue to this problem is seen in relation to Kalyani's love of roses and Ranga's dislike of them.

In the name of true love Ranga demands that she must give up her interest in roses for the purpose of satisfying his particular turn of mind. For Kalyani, there is no link between her giving up her love for roses and loving Ranga. Ranga is a symbol of old tradition and for him true love means sacrifice of individual self. But Kalyani acts as a voice of modernity. True love can survive and flourish according to her even in an act of retention of individuality: "She was interested only in him and not about their relationship and the gossip around."[6]

She is a strong individual and her opinion about Ranga is more important than other people's views about them. Kalyani echoes the view of an emancipated woman that marriage and love should not destroy the individuality of persons. Each person chooses a line of his own in accordance with his personal temperament. She asks Ranga, "Why do I engage myself in drama? Why have you turned a critic?" (137)

The marriage of Pattammal and Thamu, servants of the family, creates another ground for a debate on the true nature of love. Either marriage on earth or union in death seems to be the slogan and motivating force of Pattu and Thamu. Ranga praises their slogan as a high ideal.

Kalyani dismisses it as cheap sentimentality. She opens her mind and speaks firmly, "no one would die for love and if they did so that would be unwise." (145) But Ranga resumes his debate and states that death due to love deserves appreciation. Kalyani says that act of dying for love is an act of refusing to live. Ranga interprets their love as a noble sacrifice for each other and the glory of love in death is what impresses him. Kalyani refutes him saying, "But the real glory of love has to be proved by their way of living." (155)

Some insights are gained from the passages cited from the controversial discussion between Ranga and Kalyani. For Ranga love means sacrifice of individual self and merging of woman in man. He is of the view that if love is not fulfilled death can be embraced and that death indeed expresses the glory of love. Kalyani's unique answers make her an emancipated woman. She warns that one should be on guard against sentimentalism and emotionalism in love. She argues as a new woman that love on the basis of sentimentalism cannot have long-standing basis and all the emotions will evaporate.

Kalyani suggests that apart from emotion, love involves serious thought and critical consideration. Her complaint against sentimental love is that emotions are not supported by thought and so they will disappear betraying the cause of love. For her, death does not express the glory of love for the simple reason that death is a negative state and it represents the annihilation of life. The liberated woman in Kalyani forces her to say that love must involve living and not dying.

Love must express life and end in exalting life. She feels that unfulfilled or unaccepted love need not terminate life. It is the act of retaining the life of the individual self which does not allow anyone to surrender anything foolishly in an emotional state. A thoughtful love involves the retaining of the individual self, while emotional love can erase the individual self. So Kalyani says that a thoughtful love is preferable to an emotional love. She is of the view that individuals come together in love and they must remain so in order to make love a living reality.

Again a heated argument ensues when Ranga asks her what she considers essential for life, "Are they roses or make-up? or drama? or the togetherness of man and woman?" Ranga as a traditionalist believes that love is an expression of something highly unreachable. But for Kalyani love is a natural feeling which must have a firm foundation in the reality of life. She thinks that Ranga's view of love as an expression of high idealism has no relation to human nature and moreover it can get itself falsified in the actual conditions of life. Therefore Kalyani gives a new definition of love in the spirit of a modern woman: "Life is a serious affair. . . . They have to lead a life of sincerity, honesty and compassion. If that is not life with love, let that glorified love be placed on high pedestal. They do not need it." (167) This remark of Kalyani should be taken as the text of the new woman. Her argument is that all high ideal love lacks realism. She says that human love requires to be nourished by honesty and compassion.

Kalyani wants life to be erected on the foundation of honesty, sincerity and compassion; Ranga identifies the whole of life with love. For Kalyani, love is subordinate to life. When life is lived honestly love will flourish without any ideal embellishment. Kalyani is very shrewd when she says that the quality of love depends upon the quality of life. When one's attitude to life is unsound, love will have a flippant dimension. Without a firm basis in the reality, any love as an expression of high ideal is bound to evaporate. The initial enthusiasm found in Pattu and Thamu is not sustained and there are frequent quarrels between the two. Therefore Kalyani is right that a serious attitude to life alone can give a better basis for love.

Much against Ranga Kalyani feels that there is no need of emotional love for life. She feels that for Ranga love is a romantic feeling and ecstasy. For Kalyani love is a natural feeling and she thinks that Ranga's romantic exaggeration of love will lead to falsity without any basis in life. She gives an example to prove the truth of her statement. Pattu and Thamu are not happy with each other. When true love passes through the test of life, it suffers. She points out that such emotional upheavals of love will not last long. For Ranga love is an uncritical and emotional state. But for Kalyani love involves a thoughtful process and she feels that lovers must use their wits. Kalyani is a realist with a practical bent of mind. She feels that Ranga is more emotional than rational. Love is not simply an emotional state; it must have a rational basis.

The most crucial tenet of an emancipated Kalyani is that love is an intense awareness of individual self without any loss of mutual identity. Ranga is on the other end considering love as an expression of the loss of individual self on the part of a woman. Jayakanthan explains in his Preface to this novel that men want to impose their views on others. (5) People conquer countries by invasion. In the same way, men establish their domination over women. The act of conquering a country by invasion involves physical violence while the act of one mind conquering another by the power of domination involves mental violence. Ranga, according to him, is an example of the second category. He encroaches upon the mental territory of Kalyani and demands her individual self to be surrendered to him. Kalyani calls him an invader and not a lover.

Kalyani does not want to give up her self as demanded by Ranga. For her to give up her self is to give up her being. Ranga as a typical traditionalist thinks of love as total loss of self and identity. But to Kalyani to demand surrender of self and individuality is nothing but to pronounce extinction of life. Kalyani as a new woman gives a new definition of love. Love is not merging of self but an act of sharing of emotions, feelings and thoughts. In the process of merging of self, the loss of Individual identity becomes a necessity. But in the act of sharing the existence of individual self remains undisturbed. One of the qualities of an emancipated woman, according to Jayakanthan, is that she must remain a distinct individual. For him, human love implies human equality.

In the novel, *Kokila Enna Ceitu Vittal*, Jayakanthan presents a revolutionary Kokila, comparable to Anand's Maya. Kokila marries Ananta Raman on account of her admiration for his intellectual charm and excellence. In the first instance Kokila breaks an old tradition and creates a new one in its place. Jayakanthan writes: "Kokila had gone out of her family of Iyengar tradition to marry Ananta Raman, an Iyer. That was considered a great sacrilege and her registered marriage was viewed as a marriage out of caste."[7]

For an Iyengar woman, to marry an Iyer boy is almost an act of impossibility. But Kokila by her revolutionary courage makes it a reality. She is one of the forerunners of inter-caste marriage. Some complications arise in her family and they are due to the occasional visits of a thirty-five-year-old family friend, former classmate and a distant relative of Kokila. Ananta Raman is a learned intellectual who cares for the popular opinion of society. He gives no place to his individual judgement. His jealousy blinds him to the merit of Kokila. With all his scholarship, he lacks balance of mind and judgement.

But Kokila is calm and self-composed because she remains her own individual self in her judgement of anything. Ananta Raman loses his power of perception because he is influenced by the standards of society. The society-view of Ananta Raman and the individual self of Kokila come into conflict in this family drama.

Kokila's psychological power of understanding is far superior to that of Ananta Raman. An instance can be cited to prove this. The visit of her relative provokes him and she says calmly: "He won't come. I won't go and see him. But do you think our life will blossom after this? You'll think that I am always thinking about him. What shall I do then." (25) Kokila says that she is very clear about her motives and intentions. She views her family-friend in the right perspective. The problem of Ananta Raman will not disappear even if Kokila promises not to see him. As a master psychologist, she says that the problem of Ananta Raman does not lie in her or in 'his' visit but it lies in the peculiar mental make up of the editor whose eye is blinded by jealousy. When he feels that his life has become a torture with Kokila, Ananta Raman warns her that he can get remarried and that would make her a permanent loser. Immediately, Kokila comes out with a bold statement which only an emancipated woman is capable of making. As a lioness in spirit she replies, "In which age are you living? You know I can also say the same thing [of remarriage]. I can do it if I like. Is it a bigger thing to break off your relationship?" (31)

Ananta Raman thinks that woman is subservient to man and that she cannot live without him. When he talks about man's right to re-marry, Kokila raises her banner of protest like a typical new woman. According to her, the right man enjoys can be enjoyed by woman also. Her plea for remarriage is a plea for emancipation of women and a bold call for human equality.

Jayakanthan's Kokila is not a projection of a brutal woman. She has the tenderness of a deer and the courage of a lion: "She wished to submit herself as a tender flower at his feet. But when he crushed her under his feet without any consideration she has turned a thorn herself unaware of it." (35) Kokila prefers to be meek and submissive, but when the feeling of man being superior and woman being inferior comes, she resists it like a thorn which pricks. She is a mild flower, but she can also become a wild thorn when man becomes oppressive. Kokila says that marriage becomes a success only on the basis of the acceptance of human equality. Mutual respect is an indispensable quality for a happy married life. Kokila speaks about this aspect in the novel: "There is a limit to everything even in marriage. The marriage agreement should be safeguarded cautiously to pull on the relationship. They both should know to respect each other." (37) Kokila's speech reflects the declaration of the rights of man and of woman. Her spirit of the emancipated woman lies in her argument that man-woman relationship must be based on equality and mutual respect.

Kokila makes it clear that when the right of a woman is not recognized, she must raise a voice of protest. She says that woman must assume more and more the spirit of an individual to prepare herself for a fight for her right and justice. Jayakanthan says that it is not bad ethics. When the old ethics becomes bad, new ethics of protest and plea for human equality must be made. The novelist feels that woman gains her individuality through education, knowledge, awareness and exposure to life and society. Jayakanthan says in his preface that till man does not recognize the independence and self-respect of woman, there is no possibility for peace and harmony in marriage.

Kalyani and Kokila appear to be emancipated in different ways. The spirit of individual self is expressed in Kalyani on an intellectual plane. Kokila, like Kalyani, expresses her spirit of individual self on an intellectual plane. But she has psychological power of perception also. She is very level-headed in her approach to life. Kalyani accepts Ranga's suggestion of divorce as a solution to their problems. Her reaction is typically intellectual. She says that their relationship will continue despite divorce. Kokila seems to be different from Kalyani because any mischief in marital relation will involve a tit for tat. Kalyani's intellectual bent of mind restrains her from resorting to any drastic action.

But what does Kokila, whose animated spirit will not keep her to remain indifferent to injustice at the hands of her husband, do ultimately? Kokila does unite with her husband in spite of her wild protests earlier. Similarly in the end Kalyani who has paralytic attack accepts the hands of the estranged husband Ranga when he comes and consoles her. They talk to each other, understand each other and feel the need of living together and finally decide to live together. Do not the endings of these two novels reflect the attitude of Jayakanthan towards man-woman relationship, marriage and in the process the emancipation of woman?

Anand in his novel *The Big Heart* portrays Janki as a non-conformist. She lives with the hero of the novel Ananta as a mistress. Premila Paul points out the complex conditions in which Janki finds herself:

> After the death of her elderly husband the society expects her to be dead to all impulses and live only to worship the memory of him, her lord and master. It is said "her life would have remained a series of insults if she had been condemned to mourn the death of an elderly husband to whom she had been married by arrangement." (115)

Janki disproves the truth of the traditional axiom of the Hindu religion that there is no life after the death of the husband. Anand reviews the value of this axiom and projects through Janki the lesson that the death of the husband need not terminate all the possibilities of life. Anand feels that it is the ban on the enjoyment of life which reduces the human being to the status of an inanimate thing. The act of self-imposed denial of all pleasures of life because of widowhood takes away the value of one being a human being. The right of a human being to enjoy life in all conditions should not be denied. Why shouldn't a widow enjoy the pleasures of life? The question is taken up by Anand for critical examination.

Janki's life proves the truth that a woman becomes a widow only through wrong human attribution. The so-called widow is still a woman who wishes to live. Janki gives up widowhood because she finds no meaning in it. Anand perhaps feels that a long-established habit does not easily disappear in a day. It is the attempt at resistance of such a time-honoured habit which makes life human. Without the love of human beings, it is not possible to become a reformist. Anand's humanism is nothing but an expression of his love of man.

As religion advocates control of man by laws and axioms, there is no human dimension in such a scheme. The concept of widowhood is the outcome of such a religious axiom which evicts human dimension. Anand has seen the danger of widowhood which means denial of life. Denial of life is denial of existence. It is the absence of human dimension which is found in the denial of life. To increase humanness of a thing is the permanent endeavour of a reformist. The greatest tragedy in human civilization is to deny to the widow the joy of living. Janki's wish to live as a mistress to Ananta is a revolt against the religious concept of widowhood. Through Janki one learns that widows can dedicate themselves to the task of world building.

By making Janki live with Ananta as a mistress, Anand wants to point out the factors which pave the way for the rise of a new woman. The right of the individual to determine his own destiny, the act of glorifying freedom of choice, the tendency to keep aside any norm which diverts one from the stream of life, the value of appreciating all pleasures of life, the attempt at resisting tradition which blocks the growth of human life, the call for strengthening humanness of things are largely different factors which pave the way for the rise of a new woman like Janki.

Janki's desire is to live even after the death of her husband. She feels that a woman can live only when she breaks away from the cobwebs of tradition. Without the freedom of living, human life cannot express itself. The value system created by society is what poses a threat to life and human dignity. Janki is an ailing woman suffering from dreadful tuberculosis and yet her joy of living is not fully suppressed. But the problem with Janki is that her life with Ananta is not recognized by society. Although society becomes the greatest monster, she quietly ignores it. Either she is insensitive to the society or the society is dead to her.

Janki adds charm to the life of Ananta by sharing deep affinity with his ideals. It is this quality of sharing affinity with Ananta's ideal and becoming kindred souls which put Janki one step above Maya as a revolutionary woman. Ananta becomes a machine-man. Janki puts him in touch with the practical issues of life. Her illness and sickness act as no bar in her appreciation of Ananta's life. Janki prefers to live with Ananta as he happens to be an idealist. Ananta believes that human life must be transformed through machine. But Janki believes that human life must be altered through display of human tenderness. Janki is an individual but her approach to life is universal. The fundamental strength of her character lies in her goodness which prompts her to promote the progress of human race.

Anand feels that in the case of Janki, the lawfully arranged marriage is a failure but her life as mistress to Ananta is a roaring success. Janki becomes a new woman in the light of this complex factor: "Janki ranks higher than a wife in devotion which is seen throughout the novel and is further proved after Ananta's death." (115) The life of Janki proves that marriage by arrangement has no relation to human temperament. Its success is a matter of accident and its failure seems to be a matter of principle which shows that the individuals concerned have not exercised their option. Janki's later life is a phase of joy because she exercises her power of individual option.

Janki turns into a new woman for her life of a mistress to the protagonist puts her on the road to a new revolution. Janki experiences the pain of real widowhood only after the death of Ananta. To mourn the death of Ananta in the manner of a widow is a mark of irony for the society. But Janki's mental affinity with Ananta is so great that she experiences the loss only in his death. It is the purpose which determines the value of human existence. Janki discovers a purpose in conjunction with Ananta. It is this attempt of Janki to find her purpose in life and her desire to seek alliance with Ananta which make Janki an emancipated woman. Janki's dedicating herself to the project of Ananta after his death brings on her a new scene where she walks with the noble ideal of improving the human race.

Janki knows that in the eyes of the society she is a prostitute. She is able to bear this ignominy as the background for the rise of an emancipated woman is surrounded by thorns. "Her social status as a mere prostitute does not diminish her evangelical glory."[8] An orthodox society fails to appreciate Janki as she is a non-conformist. The merit of Janki lies in her giving a new dimension to life by leading an ideal life with Ananta. Anand is of the view that the traditional woman is a victim of society and its beliefs whereas the emancipated new woman is free from any restrictions.

Maya breaks her widowhood and elopes with Lal Singh. Janki lives as a mistress with Ananta and allows herself to experience widowhood after the death of her unofficial husband. Maya's avoidance of widowhood and Janki's acceptance of the name make them new women. Anand can proudly say that Maya and Janki are the forerunners of widow remarriage. Widow remarriage is a telling example of the liberation of woman.

Anand's Janki is presented as a non-conformist woman while Jayakanthan's Gaṇga is portrayed as a non-conformist protagonist with a difference in his *Cila Nērankalil Cila Manitarkal*. On a rainy evening Ganga, who is waiting for a bus to return home after the classes are over in the college, is suddenly offered a seat in a car and is taken away to a far off place and is raped by a stranger. The innocent Ganga on reaching home confesses her loss of virginity to her mother. The traditional mother Kanakam unfortunately makes it public with the result that Ganga has to leave the house. Her uncle Venku takes her to his place, educates her and gets her a job in an office. Venku, another traditional old man, declares once to Ganga, "You can be a concubine to some one, but not a wife to anyone."[9]

Ganga knows her uncle's malicious motive to keep her as his concubine. Her strength of mind and character resists such a plan. The novelist pictures the attitude of society towards a woman who is living alone: "in this society a single woman receives scant respect.

People don't believe the fact that a woman can remain single, unmarried without a man to support her." (140) But Ganga is living alone, of course with her aged mother, unsupported by anyone. She is bold enough not to expect support from anyone. Self-reliance is her motto in life.

Provoked by her uncle Venku, one day Ganga after many efforts and investigations identifies that mysterious stranger in the car as Prabu, a well-to-do man with two grown up children. She meets him one day and their meeting each other becomes a routine. She is very much pleased about it and her hope of getting Prabu as her friend is only an expression of her ideal relationship. She does not have sex motive in her mind. Ganga and Prabu know this fact and she expresses this view:

> Prabu though not a man of morality does not approach her for sex. . . . She too does not have such intentions towards him. She feels that she can never have such desires and he too is directed in a different line of friendship. (216)

Ganga regards her relationship with him as an ideal form of friendship. It is a kind of Platonic love where men commune with women through minds. Moreover Ganga is not a woman who allows herself to be carried away by the views of the society. Ganga's developing a genuine friendship with Prabu may perhaps be taken as a result of pricking of her conscience. Any other worldly woman would have ignored the car incident by simply embarking upon marriage. Ganga is not a simple woman who will accept expediency as her policy. Her primary preference is for truth. She has been talking about marriage in slighting terms. The spirit of independence is nurtured in her. She does not want to be a slave to anyone or anything. Prabu's proposal of Ganga's marriage with a fitting bridegroom is at once rejected by her. This incident shows that her interest is different. Her mental commitment to Prabu is mainly an outcome of that car-incident. Otherwise as a non-conformist, she is not attracted by love and marriage.

The most peculiar thing about Ganga-Prabu relationship is that she looks upon Prabu as a father. This shows that what Ganga wants is only an abiding relationship. She wants to transform the car incident and give it a different basis for developing a new form of relationship. Commenting on their relationship the novelist says, "Their relationship is a mystery. . . . Their relationship had turned to be a responsible, dignified relationship that has ended up in love." (276) What Ganga expects from Prabu is not a physical tie but a different grade of love. But circumstances and their family conditions do not permit even this relationship. When it is learnt that Ganga has no personal motive in dealing with Prabu, the misconceptions are removed. But Prabu is found in a sinking ship, and Ganga embraces the same destiny. Their life is a failure by any set of worldly standards. But the satisfaction they derive from their meeting elevates them to a realm of joy. This is the test for measuring the merit of their relationship.

Prabu confesses that he sees a new dimension of reality only after he has seen and come into contact with Ganga. This fact shows that Ganga is a new woman not in terms of inciting physical urges but in terms of her inspiring liveliness and intellectual charm. When Prabu says that Ganga is unnecessarily ruining her life, she simply ignores and looks for fertilizing a different form of relationship with Prabu.

Ganga ends her life in the Ganges, a holy river which divines their relationship. Their life is only a search for a new form of awareness. It is only human relationship which imparts joy to life. But this kind of human relation which Ganga and Prabu seek has no name at all. Ganga becomes an emancipated woman as she lays emphasis upon the fact that the meaning of life lies in a search for friendship and profound relationship without physical ties. Ganga's message as a new woman is that life is a dignified affair and the search for worthwhile human relationship is what gives meaning to life.

Ganga's life is not a happily shaped one. She is in a shambles but even in this state, she represents a vital message that mystery of life is known only through human love. For her life is like the mellifluous flow of a stream. One learns from the life of Ganga that human life is a search for some meaning. The actual purpose of life, according to her, lies in sharing love with human beings.

Ganga has kept away from those people who possess malicious motives. Her life does not exist for cheap satisfaction. Ganga's life has been side-tracked but even in this odd and nebulous state she wants to discover a meaning. It is this relentless search of the individual which moves Ganga to explore the reality of life. Ganga has a tremendous energy and a new spirit in her to tackle anomaly, anarchy, confusion and chaos in human relationship from the impersonal standpoint of a committed explorer of life. In keeping with her non-conformist attitude, Janki remains a mistress to Ananta till the end. Ganga's attitude to society is also a non-conformist one, but her dignified relationship with Prabu which ends up in love is throughout non-physical; there lies the difference between Janki and Ganga.

Anand's novel *The Old Woman and the Cow* traces the growth and evolution of the heroine Gauri. Gauri is married to Panchi who is an orphan owning a small mortgaged land. The marriage of Gauri and Panchi carries no luck. The break up of the joint family of Panchi and his uncle Mola Ram and the coming of drought and famine in the villages are the immediate misfortunes for which the coming of Gauri is held responsible according to Kesaro, Panchi's aunt. Panchi's mind is slowly poisoned by Kesaro.

Gauri's life is a life of hard drudgery. Her husband is no source of consolation for her as he has no independent mind. It is when Gauri becomes pregnant that the whole tragedy starts. Panchi has no sense of appreciation and judgement. Moreover he is submerged in poverty. Gauri's pregnancy does not bring relief and happiness to Panchi.

Panchi is temperamentally wild and his brutal nature is indicated by the novelist: "there was the prospect of the prize of a girl--a girl whom he could fold in his arms at night and kick during the day."[10] With his monstrous nature he reduces Gauri to an object of inanimate existence. There is no sharing of love or exchange of feelings in them. Gauri is true to the tradition in being loyal and devoted to Panchi. Marriage is essentially a union of hearts. Panchi falsifies this axiom and looks upon as an object of sexual fulfillment only. His brutal nature coupled with his passion for sex makes him a crude character. The indoctrination of Kesari poisons the mind of

Panchi and he sees Gauri only in the light of the evil teaching of his aunt. The greatest mistake which Panchi commits lies in his treating Gauri as his property. His attitude of reducing his wife to the status of an object is nothing but an expression of human brutality.

Gauri endures the ill-treatment of Panchi and sticks to him like a cow in a true traditional spirit. But this goodness of Gauri does not arouse a corresponding element of goodness in Panchi. The reason lies in his rough and unrefined being. The wrong-doing of Panchi is an indication of his undeveloped mind and perverted consciousness. Marlene Fisher examines the mind of Panchi in the following statement: "He can't get beyond the notion that Gauri is an extension of himself and that she should behave always even under his kicks and blows, as the cow-like submissive, and infinitely 'good' Hindu wife."[11]

Panchi will act like a tyrant and his wrong and unethical expectation is that Gauri must behave like a tender cow. The law of Manu Dharma enjoins strict obedience on the part of woman to man even in times of crisis. In the evolution of the Hindu religion the laws of Manu Dharma occupy an intermediary phase and they do not represent the totality of things as conceived by Vedic Rishis. When a human being is denied freedom, she is given a chance to seek remedy. She can always rebel against the person in a righteous manner. A law need not be followed or opposed blindly.

In the case of Panchi there is nothing to guide him. He is led by evil forces like his unruly emotions and the bad counsel of her aunt. When Panchi comes to know that Gauri has become pregnant, he thrashes her like a brute and sends her out of the house. It is poverty due to drought which drives Panchi to a mad behaviour of this kind. Panchi has no sense of balance. The joy of becoming a father is not felt by him. He asks foolishly, "How did this happen, when." (103) The greatest act of cruelty is expressed by Panchi in his uncouth manner of slandering her character: "Whose is it? Mine or someone else's?" (103)

Gauri's mother is much worse than Panchi's aunt Kesaro. Lakshmi's self-interest and her mortgage loan binding two houses create a desire in her to sell Gauri to Seth Jai Ram Das. She is not willing to sell the cow because it is more useful and lucrative than her daughter Gauri. To sell Gauri to clear the debt is an unrighteous transaction. M.K. Naik comments on this outrageous bartering in a pungent way, "In Lakshmi's scale of values, the four-footed variety obviously ranks far higher." (90)

In the house of Seth Jai Ram Das, Gauri's chastity is threatened. The greatness of Gauri's character lies in her mental strength and power of endurance. She maintains her integrity by resisting the advances of Seth. Subsequently she develops fever. Her serious illness leads to her being admitted in a hospital in Hoshiyarpur.

Dr. Colonel Mahindra is the doctor who treats Gauri and paves the way for her recovery. Apart from being a doctor, he is a spiritual healer also. Naik calls him a selfless, high-souled and philanthropic physician. He sees in him a self-projection of Anand himself. His spokesman here is Colonel Mahindra, in whose mouth the author puts his own denunciation of effete traditionalism and post-Independence materialism. (95) Dr. Mahindra is a humanist who believes in the intrinsic goodness and worth of all individuals. He believes in people becoming independent in their mental outlook. Under his benign guidance, Gauri learns to behave like a spirited individual. The traditional spirit of dissolving of her individual in the self of Panchi brought her no credit. Dr. Mahindra's association awakens a new dimension in her consciousness. She learns a lesson from him that self-independence is the real independence.

Her beauty becomes a source of attraction for the colonel's assistant Dr. Ratan Chandra Batra. Her character endowed with integrity and power of resistance saves her from the danger. Though she has now grown self-reliant, she looks for a place of safety. Batra's eye on her has created a scandal and it makes her restless. Gauri thinks that Panchi will accept her.

When Colonel Mahindra asks her what she proposes to do, she gives a resolute reply, "I want my husband. . . . I am with child by my husband, and I want to go back to him. . . . I want to go back home." (190-91) Her hope of union with Panchi is shattered to pieces when he becomes a prey to the village gossip, about the purity of Gauri. Her stay in the house of Seth Ram Dass leads to spinning of stories about her. Her stay at the hospital is another source of suspicion about her chastity. Panchi is a rough and unpolished young man who has no mature inward sensibility to guide his dealings with Gauri. A mark of excellence in Gauri's character is that she is deeply rooted in the traditional sensibility which informs her that devotion to husband should be a matter of habit. Naik says, "It is, however, in Gauri that we find the ancient Indian tradition at its best." (91)

Gauri's consciousness tells her that the beauty of wife lies in being with her husband at all costs and under all circumstances. Gauri is not accepted by Panchi on the ground that her chastity is a matter of doubt. He is determined by the voice of the village to arrive at an independent opinion about her. Saros Cowasjee sums up the crucial part of her life in a telling manner: "The villagers encouraged by the local mid-wife Rakhi, cast aspersions on Gauri's life at the nursing home and insinuate that the child she is carrying is not her husband's. Panchi demands from her proof of fidelity. But what proof can she offer? I am not Sita that the earth will open up and swallow me, she says as she takes the road back to Hoshiarpur to begin life anew."[12]

Gauri's faith in the traditional norm of obedience to her husband is put under trial. She knows that it is Panchi who falsifies tradition and life. This slowly brings Gauri into contact with a new awareness of modernity. Her existential crisis cannot force her to follow the path of Sita. She has acquired courage through her contact with the urban world. "Acha, if I am curse on you, I will go away. . . . And if you strike me again, I will hit you back." (282-83)

Gauri's farewell to Panchi must be taken as a good bye to tradition. Gauri's rebellion is against a mangled form of tradition which gets expressed in antiquated customs and corrupt religious practices. The degeneration of tradition as it is found in Panchi produces in her an element of disgust. All the earlier incidents of the novel describe Gauri as a cow symbolizing devotion, love and unquestioning surrender. But even in the phase of her as a cow, she shows formidable qualities in resisting the advances of Seth Ram Das and Dr. Batra. When her chastity is in danger, she has the power to be a lioness.

She trusts and follows a foolish and undiscriminating husband. Her desire to follow a life of harmony gets fully frustrated by Panchi who has no will of his own. Then he takes a decision to live independently. Her firm resolve to live alone is traceable to the humanizing influence of Dr. Mahindra who acts as "an eye-opener to her: "When religion, society and tradition become corrupt, it is only the spirit of a meaningful individuality which can reshape life. The decision to leave Panchi makes her an emancipated new woman because she realises her distinct status as an individual.

Gauri's crucial question as an emancipated woman is: why should an unjust husband be obeyed? The law of Manu states that devotion to husband is a divine necessity. Gauri reviews this law as she feels that this law has lost its efficacy and viability. Her life proves that life with a roguish husband is impossible. Manu does not provide a choice or an alternative and he only advises an undeviating wife to follow a deviating husband sincerely. For Gauri, this is an unjust law which can be flouted.

Anand here feels that Manu's law does not take care of Gauri's anguished spiritual cry and question. Does Manu approve of a wife-beater? He simply advises total obedience on the part of women without going into the particulars of the situations. Gauri gathers new experience and courage to disapprove of the virtue of unquestioning obedience enjoined on women by Manu. Anand is of the view that either Manu's law has no wider application or it remains insensitive to human issues. Therefore old laws become irrelevant to modern situations and the need to make the individual a court of his own enquiry becomes urgent. Gauri's wish is that a life of peace is preferable to a life of torture. This is the new law of Gauri which makes her "a woman of tomorrow."[14] Her departure from Panchi is not disobedience but dedication to a new way of life.

The story of *Ramayana* picturing a different life of an ideal relationship between Rama and Sita carries a different dimension of meaning. Rama's willingness to give credence to people's doubts about Sita's chastity as a result of her stay at Ravana's Ashok Vana is simply an expression of his special urge and duty as a king to obey the voice of public opinion. Rama as a king has to experience greater burden and his role as a husband is not independent of his role as a king. His responsibility is two-fold: to be a good king and a good husband. He listened to the public opinion in his role as a king which is not independent of his role as a husband. To argue that people should be guided by the public opinion about the chastity of wives is an unsound analogy.

A wrong form of tradition by passage of time has come into existence and it favours cruelty towards women on the basis of an unsound analogy. Everyone knows that private and personal understanding of one's own wife is more important than public opinion. There is no need for an open comparison between the pairs, namely Rama-Sita and Panchi-Gauri. Anand's plan is to modify this old myth which means that the traditional virtue of a wife obeying the husband who tests her chastity in relation to the standards of the society need not be followed.

Gauri demonstrates a new lesson to the world, that the right of the woman to revolt against an intolerably erring husband cannot be called into question. When a shirt is worn out, man has to alter it. In case the shirt is beyond repair, the only choice is to dispense with it and go for a new one. Similarly when the laws of Manu become inapplicable due to the degenerate practice of religious morals and complexity of times, the only way to safety lies in coming into contact with modernity.

In the past, laws and values shaped society and people but in the present, individuals have the right to determine their choice of life. Gauri becomes an emancipated woman in the sense that she relies on her own resources to guide her life. She is in search of a meaningful way of life. When the possibility of a good family life is closed, she decides that her destiny is to take care of the sick and suffering. This is a great ideal for an emancipated noble woman.

The theme of woman fleeing home, handled by Anand in his *Old Woman and the Cow*, is taken up by Jayakanthan in his *Suntara Kāntam*, where he also makes a powerful plea for emancipation of women. The heroine actively engages herself in a research on Indian women and marriage. The article 'Heh! Sita' in the magazine Sundari induces in her some reflections on women: the history of the Indian society reveals that marriage in principle is a sacred relationship. The Hindu religion regards woman as a Goddess. How do then women come to be treated as slaves in a society which looks upon marriage as a sacred relationship? Why do then women come to be beaten and treated as flies when the religion exalts woman to the status of a Goddess?

Sita sees the article describing men as Ravanas in many forms. Her own experience as a researcher confirms the truth that marriage has been reduced to a state of bonded slavery. The novel builds tempo when Sundara Sharma, Sita's father, arranges to get her married to Sukumaran who is a very rich Brahmin. The very first appearance of Sukumaran in Sita's house is an unpleasant one as he displays his vulgar taste in his enquiry about the authorship of the sexy articles written in the name of Miss Sundari. She sees in that comment that he has no aesthetic and intellectual taste.

Sita's marriage with Sukumaran is planned and arranged without her consent. For her father it is a marriage of convenience for repaying loan, making up the loss incurred and for promoting business interests. For Sita her marriage is the outcome of a peculiar circumstantial compulsion, "They are bent on arranging this marriage irrespective of my feelings. It is money, Mariam, everything is for money." (60) Sita always speculates about the state of women and her marriage is a contradiction of her own hopes about the plight of women. Her marriage is arranged after confirming the agreement in the horoscope of Sita and Sukumaran. Sita comes out with a revolutionary question:

> Does it suffice in a marriage that the two horoscopes perfectly match with each other? Don't you think that the minds should match? (79)

Sita's questions are relevant as the horoscope is a matter external to the human mind and so its significance has no relevance. Therefore this marriage without consent is comparable to the abduction of Sita by Ravana. Her personal happiness is at stake and there is no way out and the rat is therefore caught in a trap.

Sita seeks an interview with Sukumaran in order to find out his attitude to life. He says that he is happy about his partnership with her as a life-companion. He adds that his mother's treasure-house of jewellery is meant for Sita. She asks him a pertinent question, "Are money, jewels and silks that much essential for life?" (100) When he assures Sita that he will give up his bad habits, she gives him a bit of her mind in the capacity of an emancipated woman: "She looks at his face to say that she does not wish him to sacrifice anything for her sake. Similarly she won't certainly sacrifice anything for him." (101) Sita knows as a shrewd researcher that it is the sacrifice of individual freedom which has led women to a degenerate state. The emancipation of women lies in gaining their individual freedom.

Sukumaran claims his right from Sita through the legality of marriage and the virtue of matrimonial rituals. But Sita thinks that her marriage is a mechanical ritual without the required element of mental concurrence. Sita's crisis is seen when Mariam sees her neck without 'the sacred thali' and she puts some illuminating questions to her:

> What is the use of safeguarding anything at this stage? You should have refused stubbornly despite the threats from anyone or else you should have changed your mind and accepted the marriage wholeheartedly. (157)

Finding fault with Sita, Mariam gives her verdict conclusively: "Marrying a man of wealth for the sake of your parents without love is an immoral act." (159) She adds that to shatter the marriage after achieving the aim is itself a crime. Sita is bold enough and reflects along the line of separation from Sukumaran, her husband.

Sita sees Ramdoss who offers interesting views on women and marriage. He tells Sita plainly: "A woman loving a man is like desiring the golden deer impersonation of the demon Mareesan." (178) Man is conceived as a juggler and a magician trying to enslave women. Ramdoss tells her that men are agents of social evils and that they are Ravanas.

Jayakanthan puts forth his message for emancipation of women through Ramdoss. In response to Sita's question, he says:

> As women are abducted by men as wives, as children, they are viewed as pure Sitas. As they fall a prey to the false relationship they are called "Maya Sitas." Who is Rama then? We can see Ramas in the future youth that are going to destroy this social injustice. After this destruction only there will blossom, real justice, affection and love. (178)

Jayakanthan looks forward to a new cultural revolution in the minds of men. The salvation for the tragic plight of women depends on the reformation in the minds of men. The individual freedom of woman does not give the complete solution. Women will awaken themselves to their real position through learning and individual freedom. Women simply becoming rebels is not enough, because such a militant posture only liberates them from the tyranny of husbands. Unlike Anand, Jayakanthan feels that leaving the husband, seeking divorce and opting for remarriage are not solutions. They only show some form of protest against injustice. He therefore says that the real solution has to come from men who must experience changes in their outlook. Unless men become mature, marriage will remain bondage.

While writing about the emancipation of woman in this novel, Jayakanthan speaks of human liberation which includes men and women. The awareness that women are the victims at the cruel hands of men and the realisation that they can improve their state through learning and freedom are indispensable for the emancipation of women. Similarly men must give up their act of oppression and cultivate their minds in achieving knowledge and inwardness. Women cannot become free unless men free themselves from wretchedness in order to make women free. When men do not undergo any change in outlook, woman's act of rebellion is of no avail.

Therefore one has to associate liberation with the mental changes in both men and women. The injustice is perpetuated by man on woman. Woman must become alert and oppose it. This is one step in the scheme. But men must realise their flaw and give up their evil ways of treating women. Jayakanthan says that men must evolve themselves in order to become refined. Woman is part of man and man is part of society. What is important is that woman cannot achieve emancipation by claiming independence. Can they live alone? They cannot run away from wrong men and live in .a forest. Such a life is unnatural but life without man is impossible for a woman. Running away from the oppressor is no solution.

Sita's decision to launch into a life of separation and her plan to stay in the women's hostel are only measures by which she seeks compensation for her marriage with Sukumaran. The tragic plight of women as wives will change only when they receive high level of education and economic independence. Marriage makes women slaves and unpaid servants. Their independence depends on their power to act in a spirit of opposition. Their power of resistance, possession of knowledge and gaining of individual freedom create favourable conditions for them to achieve dignity and status in society. Education is an important condition for their emancipation. Sita is of the opinion that along with education they must secure jobs also.

Jayakanthan is different in his perspective when he explains in his preface that women cannot live alone, men cannot live alone and that none can live alone. (3) The plausible reason is that they are all members of society. When a particular unit stays out of society in order to lead a life of independence, he calls it an unnatural state. According to him, life can be lived within the framework of society with a spirit of mingling with others.

Jayakanthan believes that Sita's act of complete separation from Sukumaran is an expression of relief but it is not an indication of permanent solution. To dispense with the institution of marriage and remain independent is no solution for women. To seek separation from men for correcting the wrong choice of marriage is only a partial solution. For women to achieve emancipation through learning and job is only one phase in the process of liberation and the other phase lies in men who must evolve into mature beings endowed with inwardness. Apart from women's gaining education and job they are really emancipated, according to Jayakanthan only when men make themselves cultured beings.

Real emancipation for women is to be achieved within the framework of society. The truth is that woman has to live with man. The reciprocal relation between man and woman is an inevitable part of society. Jayakanthan says that society is not a structure hanging in the clouds. Men and women live together and they constitute society. Men have become monsters and women want to live away from them; this is an abnormal state inevitable for some time. In the long run, men must reform themselves fully and give due dignity to women.

Thus Anand and Jayakanthan examine the issue of the emancipation of women. In these novels one finds in women the spirit of high individualism and the novelists advocate the acquisition of knowledge and attainment of economic freedom as measures by which women can increasingly grow in their sensibility and consciousness and feel the spirit of inherent dignity and self-respect. They feel that woman is as important as man. But in virtual practice, woman is found in a pitiable state without any spirit of equality and social importance. The sad state in which women are found is what motivates these novelists to engage their attention upon this issue.

These two novelists feel that without the actual possession of individual freedom, women will always be objects of cruelty and torture. Their plea for individual freedom arises because most women are treated as having no independent existence or status of human beings. The choice of women to determine the nature of their marriage and mode of life is approved by them. They hold the view that women can assume greater power and responsibility in shaping their life. It is the deeply ingrained traditional habit of living as dependent creatures which gives a blow to their dignity making their life sad. The emancipation of women is based on two factors which lead to the simultaneous process of their learning and earning.

While these two novelists project the concept of new woman, they have their own suppositions which are derived from their preoccupations. For Anand it is the Hindu religion which has led to a strong spirit of inequality among men and women. Jayakanthan does not ignore an external factor like the Hindu religion which has led to some imbalance in the relationship between men and women. He says that men must emancipate themselves from wrong traditional assumptions and that women must gain a new awareness.

Jayakanthan says that man and woman must together reform themselves in order to make a happy living. The greatest advantage, according to him, in this process of woman's emancipation is education. Anand maintains the view that all social aspects of life must be revolutionised by the spirit of modernity. This suggestion of Anand has a humanistic background where religion and tradition have no place. Anand means by modernity an increasing awareness of a rational, scientific view of life. He believes that woman will be viewed in a different perspective in this modernist scheme of life. Jayakanthan gives due place to modernity. But he is of the opinion that the extreme forms of tradition and modernity have their own limitations.

He thinks that good values of the past have not become facts of life and that the wrong elements from it have assumed monstrous shape and existence. He reveals a new dimension to the problem. For Jayakanthan, mere plea for woman's emancipation on the basis of education and economic freedom is only one side; the other side lies in the voluntary reformation of the individual. Therefore he argues that the full emancipation of woman depends on the change in the outlook of men. He says in the preface to *Suntara Kāntam* that in the scheme of creation, woman's existence is not meant to be separate. (3)

Women have to marry men and this venture is a cooperative enterprise. He says that women can gain independence with education and economic freedom but they cannot remain without entering into the framework of marriage. For women to remain alone is unsound. The extreme form of woman's liberation movement recommends a life of isolation. Jayakanthan generally does not approve of this and says that women have to marry and this enterprise of marriage involves association with men. At the same time, he impresses upon men the need to reform themselves, to treat women with dignity and equality. Therefore women cannot live alone and they have to live with men.

Anand works out a different line and he says that women must possess courage and conviction to face all eventualities. He opposes the society dominated by tradition and religion. He concludes that religion and tradition give priority and primacy to men and this special privilege leads to the suppression of women's dignity and equality. Therefore Anand sees the possibility of women's emancipation through protest, resistance and revolution. What opposes women is the society dominated by tradition and religion. He feels that tradition and religion in some form or other have led to male chauvinism. Jayakanthan also deals with this question and says that male chauvinism is a denial of human equality. He states that male chauvinism is an expression of human superiority arising out of lack of culture and inwardness. For him, marriage must create the enlightened idea of friendship which will nurture the feeling of mutual respect basically implying human equality.

The women in Anand's novels are women with keen and critical sensibility. Circumstances induce in them courage to accept a new line of thinking. Gauri is an example of this type of woman. Maya and Janki are individuals who have boldness and the spirit of independence and for them circumstances are subordinate as they create a new history. Jayakanthan's Kalyani, Kokila, Ganga and Sita are learned intellectuals who express themselves freely without any inhibition. Even in their highest state of happiness, they never surrender their individuality. Anand's Maya and Janki are formidable rebels and their capacity to manifest hostile reaction to the society is easily discernible. But they are not essentially intellectual characters like Jayakanthan's.

The reason is that Jayakanthan has developed the view that emancipation of woman is possible only through their endeavour to acquire knowledge and learning. Anand also believes in the same tenet. But in his novels his emphasis is different and he is concerned with characters like Maya, Janki and Gauri who are not intellectuals but are deeply sensitive to human issues by virtue of their critical awareness. For example, Maya disregards class consciousness and she accepts a poor peasant Lal Singh as her lover. A revolutionary idealism found in him becomes a source of her joy. Maya strikes at the very root of tradition when she gives up widowhood and contracts a runaway marriage with Lal Singh. Maya is an activist while Kokila is an aesthetically oriented intellectual.

Kokila resembles Maya in her courage of opting for remarriage in a spirit of challenge. Kalyani and Kokila believe that as emancipated women they are distinct individuals and they claim equality with men. In Maya and Janki there is a spirit of surrender to their men and merging into a state of oneness with them. Probably they are carried away by their ideals. But Kalyani, Kokila, Ganga and Sita claim equality with men as a matter of right.

Anand disbelieves in the traditional concept of arranged marriage where men and women are forced into a close shell. He says that marriage should be the spontaneous choice of the individuals.

Maya and Janki happen to be good examples in the later phase. The widowed Maya and Janki living with Lal Singh and Ananta respectively create the biggest sign of revolt. Anand is aware of the pain of widowhood and he has seen the practical impossibility of widow remarriage in a corrupt society. Jayakanthan deals with this question and he has made this problem the concern of an intellectual who has the capacity to think and resist the currents of the prevailing traditional social forces.

Maya and Janki live up to their own individual expectations and the image of the society sinks very low in their estimate. Anand says that their new venture as "widowed wives and lovers" resists the force of tradition and religion. As Jayakanthan has made a different historical study of the Hindu religion, his argument on woman's emancipation goes in a new direction. He says that he is not for a degenerate tradition. But he is interested in a genuine form of life-giving tradition which does not contradict progressive measures like widow remarriage. The simplest solution of Jayakanthan for woman's emancipation is that when individuals become intellectuals they solve the problems themselves.

## NOTES

1. Swami Vivekananda, qtd. Jayakanthan, *Suntara Kāntam* (Madurai: Meenakshi Puthaka Nilayam, 1982), p. 5.
2. Milton, *Paradise Lost*, Book IV (New York: Longman, 1984), p. 213.
3. Premila Paul, *The Novels of Mulk Raj Anand: A Thematic Study* (New Delhi: Sterling, 1983), p. 114.
4. Mulk Raj Anand, *The Sword and the Sickle* (Bombay: Kutub-Popular, 1942), p. 80.
5. Mulk Raj Anand, qtd. Marlene Fisher, *The Wisdom of the Heart: A Study of the Works of Mulk Raj Anand* (New Delhi, Sterling, 1985), p. 96.
6. Jayakanthan, *Oru Natikai Nātakam Pārkirāl* (Madurai: Meenakshi Puthaka Nilayam, 1988), p. 108.
7. Jayakanthan, *Kokila Enna Ceytuvittal*? (Madurai: Meenakshi Puthaka Nilayam, 1988), p. 33.
8. Krishna Nandan Sinha, *Mulk Raj Anand* (New York: Twayne, 1972), p. 56.
9. Jayakanthan, *Cila Nērankalil Cila Manitarkal*, p. 65.

10. Mulk Raj Anand, *Old Woman and the Cow* (Bombay: Kutub-Popular, 1960), p. 5.
11. Marlene Fisher, p. 100
12. Saros Cowasjee, *So Many Freedoms* (Delhi: Oxford University Press, 1977), p. 155
13. Premila Paul, *The Novels of Mulk Raj Anand: A Thematic Study*, p. 118.
14. C.K. Rajan, "Myth in Mulk Raj Anand's *Gauri*," *Littcrit*, Vol. 17, No. 1 and 2 (June and December 1991), p. 55

# Tradition Versus Modernity

> The new philosophy is to perceive the Old Glory and sympathetically understand the modern ideas.[1]

The subject 'Tradition and Modernity' is a burning issue. The general atmosphere today is to revise and reexamine old things. The main reason for this comes from the changes in the times. Tradition seems to have lost its capacity to arrest and stop the degeneration in life. This assumption creates the possibility for two different approaches. From the first approach one understands that the degeneration in life is not prevented by tradition and so it should be ignored in preference for something else. The other school of thought is of the view that the disappearance of good life indicates the fact that there is a pressing need to renew the old tradition and interpret it in accordance with the forces of modernity. All people prefer one approach or the other in agreement with their education, upbringing and cultural preconceptions.

A group inspired by the European Enlightenment treats tradition as a hindrance to the progress of anything. Reason must establish its triumph over tradition and throw light on illuminating life. Anand belongs to this group which thinks that much of the progress of society depends on the supreme role of reason. According to it, it is the evil of conservatism which has killed the springs of life.

Therefore the major idea of modernity lies in discounting religion, tradition and convention. Scientific outlook, intellectual change, avoidance of class consciousness, abolishing the gap between the rich and the poor, acceptance of Marx for the purpose of uplifting the humanity, and dispensing with religion are some of the chief sources of his modernity.

Jayakanthan belongs to the second group which says that the degeneration in life must make one critical and watchful and enable him to reassess the relationship between tradition and modernity.

The European Enlightenment has placed heavy premium on modernity and it has kept tradition at the altar of sacrifice. The second group thinks that the essence of tradition is dead and that only conservative people preserve the external form of tradition and not the spirit of it. Jayakanthan believes that each age reflects the spirit and essence of tradition by giving new form to it and rejecting the old one. This act which makes a distinction between the spirit of tradition and the external form of it must indicate that the essence of the old outlook is relevant to the present times. Therefore a critical and cautious review of tradition constitutes Jayakanthan's conception of modernity.

Sharma representing tradition and Seshadri celebrating modernity are seen in relation to each other in Jayakanthan's novel, *Pirammōpatēcam*. There is a debate between the two without the possibilities of triumph or defeat. In *Pārisukku Pō*, Jayakanthan declares that modernity does not mean acceptance of divorce and rejection of marriage and does not imply imitating the West in external form. Real modernity means change in outlook and in perception of life and its values.

The village Trilogy of Anand is unlike this in spirit. His protagonist Lal Singh thinks that scientific knowledge is absolutely necessary to change the people in *The Village*. Anand's next novel *Across the Black Waters* gives Lal Singh's experience of exposure to the West. It is very useful in reorganizing his society. Through *The Sword and the Sickle*, Anand lays emphasis upon mass movement and investigates the pros and cons of the organized rebellion as a way of controlling the traditional feudal autocracy.

Like the tetralogy of Shakespeare's History plays, the Lal Singh Trilogy, "a comprehensive major work"[2] of Anand, has its own profound moral significance. The purpose of Shakespeare is to show the consequence of the rejection of tradition and ethically established order. The main motive of Anand is different as he happens to be an active exposer of the corrupt tradition and false morals. Technically his idea is to build up the story of a hero and project his life in three different novels which lay emphasis upon a basic theme. In the renowned village Trilogy, "an impressive work,"[3] *The Village*, *Across the Black Waters* and *The Sword and the Sickle* with

Lal Singh as the central figure, Anand discusses the theme of tradition versus modernity.

These three novels have the conflict between tradition and modernity in the life of the hero Lal Singh, who belongs to an agricultural family of Nandpur, a village in Punjab. This village is deeply steeped in social conventions, rituals and taboos which curtail the growth of human sensibility. But here one finds Lalu, "a sensitive lad who early comes into collision with the codes and customs of the village."[4] So "the village is symbolic at once of the tragedy as well as the hope of India."[5] A long established tradition becomes corrupt when it does not show the capacity for a fresh renewal. Men in such a village imitate conventions meaninglessly. No problem arises when people follow these conventions mechanically in a spirit of unquestioning submission. Anand creates certain situations wherein he dramatizes the life of the hero. These situations are not simply imaginary but are highly realistic as they draw their strength from the novelist's power of observation and depth of experience. The central figure of the trilogy, Lal Singh, is the spokesman of the novelist. He is not able to identify himself with the native conventions and rituals of the village. M.K. Naik rightly calls him "an insider turned outsider."[6]

The hero is not at home with anything that prevails in the village. This builds up in him a feeling of dissatisfaction. His first note of protest is registered when he sees an innocent villager accepting a particular prescription of a quack doctor as an Elixir of life. The ignorance of the villager is a stumbling block in the perception of anything worthwhile. The sad feeling of the hero is that when the villager does not possess knowledge to see things he ceases to be alive and it is a sure sign of doom. The reaction of the hero is described, "Suddenly the figure of the foolish peasant loomed large before his mind."[7]

A deeply ingrained convention cannot be thrown overnight and so the hero makes attempts at showing his resistance to such corrupt practices. Anand sees in Nihal Singh, the father of Lal Singh, a humble figure who obeys the norms of tradition and spontaneously believes that obedience to the value of the past must become a matter of habit as it produces harmony and health. Lal Singh with his critical awareness discovers the need for improving the destiny of the villagers who live amidst dust and dirt without possessing the notion of sanitation and scientific hygiene. Anand welcomes the benefit of the science of the West as it will bring out a revolution in the life of people. The hero, being the self-projection of Anand, believes that healthy human beings are possible only in healthy surroundings and clean environment. The irony is that Nihal Singh is an antithesis to Lal Singh because the former thinks that the modern machine is like the devil and the age of science is unwelcome for him as it produces a faith which disturbs the past. Science, for Nihal Singh, is a creator of darkness and not a bringer of light. Hard physical work was what the old agricultural age required and there is no place for intelligence in such a scheme of life. Big feet with wide palms and long fingers are the sign of hard work put on the land. While looking upon these human features as odd and eccentric, "Lal Singh pities his father, Nihal Singh, who represents the deeply orthodox and superstitious values and beliefs."[8]

Anand points out a mild difference of opinion between Nihal Singh and Lal Singh in terms of their approach to tradition. The novelist treats Nihal Singh as a healthy symbol of tradition as he is free from maliciousness and mean motives. But his disapproval of what prevails as an old custom in the village is firm, although he sees the good qualities of men like Nihal Singh. Lal Singh respects his father but differs from him sharply on many issues. Men like Nihal Singh represent an old tradition and a conventional wisdom which are no longer suitable to the present age.

Lal Singh's elders look upon education as a threat to their agricultural way of life which requires enormous physical energy without the necessity for mental work. Any loss of physical energy is accepted as loss of life. To Lal Singh, such an opinion of the elders is a sign of ignorance and uncritical submission to the old agricultural tradition. That education weakens the physical limbs and its advancement brings death is a view which has got itself embedded in the minds of old people. Lal Singh is very much annoyed to see these meaningless attitudes of the elders who have absolute reverence for tradition. He therefore concludes that real human growth is impossible in such a conservative cultural set-up.

Lal Singh believes that the conditions of the village life cannot be improved without the assistance of science. For Anand the meaning of modernity lies in the use of science. Lal Singh's longing for modernizing the village can be seen from the following passage:

> Lalu hates the dirt and the stench of the village and thinks, 'If only a fire could come and burn these wretched hovels to the ground! He would like to see the village rebuilt with brick, as the houses of the mechanics near the Power House were built.' (35)

There is no doubt, for Lal Singh, that the village has its own beauty for this does not keep him blind to the ghastly picture of ugliness seen in the stench and the dirt. Therefore his plea for using the benefit of science becomes the basis for expressing his theory of modernity. An increased awareness of the actual conditions of life and envisioning the means for improving them constitutes the theme of modernity. Lal Singh is an instrument for an expression of this critical faith. As Balarama Gupta observes, "One finds Anand's faith in the eventual awakening and emancipation of peasantry, easily discernible in the dashing, rebellious character of the hero who fights against all hypocrisy and tries to emerge into a richer and more honest world." (53)

Lal Singh sees no meaning in the rigid conventions of Sikhism. To eat in a Muslim cook-shop is a sign of violation of that sacred convention. He also gets his long hair removed which is an act of sin, according to the Sikh tradition. But the hero concludes because of his modern faith that human brotherhood is an important ideal of life. He feels that all human beings are one and to discriminate a Sikh from a Muslim is the greatest mark of blunder. A broad vision which embraces all human beings in one fold is a major part of Anand's faith which gets expressed in the act of Lal Singh eating in a Muslim hotel.

The same modern spirit enables the hero to review the meaning of certain conventions which are born out of specific cultural climates and environmental necessities. There is a long passage from the novel indicating the circumstantial compulsions leading to the rise of certain peculiar conventions. The novelist proceeds to make a severe rational criticism of these conventions. He places himself in the context of pre-independence and tries to prove the futility of these rituals. Anand refers to a phase in the Indian history when religious conventions passed through a state of degeneration.

Lalu's condemnation of the Sikh religion takes a vigorous form when he describes it as "A religion of donkeys; a religion of bullocks." (28) As this is an extreme criticism, the relevant passage is quoted for examination:

> The Katch, Kara, Kirpan, Kesh and Ganga might well have been necessary when Guru Govind was fighting Aurangzeb. Then it was said he enjoined his men to wear shorts because he couldn't get clothes, bangles and swords for symbols, and long hair because he couldn't get barbers to shave them, and combs to tidy their hair. Such provisions were dictated by necessity and common sense. But as everyone with a grain of intelligence said, what was the use of observing these conventions now that there was no further need for them? There was no religion in doing so. He had always felt impatient and embarrassed at having to wear long hair. The other K's he didn't mind. They were unnecessary and superstitious but they did not involve any active inconvenience. (28)

In this passage Anand points out that the Sikh religion has lost its capacity for adapting itself to the changes of the times. Reason brought about a revolution in the West and it was useful in dislodging many superstitions and false beliefs. The spirit of modernity draws its inspiration from the purifying influence of reason.

Anand's profound conviction is that life must be revolutionized by the rational spirit of modernity. The old customs like wearing shorts and having long hair have lost their value and to stick to them in the name of tradition is a sign of cultural misconception, according to the novelist. He thinks that the whole weight of religion should not be made to depend upon adherence to external customs. For the novelist, freedom is the main moving spring of life and a religion of conservatism is a hindrance to any development. There is no question of denying the fact that the birth of a religion has a strong climatic and geographical background. When man remains good in spirit, customs and conventions become secondary. This is the basic meaning of Anand's spirit of modernity. Lal Singh therefore believes that the development of society requires the adoption of scientific inventions. The novelist affirms the view that traditions and conventions have made life wretched and inhuman. So Lal Singh thinks that science humanizes man and life and it provides materials for keeping the surroundings clean and healthy. Anand feels that improving the external aspect of life in terms of sanitation and hygiene and dislodging meaningless conventions with the help of scientific rationalism constitutes the theme of modernity.

The portrait of Mahant Nandgir, the false priest of the village, is a masterstroke of Anand in exposing the religious people who do not lead a life of piety and devotion. The life of a priest is an example for a common man to emulate but here Mahant observes no meaningful religious principle in matters of eating and controlling the senses. Although the village people know the priest to be a pretender, they find no way of checking him as religion has its strong impact on people. The cure for snakebite, according to the village priest, is to recite a Mantra in the name of God. Anand is very critical of this kind of religion which comes to be identified with superstition.

When Maulvi, the Muslim 'medicine man,' tells Lalu's father that he can never be blessed with the vision of heaven since he happens to be a non-believer, Lal Singh bursts out, surely there is no favouritism shown to men in heaven, if there be such a place, just because men belong to one religion or other." (218) Lal Singh thinks rightly that it is improper to deny the benefit of reaching heaven on account of one being a follower of a particular religion. He also says that God, if there were one, should be impartial and that he should not become a victim of favouritism. Anand here points out how religion has become a tool for promoting wrong practices and false beliefs.

Anand gives a graphic description of the village elders and priests who devise several means by which the freedom of the people is curbed. An action cannot be performed in this village because it needs to be reviewed by religion. Any action which carries no sanction of religion is a matter of sin. The influence of religion is so strong in the minds of people that they cannot even laugh in the presence of elders. To laugh in the presence of elders is construed as a mark of disrespect. Anand feels that the growth of life does not depend upon the injunctions of religion to repress individual freedom. The elders and priests have become mechanical in their attitude to religion and tradition. Lal Singh says that such people are not really bad but it is religion which undeniably safeguards their false and hypocritical life. To question their spurious life is a mark of sin arising out of disobedience. In this way religion and convention perpetuate a false way of life and any denunciation of it is treated as heresy. Anand sees how truth is sacrificed by the elders and the priests. This is because the real spirit of religion has disappeared and only the empty form with its pompous ritualism prevails. Anand says that real life must be valued and appreciated and, for that purpose, truth must be discriminated from falsehood.

Jayakanthan, in his preface to the novel *Pirammōpatēcam*, makes a valiant attempt at clarifying his position and clearing up some misconception and misunderstandings. For instance, K.N. Subramanian points out, "Jayakanthan is a radical in his mental outlook but his novels have a conservative overtone."[9] Similarly Jayakanthan says that his communist critics wanted him to stick to their ideology and that the non-Brahmin observers did not like his exalting the character of Sharma. His primary duty as a novelist is to make his position intelligible to them. He is therefore forced to define what he means by forward-looking attitude. Two passages are quoted from the preface:

> He who has a tuft is a conservative, he who goes to the temple is an orthodox. All our Puranas are terribly unprogressive. When one condemns our Shastras as backward and conservative, one is extolled as being forward and progressive.
>
> Changing the name of a person is an act of progressiveness; to eat biriyani is a sign of forwardness; to talk about the West while discussing any subject is a cultural progression. Another theory of progress is to debunk our culture and become an iconoclast. (4-5)

Jayakanthan, while attacking such notions of a conservative and a liberal, says that these two ways of classifying backwardness and forwardness do not indicate any wisdom. There are two categories of people, namely, liberals and conservatives. But according to the novelist they miss much in being exclusive and partisan.

Jayakanthan clearly says in the preface that a section-follower or a party-follower of any kind is not a seeker of truth. (4-5) One of the qualifications of a real forward-looking person is not to hate any section or anything but to give up mental prejudice and preconception. Such a person works for the uplift of the human race. The follower of a communist denomination is pained to see Jayakanthan praising the virtues of real orthodoxy. Jayakanthan's unilateral answer is that a man who fixes himself either in Marxist dogma or religious orthodoxy cannot see the truth, he tries to aim at. He has in his mind the picture of a balanced thinker who is just and fair in all his dealings. Therefore the novelist concludes that a forward-looking person with progressive zeal is not a party or section-follower, but a seeker of truth.

Jayakanthan's notion of a forward-looking person as a truth seeker softens the opposition between tradition and modernity. The novelist again distinguishes the dissembler and pretender in religion from a truth-seeker. In this respect Sankara Sharma is a great revolutionary hero. (5) He not only believes in rituals but also in work. He is unorthodox in accepting a non-Brahmin as his son. His mind has no predominant caste-orientation. His rejection of Seshadri and acceptance of Sadhanandan is a sign of his being true to his inner ideal. When someone says that a pronounced atheist like him cannot and should not be an admirer of Sharma, Jayakanthan replies that it is not an act of courtesy and ethics. (6)

Jayakanthan describes his moral and spiritual vision in the preface when he says that there is no wisdom in attacking a person of some persuasion just because he does not seem to be in alliance with his point of view. The world destroys itself by a block-thinking tendency. Therefore Jayakanthan describes Sharma as an exemplary character. His broad vision is reflected in the character of Sharma who has a passion for imparting knowledge to people and doing service to humanity. No real forward-looking person can afford to dismiss Sharma because his ideal is to help humanity and this is no different from the policy of any progressivist. Sharma has a genuine zeal to reform life and he projects in himself the outlook of a spiritualist. Moreover this ethical and spiritual orientation of Sharma is acceptable to Seshadri. Sharma is a reformist, as he wants to be responsive to the spirit of times. The novelist makes Seshadri an ideal character. He never attacks Sharma. His aim is not to exalt his notion of atheism and communism in the presence of Sharma. Sharma does not dismiss Seshadri but he treats him with patience and due respect. Seshadri also does not disregard Sharma but he treats him with respect and humility. Jayakanthan sees the highest mark of culture in the interaction between the two characters. The novelist believes that creeds and ideologies need not create conflict and ill-temper. He who wants to transform life should not become a meaningless slave to ideology.

Jayakanthan believes in a cooperative spirit of partnership between people like Sharma and Seshadri who belong to different schools of thought. For the novelist, atheism does not mean simply denial of God. It means the emergence of a new critical force and spirit which reviews and reassesses life in accordance with the changing spirit of the times. In fact, Sharma has a greater critical force and spirit than Seshadri. Sharma shows his dissatisfaction with the clan of his own people who lead a degenerate life. Seshadri's atheism is an outcome of his critical awareness. While the ideal of social well being is at the heart of Sharma, the concept of social justice is at the heart of Seshadri. Jayakanthan says that Sharma and Seshadri work for the same ideal with new ideological backgrounds. Many critics consider *Pirammōpatēcam* a novel of compromise. (7)

It is certainly not so because no character is allowed to give up his specific cultural point of view. Sharma's dismissal of Seshadri and acceptance of Sadhanandhan is not a policy of compromise. For Jayakanthan it is a sign of the biggest revolution. Here the novelist's guiding canon is that a forward-looking person like Sharma gives up his partisan bias and rises to the new vision and perception of truth. If a critic believes in the usual distinction between tradition and modernity, he will call Jayakanthan a novelist of compromise. But Jayakanthan does not believe in such an invidious distinction between old and new because he believes that a progressivist is a highly cultured man and he rises above these divisions.

Jayakanthan's novel, *Pirammōpatēcam*, raises certain key issues in modern society. What are the standards by which a modern man must judge very complicated questions like the place and status of the creed of Brahminism and the modern concept of Communism and Atheism? The novelist's intention is to approach these problems from a balanced and impartial standpoint. Jayakanthan at the time of the publication of this novel was a Communist and he was correspondingly an atheist. Even while he was a Communist and an atheist he as an artist was something morc than all these labels could describe. The major reason for his being something more than these labels lies in his firm and passionate attitude as a creative artist. As an imaginative thinker, he explores these different questions by creating a story and investing the characters with specific attitudes and dispositions. The story of the novel can be taken as a cover for unravelling the complex nature of the problems. The novelist wants to be true to life and prefers to be realistic and frank in his perception of the age-old controversies.

The hero of the novel, *Pirammōpatēcam*, Shankara Sharma is a dynamic character. He was originally a native of Trichy. His mind was pained when he could not tolerate the sight of people following superstitions and customs. He was more interested in seeing the truth and real nature of things and so he embarked upon a far voyage. His life-journey brought him face-to-face with two things. He felt that the entire world was in the grip of atheism and ignorance. Sharma is one who belongs to the rich old Vedic tradition. Therefore he believes that evil will be found on a large scale when the Kaliyuga will come to an end. (10) According to him, the virtuous Brahmin who knows this law of life and when he surrenders himself to these corrupt influences forgetting his mission and Dharma, how can one overcome the evil effect of Kaliyuga? A Brahmin is supposed to be a custodian of knowledge. Sharma affirms the view that a Brahmin has no privilege of being a fool. (11) His life-travel brings him to two conclusions. He discovers himself to be disheartened by the prevalence of atheism which will not improve the world, according to his estimate. At the same time he sees that the Brahmins are Brahmins only in name and not in their observance of ethics and high ideals. (11)

Jayakanthan reveals his inner mind in his creation of Shankara Sharma. The novelist develops a new ethics in his life-vision and, that is, he does not want to show partisan interest in anything. For him, there is no wisdom in ignoring the truth or deliberately distorting it, in accordance with one's own mental preconceptions. The business of a creative artist is not to fabricate things and indulge in perpetuating the existence of untruths. It is this disinterested spirit of an observer which controls the mind of the novelist in his judgement. All the characters in this novel are the spokesmen of Jayakanthan. He reveals his truth-speaking tendency when he is for an impartial investigation of important life-issues.

He makes Shankara Sharma a revolutionary Brahmin. The Brahminical way of life involves special duties and responsibilities. Sharma sees deep degeneration in the life of Brahmins who no longer have the temperament to follow the Vedic way of life. He is angry with them for their failures and shortcomings. With the help of Sharma, Jayakanthan is able to distinguish and say that the virtue of Brahminism is one thing and its degeneration is another. Sharma says to himself:

> Chanting Vedic Mantras and delivering discourse on Puranas is not the only function and vocation of a Brahmin. He can do some work and earn his livelihood and thereby he gains an opportunity to be close to life. (12)

Sharma knows that for an orthodox Brahmin, to earn livelihood by work and not by chanting Mantra is an act of sin. This is the first incident in the novel, where the novelist starts showing the conflict between tradition and modernity. Sharma has in him the courage to revise the old values and make it suitable to the prevailing spirit of the age. It is very clear for Sharma and his creator that old values do not have the structure of a dead stone. Sharma's preparedness to reassess the old values is a sign of his being alive to the forces and complex currents of life. The old is bad and the new is good: this seems to be the voice of modernity. The old is good and the new is bad: this happens to be the voice of tradition. Jayakanthan is not caught in any one of these two blocks. He prefers to stand midway between the two groups.

Sharma and his daughter Maitrei live in the back-portion of a house in which Rayar and Gangabhai, a Kannada Brahmin couple, live. Though Rayar is much older than Sharma, there is a spirited intimacy and relation between the two. Jayakanthan uses this situation to develop a dialectical debate between tradition and modernity. Sharma is a headcook who delights in preparing many food items. The novel gains momentum when Rayar introduces a communist worker Seshadri to Sharma telling him that because of his participation in labour union activity he could not continue his service in a hotel. Sharma reveals his real character when he explains that his delay in getting Maitrei married is due to his inability to come across a real Brahmin. If Sharma cannot get a virtuous Brahmin as a match for Maitrei, he is prepared to keep his daughter a spinster. This attitude of Sharma gives a clue to his intentions. Merely being a Brahmin is not enough for Sharma. What is important for him is that a Brahmin has the duty to avoid inconsistency and contradictions in life and lead a life of ethical perfection.

The dialectical debate between tradition and modernity is introduced by Jayakanthan when he shows a very heated and lively conversation between Sharma and Seshadri. Sharma asks Seshadri: "you say you are a Brahmin boy. You have no sacred ash on your forehead." Seshadri replies, "I have no faith in such a ritual." Sharma again interrogates him, "have you no faith in being a Brahmin?" Seshadri gives a fitting answer, "I have no faith in being a Brahmin by having sacred ash on my forehead." (16)

It is clear for Sharma that one cannot be a Brahmin without observing rituals and applying ash on the brow. But for Seshadri one can be a Brahmin even without these rituals. Perhaps Jayakanthan agrees with Seshadri and says that it is not ritualism that makes a Brahmin a real Brahmin. Seshadri is of the opinion that the virtue of Brahminism does not lie in observance of rituals, but in having a noble and compassionate heart.

Jayakanthan makes use of all his artistic energies in depicting a conflict between two diametrically opposed views. Sharma and Seshadri represent two poles of human existence. The novelist makes special effort in creating an awareness of the complexity of the conflict. The artist builds up a climax when he engages these two characters in a deep conversation. it is worthwhile to record the conversation in order to show the full force of the debate between tradition and modernity.

Sharma sees a book in the hands of Seshadri and goes through it very carefully for sometime. It is a book which refutes the value of religion and preaches atheism. Sharma tells him that the book is written from an atheist standpoint. Seshadri admits that the book contains the seed of atheism as it is written by a Communist. Sharma asks Seshadri whether he belongs to the same Communist movement. This question troubles the mind of Seshadri and he admits with great hesitation that he belongs to the same Communist Block. Sharma has an open mind and does not judge people merely by their views.

The masterstroke of Jayakanthan lies in Sharma's reply to him: "It is better to be an atheist than to call oneself a Brahmin and lead a degenerate life." (19) Seshadri puts the opposite question to him and asks whether a Brahmin should not be an atheist. But for Jayakanthan, Sharma seems to be more interesting because of his view that it is better to be an honest atheist than a corrupt Brahmin. Seshadri's reply is less attractive in its dimension. Sharma goes on to give a definite reply to the crucial question of Seshadri, "It is not that a Brahmin should not be an atheist. Not that he cannot be but that it is impossible for him to be like that." (20) Sharma concludes in this speech that when a Brahmin becomes an atheist, he ceases to be a Brahmin. It is almost a foregone conclusion for Sharma that an atheist cannot be a Brahmin. For him, Brahminism and atheism are sharply opposed and logically distinguishable terms.

Jayakanthan pays great attention to the reply of Sharma. The novelist tries to be fair in his analysis. Sharma holds the view that an atheist cannot be a Brahmin because he denies any belief in Brahman and refuses to follow rituals and conventions. To become a Brahmin, birth and caste are not necessary. A man does not become a Brahmin just because he is born to a Brahmin husband and a Brahmin wife. Like any other man he is born like an animal and becomes a man by developing his character and performing his duty. Later on he is initiated into the Brahmin-knowledge and instructed to wear the sacred thread. According to Sharma, propagating knowledge and doing service to humanity should become the sole duty of a Brahmin. He will be judged to be a real Brahmin so long as he performs this duty. Therefore atheism is untenable and it is certainly a contradiction of Brahminism. Jayakanthan's intention is not to uphold whatever Sharma says. But he certainly appreciates him because Sharma is clear-headed in his views and does not confuse the issue. He is sincerely interested in improving mankind. His policy needs to be respected.

This intricate discussion shows one particular attitude of Jayakanthan very distinctly. According to the novelist, Sharma is not an orthodox Brahmin. It shows that Jayakanthan does not work with bias for anything. He scores an initial victory in the realm of ideas when he makes Sharma an unorthodox Brahmin who chants not only mantras but works as a head cook. Sharma shows his readiness to alter the old value and this shows his forward-looking tendency. Jayakanthan believes with Sharma that without making modifications, old values will lose their force and outlive their usefulness. Jayakanthan has admiration for Sharma not because he is a Brahmin but because he is a Brahmin who sees life openly without any prejudice and is prepared to reassess things. What the novelist wants to convey is that Sharma's attitude to life is appreciably healthy. It is this perspective of Sharma which attracts Jayakanthan. A good society requires an enlightened person like Sharma and his presence is a source of inspiration to many people. The novelist knows and sees that a character like Sharma inspires people, creates a taste for knowing truth and puts them on the right path.

Jayakanthan brings out the nobility and disinterestedness of Sharma in another manner when Seshadri confesses that it is a sign of impudence to debate with elders like Sharma. The novelist does not fail to introduce a new dimension in the character of Sharma. To the apologetic tone of Seshadri's humility and his endeavour to discuss freely, Sharma exclaims that it is no sin for a man to feel apologetic for expressing his views forthrightly:

> If I am afraid of facing intellectual enquiry then I have no belief in the Dharma I follow. He who clings to a weak and ineffective philosophy may think that others should not speak about their views freely. (21)

Sharma deserves appreciation when he says that the right to listen to any man's view forms part of his Dharma. Jayakanthan says that Sharma does not prematurely dismiss any man's view without giving a patient hearing to him. This ideal of objectivity which the novelist attributes to the character of Sharma endears the latter to the readers. Seshadri is allowed to have his say:

> The fact that you did not accept me as a Brahmin is quite right. I have not come here to claim that right as you point out. But looking at the vast changes taking place in the world, I think that this new gospel of social justice [Communism] is better than the old Vedic Dharma and I have accepted this gospel as my new Veda. Even otherwise, the Brahmin community treats these rituals and conventions as imprisoning chains and fetters and they do them mechanically and inevitably much against their heart. At the same time he who accepts the new Veda discovers fresh insights, acquires enlightenment and develops knowledge based on free and independent enquiry. The most important thing that you pointed out, imparting knowledge to people and society, even that the followers of the new Veda do. They serve in other matters also. I hope, it is not a mistake if I call myself to be such a Brahmin who follows this new Veda and imparts knowledge to society in many ways. (21-22)

Sharma is under the impression that his old Veda and its message can improve society. But Seshadri thinks that the old Veda has lost its utility and problems in the society arise from different angles. The Communist philosophy, according to Seshadri, aims at transforming the conditions of social life. His deep interest in labour union activity indicates that social justice needs to be gained on the basis of organized mass movement and protest. Naturally such labour union preoccupations create a demand for looking at the world and its structure much more realistically. Seshadri's allegiance to Communist ideology is a sign of his being alive to the pressure of time which calls for a new way of organizing the society. There is therefore a strong tendency in a Communist like Seshadri to interpret improvement from a materialistic point of view. He deeply believes that the old Veda is excellent but it remains unconcerned with the new problems and changes which take place in the society. His intense awareness of what happens in society leads him to give up belief in the old Veda and accept in its place a new one.

Seshadri thinks that worshipping God, chanting Mantra, delivering discourses on Puranas belong to the old world civilization.

These activities have their own meaning and relevance. But their role is different from what a typical Communist like Seshadri has in mind. When Sharma connects Communism with atheism and says that both are identical in their outlook, Seshadri reacts to his act of mingling these two things and raises the question as to why a Brahmin should not be an atheist and Communist. For Sharma Brahminism and Atheism are polar opposites; but for Seshadri there seems to be no opposition between these two because he thinks that a good Brahmin should be alive to the spirit of the times. This consciousness of being alive to the spirit of the times produces in him a new awareness of the social problems. The necessity for change is realized and it leads to a review of everything.

It is this critical spirit which makes a Brahmin like Seshadri an atheist. Sharma grows sceptical of the value of this critical spirit which destroys the old values. Seshadri is equally sceptical of the values of the old Veda and he thinks that the new social problems cannot be tackled from the standpoint of Sharma.

Sharma is a revolutionary, in the sense that he has enlarged his idea of the old Brahminism to include belief in work as an inseparable ideal of a good Brahmin. Seshadri feels that this is not enough, because his religious sensibility does not enable him to perceive the actual problems of life which cry for social justice. It is this thought of establishing social justice which engenders in Seshadri a feeling of disappointment with the old values of tradition. Sharma provides dialectically an answer to the question of atheism in a long passage:

> Yes I agree with you. Just as theism is the basis for the old Veda so also atheism is the foundation for the new Veda. However much you try to talk about the old and the new, you should know one thing. Atheism is as old as theism. But for the purpose of living and the improvement of the human race, culture which is spoken of as essential is developed by theism. Even at that time only a few knowledgeable individuals preached and spoke atheism. People never accepted it. It is only because of this wise disapproval of atheism that the society grew. If people accept atheism, the world will be in doldrums. Therefore the world should be saved from the onslaught of atheism. (22)

Sharma utters these words in a raised tone. He believes that atheism makes the society and the world godless. Sharma takes into account what Seshadri says: but his firm belief is that the organization of social order is impossible without theist-orientation. For him, the past history shows theism as the greatest inspirer of everything existing in the society.

Sharma strongly believes that the very existence of life is sustained by theism. The ideas of home, family, parental affection, marriage, living together, helping others, observing one's own mission and duty, consideration for the poor and the disabled, humanising man's aggressive and brutal instincts and feelings, prayer for rain and avoidance of calamity were all promoted in the past by a sincere act of strengthening theism. Whatever is good and makes for order is due to the healthy influence of theism. The building up of life and the making of a civilization according to Sharma carry a long established history which is invariably nourished by theism. The disciplining of human life and energy is impossible without it. Sharma without hesitation concludes that the best things of life have been secured and made stable only by the benign influence of theism. It is visualized as the ordering principle by which everything is built up and formed. Sharma therefore continues to think that the same life-giving principle of theism will add salt and strength to things. The function of a Brahmin, according to him, is to know his heritage, learn it and make it an integral part of his consciousness. His competence to spread knowledge and do service is derived from the observance of his ethics and dedication to the noble ideal of preaching and propagating good things for the maintenance of life.

Jayakanthan's party-allegiance to Communism and his dismissal of religion at the time of writing the novel, *Pirammōpatēcam,* may lead people to conclude that he will deliver verdict in their own expected favourable terms. But Jayakanthan's business is not to take sides with the one or the other. It is the temper of the creative artist which helps him in his understanding of this problem. Brahminism is bad and atheism is good or atheism is bad and Brahminism is good: Jayakanthan is not interested in this kind of pigeonholing. The artist says that when bad Brahminism is condemned, it does not automatically invalidate the virtue of good and noble Brahminism. For him, Shankara Sharma is a good example of this kind. Similarly dishonest atheism does not altogether nullify honest atheism. The novelist takes Seshadri as a good example of this kind. Jayakanthan's atheist critics want him to condemn religion and his Communist critics expect him to uphold the Marxism of Seshadri. Jayakanthan was an atheist and a Communist. This past stand does not or even need not oblige him to support Marxism as against religion and theism. His atheism combined with Communism must be taken as a phase in the evolution of his character and personality.

Jayakanthan thinks like his character Seshadri that society must be changed and that it can be changed only on the basis of Marxist philosophy. But this work of altering the order of society does not rule out for him the existence of Vedic values. The novelist says in his preface that an ideal forward-looking person is one who is fair to everything. (5) He does not accept the stand that the atheist is forward-looking and that a theist is a backward-looking conservative. Jayakanthan does not see Sharma and Seshadri separately but he sees them in relation to each other. It shows that Jayakanthan is a believer in relating things and not separating them. When he states that he who believes in the total uplift of the entire human race without any bias and hatred is an ideal progressivist, it shows that his mind can go beyond the ordinary division between old and new. This concept of progress does not force him to sustain the polarization and the dichotomy between tradition and modernity. He gives a new meaning and dimension to the age-long conflict between tradition and modernity. He is a creative artist endowed with a liberal humanist perspective. It is this quality which makes him impartial and without his being emotionally committed to things. Jayakanthan has the wisdom to know that people like Sharma and Seshadri possess some ideal aims but their means for implementation are different.

Sharma's stern refusal to give his daughter Maitrei in marriage to Seshadri is noteworthy. There are two grounds on which he does not favour this proposal. Sharma thinks that a true Brahmin alone can marry his daughter. His inordinate delay in getting her married is only an expression of this bias in favour of finding a true Brahmin. Although Seshadri is a Brahmin by birth, he is not fit enough to marry Maitrei, as he is an atheist.

Seshadri's boldness to marry Maitrei against all odds is an indication of his firm resolve to carry out the plan. He also furnishes some standards to validate his action. He assumes that when the hearts are united, Shastras need not stand in the way. Sharma's insistence on discovering a true Brahmin is a mark of his lack of capacity for adaptability. Moreover Maitrei is not in agreement with her own father's wish and plan.

Seshadri has the intellectual shrewdness to quote the law of Manu Dharma Shastra which says that a girl has the right to marry a person of her choice three years after she comes of marriageable age. (28) This is a blow to Sharma. He recovers himself from this shock of being exposed to Manu and says that there is no condition stated that the father must necessarily approve of such a choice and act.

Sharma gets a chance to see the young twenty-year-old boy Sadhanandhan with sacred ash on the forehead chanting religious songs musically with proper stress and correct intonation. His thrill in discovering such a religiously inclined boy is remarkable. Sharma has great admiration for Sadhanandhan. But his admiration for him is not unqualified. Sharma invites him to his house and provides food to him in the front portion for he has no mind to flout his conviction by taking the non-Brahmin to the interior of the house.

Sharma's revolutionary endeavour to make the non-Brahmin Sadhanandhan a Brahmin by observing all the rituals and ceremonies and initiating him into the knowledge of the Brahman is an astounding act. Sharma does not totally reject the marriage between Seshadri and Maitrei. He gives blessings to them as he would normally give to a stranger and a third person without any real involvement. This proves his axiom that a man does not become a Brahmin by birth and caste affinity. Mere Brahminical parentage does not confer special virtue and grace on him. He has to deserve that stature of being a Brahmin by his passion for ethical discipline and perfection. The work of a true Brahmin is different from the work of an atheist and it is on this ground that Sharma does not accept Seshadri as a Brahmin. His final view is that real Brahminism enriches life and atheism destroys life.

Sharma's bold admission and acceptance of Sadhanandhan as a Brahmin indicates his large-heartedness. This also reveals the principle of Sharma that a man becomes a Brahmin only by character and not by caste and birth. Sharma himself consoles Rayar saying that Vishwamitra and Kanva Mahrishi became Brahmins by their observance of high ideals and ethics. When Rayar suggests Sadhanandhan as a match for Maitrei, Sharma sternly reminds him of the practice of only the father initiating the son into the Brahman-knowledge. Therefore Sadhanandhan becomes his son.

Jayakanthan combines in himself the various qualities of a liberal humanist, Marxist sympathizer, a refined atheist and a discriminating admirer of the past. He is no longer a believer in a partisan perspective. It is the tendency to know the truth which impels his mind to show this novel in a broad form. He says that for a partisan follower, there is a conflict between tradition and modernity. The main cause is that the partisan follower has fixed his mind in a particular way and he is determined to denounce the opposite view.

Jayakanthan says in his preface that theism and atheism are opposed terms. (5) As a creative artist, he does not approve of a mind which works in partisan terms. For him, according to the novel, the conflict between tradition and modernity is artificial and such a division between the old and the new is the result of absolute partisanship in the matter of following things. Jayakanthan feels that as a creative novelist his role is that of a truth-seeker. He believes that a sympathetic observer knows life much more comprehensively than a partisan follower. As a creative thinker, he has the patience to trace the history of any problem. He does not allow his mind to be controlled by a preconceived view. He looks at life freely and openly.

The second novel of the Lal Singh Trilogy of Anand, *Across the Black Waters*, is commonly described as a war novel. Such a critical estimate does not go without weight. It can be easily understood that war in this novel is only a background for showing complex human relations. To describe it only as a war novel does not conform to the real intention of the novelist. The hero Lal Singh is found in Europe when a false charge of theft is foisted upon him by the village landlord in *The Village*. Lalu hates the village for its blindness in following meaningless customs. His dissatisfaction with the village arises from the ignorance of the people who have no inclination to see anything in the right spirit. He therefore concludes that truth-knowing involves a critical spirit and according to him it is this freedom of perception which can lead the village on the path of truth. His scientific and critical outlook alienates him from the conventions of the village and his life becomes a life of uneasiness like a fish out of water. He is not able to identify himself with the ancient roots of the village. It is a familiar surrounding but he experiences strangeness amidst his own native background. In a sense, *The Village*, an Indian pastoral unique in character, is a study of alienation and "helplessness of its hero . . . in a predominantly callous world."[10] This psychological dissatisfaction with the village is the result of his modern progressive rational spirit.

Anand's love of modernity does not keep him blind to the traditional nobility and wisdom of the village embodied in people like Nihal Singh. His moving farewell to his son Lalu captures a new dimension in him. The dying father tells his leave-taking son that men should be explorers. His only wish is that his son must gather experience and prove to be a lion in facing life. Above all, he says, Lalu must illumine the lives of his forefathers by bringing fame and name to them. When he leaves for France, the entire village rises in a mood of jubilation and gives a warm send-off to him. There is communal harmony which is strengthened by a convention which gives meaning to the exit of Lal Singh. The last words of Nihal Singh to his son who is to rejoin the army are reflective of the wisdom of the father:

> Parents breed children not for themselves but to fight public cause. Let him go out to life and be a lion's son. Let him go out and perform deeds worthy of his forefathers. Let him go out and reap the harvest of experience. (221-22)

From the ritualistic convention one finds human solidarity. This is revealed when Lal Singh leaves his village to go back to the army. The whole village community gives him a ceremonious farewell and their affection "comes from the mainspring of a convention which had ritualized departure . . . he sensed the element of vanity that was in the attempts of his relatives to outdo one another in generosity and nobleness now towards him." (223)

The central scene of action in *Across the Black Waters* is laid in Europe covering areas like France and Germany. Here "Anand has recreated all the horror and brutality of war."[11] Lal Singh joins the army in order to escape from the charge of theft thrust on him by the landlord. The basic motive of the novelist apart from a "ruthless denunciation of war which is only a dignified name, for cruelty and cold-blooded violence"[12] is to put the protagonist in touch with foreign lands and enable him to know how people there have made their progress in regard to many things. Lalu sails to Marseilles to fight in Flanders. But the events come to turn in such a manner that he becomes a German prisoner of war. The novelist takes such incidents like the hero's escape from the village for fear of being caught on a false charge of theft, his flight to France with the mission of a soldier and subsequently becoming a German prisoner of war as a background for exposing him to the atmosphere of the West. There are three themes which are explicitly developed in the novel.

The progressive West is contrasted with the unprogressive East. One finds an expression of the novelist's pet belief in the general superiority of the modern West over the East.[13] The old ideas of tradition and convention keep the village in a state of ignorance as people never gain any glimpse of change. Secondly the act of gaining new knowledge in the encounter between the Indians and the Whites is dealt with. The idea of participating in a war without knowing the purpose is an enigma to Lal Singh and other soldiers who are resigned to their lot towards the drama of war. Lal Singh, for whom war means inevitable destruction of human race and its surroundings, is at a loss to know why war is fought at all:

> The elements of sanity in Lalu persisted in the face of guns and in the face of the insanity which had blown off the towers of the churches, and he could not believe that ordinary men and women of good sense, and the Government of France, England and Germany, which were saner and wiser than the ordinary people over whom they ruled, could be engaged in a war in which men were being wounded and houses shattered.[14]

Finally in *Across the Black Waters*, there are instances to show that the Whites are far better than the Indian officers who ill-treat the Indian soldiers.

Anand understands that the concepts of modern social reform are derived from the West. Lal Singh's exposure to the West gives him a new awareness of life and things. His experience in the foreign land imbues him with a higher knowledge. The first impression which the hero gathers is that the Indian villages live in wretched and unhealthy conditions while people in the West live in a neat and clean surrounding with their improved knowledge of hygiene. The European philosophy of progress is based upon industrialization and mechanization. These are the two scientific processes which brought about a new conception of life. Anand thinks that so long as the Indian village is not exposed to this philosophy of progress, it will remain in a state of backwardness and ignorance. It is this progressive feeling which encourages Lalu to look upon the forward-going Europe as a kind of perfect heaven. He sees that in a traditional village the young do not have the freedom to communicate with the old. The new philosophy of progress has established the idea of equality among people in the West. Lal Singh assumes on the basis of his experience that any human growth is based upon freedom. The tradition in the East treats the restriction of freedom as a sign of culture while the West considers critical enquiry of anything as a means for renewing life in a fresh and original manner.

Anand thinks that any attempt at resisting the philosophy of social progress is to strike at the idea of improving life in a more scientific manner. In the novel under discussion, one finds in Lal Singh an urge to modernise the village:

> If it was typical of Vilayati peasant households, then all his righteous indignation against his own village folk had been justified and his aspiration to live as European farmers lived a great deal. He wished some of the old fogies of his village were here, for then he could show them how true had been his task about reforming the village. (196)

Lalu denounces the conservative mentality of the villagers who live a low level of existence for want of progressive knowledge. He discovers that the rural villages in the West are completely modernized and as a result people have gained the benefit of sanitation and hygiene. The village remains undeveloped with its traditions and conventions and innumerable restrictions are imposed on life. A free expression of life is what the idea of modernism promotes and it is found in the West. When Lal Singh sees sweepers easily mingling with all people drinking wine, he observes that the feeling of equality is greater in the Whites than in the Indians as the former achieved liberation from convention and tradition.

Anand is pained to see the unprogressive mind of the Indian villagers who refuse to change their old style of life. He calls such people 'fogies'. A fogy is an old uninterested person who has no inclination to accept changes and dislikes all modern ideas of reform and progress. Lal Singh's main complaint against the village is that the traditional teachers have not thought in terms of giving a human dimension to life. This knowledge of improving human dimension comes from science and the idea of social reform. But the villagers resist this new knowledge as they think that it poses a threat to the existence of tradition. The novelist thinks that this is nothing but backward-mindedness. The villagers are trained to think that any resistance to change is what constitutes their loyalty to tradition.

Lal Singh shows in the passage quoted a glaring contrast between the European farmers and their Indian counterparts. Anand says that life is lived by the European farmers fully. This experience of fullness of life is made possible by the modern idea of progress and scientific reform of things. It is a source of sorrow for Lalu when he simply reflects on the unclean surroundings and the unprogressive condition of mind. He visualises that these old people must be told that cows must be milked by machines and the houses and hotels in the European villages are kept in a state of hygiene and the pigs, cows and horses and the sheds and stables and the bath are cleaned, washed and purified through scientific methods.

Anand proves on some substantial grounds that European way of life is far superior to the Indian way of life. Lal Singh comes across a group of White women who wear frocks showing their legs and breasts and smiling with joy and happiness. The strong tradition in the Indian villages leads people to think that concealing legs and covering the breasts fully are an expression of culture. But the

European women are carefree and they do not bother much about the external dress and its capacity to cover all parts. These women think that a free expression of human sensibility keeps them in a more natural state.

Lal Singh is of the opinion that the Indian women conceal their parts with the dress but their heart remains undeveloped. What the hero feels is that artificial care does not pave the way for real progress. Another important fact which he notices is that married women take extraordinary interest in their beauty and external appearance. Their wish is to remain young although they are past middle age. But the case with the Indian women is different. Their traditional restrictions do not permit them to beautify their face and improve their external charm. The teaching of the old tradition is that a married woman with a child must appear unimpressive. The hero thinks that such notions have no meaning. He admires the European women who express their feelings naturally and their response to life springs from affection and love. So one finds that "without much of a unified plot, this story remains interesting."[15]

Anand, like Tennyson, thinks that customs and conventions have corrupted life. Without accepting the rational spirit of modernity, there is no possibility of reforming life. The hold of past conventions is so strong on the minds of people that it is extremely difficult for them to review and accommodate new things. In an excellent passage, Anand brings out the nature of the old villagers who refuse to think freely:

> You must always put on a miserable expression and remain quiet in the presence of your elders, that is respect. And, of course, you must never commit the crime of being happy! "Always follow custom!" (44-45)

Lal Singh recollects his old memory when he returns home. His reaction is poetically expressed by Anand:

> Our elders say, 'It is not the custom to do this, it is not the custom to do that. Fools! if you are seen drinking a pot of wine you are automatically declared a drunkard, and if you look at a woman you at once become notorious as a rogue, a pimp and a whoremonger and your

> parents tell you that you have cut their nose in the brotherhood. . . . Burnt up people! Owls! (43)

Anand says that the Indian village discourages the development of critical spirit and it expects people to accept things on the basis of belief in tradition and convention. To say that respect before the elders is to remain silent is to exaggerate the importance of convention and underrate truth. Anand's idea of modernity lies in questioning the meaning of established conventions and their relevance to the present times. Lal Singh sees that respect before the elders consists in unquestioning silence. The question why should respect imply silence and meek submission is mysterious for any objective onlooker like Lalu. What is pointed out by him is that such a conventional principle of respect before the elders implying silence does not promote independent enquiry. To develop the view that the old age is a sign of wisdom and youth a symbol of immaturity is too hard and reflects the principle that human error is a natural occurrence which can happen at any stage irrespective of age.

Lal Singh refers to the conventional habit of not laughing in the presence of elders. The novelist adds to this axiom and states that they must even put on a miserable expression. Such an act involves total loss of identity and individuality. He thinks that it is a tragic mistake to call a wine addict a drunkard and to describe a woman gazer a whoremonger. Any act which is a deviation from convention is nonsense for the villagers. The only reply that the novelist provides through Lal Singh is that the aged villagers do not keep pace with the changes of the times and their rigid and firm adherence to tradition makes their sensibility lifeless and mechanical. The hero therefore becomes a severe critic who indicts the limitations of conventions.

Anand's next mission is to portray the encounter between the East and the West in terms of human relations. Lal Singh in *The Village* comes in contact with Mr. Hecules Long, the Deputy Commissioner of the district. He praises Lalu and makes him the leader of the Scouts. Long is a good Englishman who thinks of improving the conditions of the peasants. The broad-minded captain Owen saves him from prison and discovers in him the dispassionate spirit of a talented hockey player. Lalu's admiration for the Whites continues in *Across the Black Waters* and it is so great that he looks upon these people as a heavenly race without any setbacks and limitations. He develops close connections with Andre and his charming sister Marie. When he sees the French farmer's wife weeping over the loss of her son, he is impelled to think that even this heavenly race is really subject to sorrow and joy. It is a lesson for him to know that the French Sahibs shed tears and express sorrow, joy, excitement and mental confusion like any other human being. He believes that the White race is a race of self-assurance and self-control. His excessive admiration for the Whites prevents him from seeing the reality of human nature which, according to the novelist, is the same elsewhere. Lalu realises that there cannot be any basic change in the expression of human emotions. It is interesting for him to know from his observation that races may be different but their emotional expressions are the same.

As he analyses the human relationship in his East-West encounter, Anand makes his 'authentic voice',[16] Lal Singh, narrate how he was affectionately loved and treated by a French family. In the process, one finds a veiled attack on tradition in India. This is clearly seen in Lalu's letter to his mother Gujar Kaur, describing to her how the French family has showered love on him:

> The women here walk in public without purdah and look straight into the eyes of the men who should tease them. They read, write, play, ride on horses and play cards, but no one dares to call them immoral for all these things. The daughter of my Fracisi mother is a young girl whom I like. But, mother, rest assured that it is not considered wrong for men and women to like each other and there is nothing bad in it. I remember that you told me to regard every woman as a mother or sister, but, mother, that would be a lie because men do not look at all women as sisters even if they say they do, for love, fire and itch are not concealed! (228)

The third in the Lal Singh trilogy, *The Sword and the Sickle*, where one sees an intimate picture of Indian life"[17] is a social and political novel. Here 'one finds Anand carrying on his ruthless crusade against the evil of landlordism."[18] The novel describes the release of Lal Singh from the German prison camp. His life again becomes a life of struggle and he looks for some means of subsistence. The British government gave him no war benefits as a mark of his service. He can no longer look to parents as they have died. His land in the village has been confiscated. He is deprived of all help and assistance. As a result, "he is thoroughly disillusioned with the society and the state."[19] He decides to become a social fighter against all forms of injustice. It is in the process of his struggle as a revolutionary fighter that he happens to see Maya, the daughter of the landlord. His old love story is brought back to his mind. Although she is a widow, he arranges a kind of marriage with her. This leads them to a village near Allahabad.

Lal Singh sees that the peasants are the victims of the landed gentry. Chandra, the labourer, is physically ill but is forced by the Nawab of Nasirabad to cut wood despite his bad health. This forced labour leads to his death which creates a stir. "Lal Singh, the fiery adolescent of *The Village* and the sensitive observer of *Across the Black Waters* graduates here into manhood,"[20] as he sees the injustice and gathers a group of peasants as a mark of protest against tyranny. But this rebellion is crushed by force. Lalu sees that the peasants are not thoughtful enough to strengthen the needed unity for a solid protest against injustice. They are not able to free themselves from their habits and customs and so the idea of rebellion loses its force.

Anand makes Kunwar Rampal Singh leader of the revolutionary struggle. It is a mark of irony for a count to become a leader as he is fighting against his own feudal class. It is a greater sign of wonder when the peasants appreciate his leadership and acknowledge their whole-hearted loyalty to him. For the peasant to obey the lord has become a matter of habit. Lal Singh's social struggle under the leadership of the count does not go without any benefit. Lalu sees the changes in the peasants and faithfully records these:

> They had become different from the broken, demoralized, backboneless creatures who would abjectly catch hold of the feet of a policeman and grovel in the dust with joined hands, completely unlike the gentle, kindly men with bottomless souls who were forever sunk in the misery to which they always resigned themselves. The new movement seemed to have given them a new faith.[21]

Lal Singh sees in the peasants the spirit of defying and challenging the authorities. Their ignorance is removed by a new social ideology of Communism. They grow fearless and disapprove of the old ways and customs. The fruit of this social struggle is soon seen in the peasant Sukhua who jumps on the landlord with very remarkable sentences:

> The old days have gone; he kept saying, waving his hand as if the world had dissolved into insubstantial nothingness. The old days have gone. . . . Lecher! If you go teasing other people's wives I will teach you a lesson. (324-25)

The new ideology strikes at the old notion of superiority and advocates a new morality which treats all human beings as alike and equal. A new vision of life is gained in this social ideology.

Anand sees in Lal Singh a rebel and a revolutionary social reformer. Lalu's vast experience in the West, in France and Germany as a soldier and a prisoner has given him a new knowledge of social dimension. He sees the profound need for the ideology of social and political progress. His exposure to the West and his increased awareness of the problems of life have made him a greater rebel. In this mood, he reviews and recollects his old styled life involving contracts with his father and brother in this passage:

> What was the destiny of man without a sense of right or wrong? Throughout his life he himself had struggled to perfect himself, if not according to the pietistic ideas of his father who told beads of a rosary every minute of the day, or like his brother Dayal Singh who quoted the words of Guru Nanak but according to his own ideas of well-being and those which he had found good in the teaching of the church Mission High School at Sherkot. He had been in revolt against the prejudices of religion in Nandpur, and he had sought to perfect himself a man against evils though he had suffered. He had struggled and always would go on struggling to remove his own ignorance and the defects in his own nature. And, since self-perfection was not enough, he would try to cleanse the blurred minds of all the peasants, to open their eyes to the inequities which were practised on them. (242-43)

This classic passage describes the growth of his character which is achieved through various phases. Anand establishes his idea of character formation on the ground that free and independent growth is the basis for character building. Lal Singh speaks about it elaborately. He recollects and says that his father was a pious man. He says that piety does not provide scope for critical analysis. So he is in no mood to adhere to his father. His brother Dayal Singh is an avid admirer of Guru Nanak. Lalu sees in his brother a good religious spirit but feels that this kind of devotion does not invalidate free criticism of anything. What is found wanting in them is that their understanding of life is in relation to what convention and tradition dictate. Life is not explored by them freely but it is seen in restricted directions.

Lalu says that he breathes very freely in the school and it is conducive to independent thinking. He feels that religion and society have failed to shape him. He depends on his own individual resources and energies to strengthen his character. His experience in the West is a source of inspiration for him. Instead of his reliance on religion and social customs he looks to the West as a model for building up life and character. As K.N. Sinha says, "He is no longer content with reacting to the world around him; rather he takes upon himself, the responsibility to change the world." (51)

Lalu does not intend to stop with his own perfection. As a first step towards changing the world, he wants to cleanse blurred minds of the peasants. His view is that peasants must gain knowledge and enlightenment and without these tools there is no possibility for realising the injustice done to them. Lal Singh pleads like a reformist that the individual must acquire knowledge to shape his mind and fight against tyranny.

Anand's creation of the revolutionary leader Kunwar Rampal Singh is a matter of riddle and mystery. The court belongs to the feudal gentry and is opposing a group to which he is related. A feudal lord like the count becoming a revolutionary leader appears to be an act of inconsistency on the face of it. But there are deeper motives which go into the making of the character of the Count. The novelist does not make Lal Singh the leader of the revolution. In fact the protagonist makes his submission to the Count and willingly accepts his leadership. Lalu is "courageous, resourceful and dynamic" (53) enough to resist injustice. But these qualities are not enough to make him a leader. He makes the Count the leader and the most interesting aspect of it is that a feudal representative becomes anti-feudal in his campaign. Anand sees the Count as the spokesman and a fierce crusader for the revolutionary communist ideology. The novelist believes that the organization of any revolution is based on sound intellectual leadership. Anand is not for making a common peasant leader, because he feels that the leadership requires certain special qualities and perhaps the Count fulfils the profound intellectual criteria of the novelist. He also points out that the Count's love of leadership arises from his passion for gaining power and prominence. The Count is a leader and has love for power and so in the estimate of the novelist he is not an ideal character.

M.K. Naik perceives an element of comic incongruity in the revolutionary group of people. (73) Everyone wants to know the reason why he has made revolutionaries comic and clownish. Naik's assumption is that an idealized presentation would have been in accordance with the theme of modernity. Prof. Verma is described as a "quick-witted buffoon." The count looks upon the comrade Ram Din as a camel. Comrade Nandu is portrayed as a "murderer and hunter." Pandit Ram Kumar Misra is shown as a person who is beaten by his wife with a broomstick as he took a cobbler woman to bed. Such a satirical description of these revolutionary characters is ill-suited to the purpose of the novelist, according to Naik. Anand is creating a fictitious framework in which he visualizes characters. The novelist thinks that these revolutionary figures are not idealized characters. Perhaps some human dimension is imparted to them by way of comic incongruity. Moreover Anand as a liberal humanist does not fully subscribe to the action programme of the Communist ideology. He has great admiration for the Marxian attitude to life but he believes that the Marxian leadership needs to be qualified by certain other things like capacity for vision, perception and intellectual excellence. This is one reason why he makes the Count the leader of the anti-feudal revolution and campaign.

The love episode of Lal Singh with Maya is shown as a sidelight. The hero sees in Maya a source of emotional relief. The landlord's anger with Lal Singh arises out of the love relation between the hero and his daughter. Maya. His escape from the village is prompted by Maya. This novel, *The Sword and the Sickle* bring them together, again. But the hero's interest in the revolutionary struggle spares him not enough time to be with Maya. It is said that this love episode is not artistically integrated.[22] It is true in a sense but the major purpose of Anand is to show revolutionary figures in human forms with all their emotional weaknesses and limitations. It is this fact of realism which impels the novelist to project the emotional life of the protagonist. Lalu identifies himself with the cause of the revolution and so he forgets his emotional ties with Maya. Sometimes he returns to see her. It is the natural habit of a human being to keep aside the burden of work and look for relief. The behaviour of Lal Singh can be judged in this perspective. The theme of the novel is a plea for removing social injustice from the standpoint of tradition and modernity. Anand does not intend to give undue prominence to this love affair. His main interest is to show how human beings behave under natural circumstances. The revolution is not a success because he believes in the fact as a humanist that human race has to be educated to visualise a new order.

Anand does not offer a well-balanced solution to the problem of social life as visualized and portrayed by him?[23] For instance, comrade Sharshar and the Congress leader, Srijut Laldi Prashad Tiwari are presented in ambiguous terms with a "strain of irony."[24] Lal Singh and his associates do not discover any meaning from the method of the Mahatma who inspired India. They see that Mahatma Gandhi's love of simplicity and Pandit Motilal Nehru's Westernised way of life do not agree with each other. But Gandhi's philosophy of voluntary suffering and the gospel of non-violence make a profound impact upon them. There is a way of resolving this riddle in a satisfying manner. The key to unlock the mystery is to know Anand's attitude to life. Anand is a modernist who welcomes the Western influences in the form of science and mechanization. This modernist attitude distinguishes Anand from the Gandhian line of thinking which denounces machines. The novelist believes in transforming the established system and in this respect all his intellectual sympathies are with the Marxian ideology. Gandhi's system of philosophy does not advocate the overthrow of the established system. Anand is Marxian in his intellectual outlook but does not believe in the radical overthrow of the established system, as he is a liberal humanist. He is a liberal socialist who is neither with Gandhi nor fully with Marx. But the Marxian analysis of social life and problems attracts him very much.

The novel, *The Sword and the Sickle*, aims at showing different political and social ideologies. The novelist hints at certain basic truths which can be known only through the spirit of modern science and reason. The tyranny of feudalism is a specific issue handled by him. The European idea of instilling equality and its spirit in human beings is one way of reducing the graded society of feudalism. Moreover the feudal society is clubbed with conventions and traditions. The best way to lighten the effect of conventions is to inculcate into the minds of people the rational spirit of modern outlook. The third issue is that the novel is connected with the rebellion of the peasants. Here, "Anand tries to point out how the travails of landless peasants and evicted tenants have gradually awakened them to a knowledge of their plight, and how they would put up a united fight against all oppressors, if only they could be properly led."[25]

The leadership of the count presented in the novel appears to be an anomaly and the so-called revolutionary figures are shown only in a satiric vein. The failure of the leadership and the revolution is due to the fact that Anand does not believe fully in the radical revolution and its Communist ideology oriented programme of action. As Anand is a liberal humanist, he longs for some life-improving elements. He appreciates Gandhi's scheme of life, but does not approve of him. He sees the need of Marx and its relevance to the social problems. He also sees the defects in the Marxian leadership. It is his observation based on experience which leads him to make the count the leader and present the revolutionary figures in a light vein. When Lal Singh discovers the discrepancy between Gandhi's love of village life and Motilal Nehru's love of Westernisation, he only wants to know which would be the right model for the nation. Anand is convinced that India without the benefit of modern Westernisation will remain ignorant and backward. His purpose is only to project the nature of the socialist remedy which has to take into account the reality of the situation which is very complex.

The novel *Pārisukku Pō* is a good example of Jayakanthan's skill and power as a master debater[26] and an able dialectician. The novelist explains in his preface to this novel that his purpose is not to tell a story in a conventional sense but to describe a complex world where men pursue different points of view. He thinks it is very difficult to prefer one view to the other. Jayakanthan agrees that *Pārisukku Pō* is in the form of a philosophical discourse. It is difficult to judge the merit of the novel for those people who approach life with some preconceived ideas. Jayakanthan says that any dispute in the realm of ideas has to be examined in a balanced manner.

Jayakanthan wants to indicate a way by which the complex nature of modern life be understood. The novelist says that all opposite points of view must be accepted. These views may not be in accordance with one's basic faith and conviction. Nevertheless these views have their own merit. In the preface he explains his position, "Let it not be assumed that there is a conflict between Dharma and Adharma. There can be innumerable conflicts and clashes within the framework of Dharma itself."[27] What the novelist wants to say is that the idea of Dharma can be interpreted in many different ways and there need not be agreement among these approaches at all. Yet the responsibility of an artist is to discuss the value and relevance of these views, however contradictory they may appear to be.

The story of *Pārisukku Pō* is built upon the basis of a formidable figure, Seshaiah, who is the head of the family. For him, the superiority of the Indian tradition and culture and the glory of the carnatic music are the prominent things which need to be respected by everyone. Seshaiah is a man of dignity and nobility but he is very uncompromising and highly inflexible in regard to anything which goes against his personal conviction. The arrival of his son Sarangan from Paris creates a stir and excitement. He is a specialist in violin and a believer in the superiority of the Western music. His main interest is to modernise the old carnatic music. The novelist starts juxtaposing these two different characters, father and son, in the form of two opposing points of view. The Indian culture with its rich carnatic music is very valuable. Certainly it needs to be learnt and appreciated for its own merit. Such a fact of this kind need not make one blind and insensitive to the value of a different system of music. The cultural geography of the West has created a music of its own. Its range is different from the order of carnatic music. The value of carnatic music is known and established. The existence of the Western music is what is not known to many. Men who are willing to expose themselves to a new cultural climate can have the inclination and opportunity to know it.

Jayakanthan makes Mahalingam and Lalitha an antithesis to Seshaiah. Mahalingam is the close friend of Narasimhan who is the first son of Seshaiah. They start admiring Sarangan whose letters addressed to his father are read by this couple. These letters fervently express his ideals which lie in the way of changing the glorious great tradition of its music. Mahalingam and Lalitha are his admirers who see in Sarangan his profound thirst for changing things in the manner of improving them. Therefore they lend support to Sarangan's revolutionary ideas and Mahalingam goes to the extent of saying that the present society needs people like him. When Seshaiah came to know of Sarangan's interest in the Western music, he looks upon it as a mark of discontent. Lalitha knows that Seshaiah himself is a musician of merit and distinction. Sarangan's broad perception leads him to comment on his father's carnatic music. Sarangan argues that the function of any good music is to capture the sense of the infinite and the universal. For him, carnatic music is a little rigid as it involves a kind of mechanical recitation.

Jayakanthan thinks that the play and conflict among ideas is an interesting game. Seshaiah looks upon the Western music as the hooting and howling of a jackal. Sarangan does not disrespect carnatic music and he only says that it is treated as "Yoga." He thinks that when music is treated as Yoga, it loses its width and flexibility for adaptation. It is this attitude of Sarangan which irritates his father, who regards his dead son Rengaiah as his ideal son and bemoans the wayward nature of his Paris-based son.

Lalitha wants to prepare an article on Sarangan's ideas of music and publish it in a leading magazine called *Manonmani*. Mahalingam and Lalitha form a happy pair in their reaction to Sarangan's modern ideas. When they discuss Sarangan's fortunes in his house on account of his belief in modern ideas, they agree that change must fundamentally start with the individual and slowly get reflected in the family and then influence the general consciousness of the nation. Jayakanthan says that change has to occur in a gradual manner. Mahalingam and Lalitha visualise that modern ideas of Sarangan can be easily misunderstood by the people. They themselves are neither ancient nor modern, but want to be truthful and meaningful in their response to the pressures of life. They feel that the old thing must get renewed, otherwise it will die.

Jayakanthan offers a clue to the way of discovering what the concept of modernity means. This is brought out in a meeting between Sarangan and Madhavi and Lalitha who have plans to invite him for a talk in the women's Association. He appreciates the hair-style of Madhavi which is after the manner of the fashion in Paris. He also remarks that there is no evidence of the Western impact on Lalitha. (87) Lalitha gives a powerful rejoinder to this statement. She says that the Western modernist outlook does not imply an external imitation. (87) She thinks that the idea of modernity is useful only when it changes the perception of a person in a worthwhile manner. The most enduring part of a man's life lies in an inner change. To appear modern in hair-style is the greatest misconception of modernity, according to Lalitha. This incident shows very clearly that Lalitha is not an indiscriminate admirer of the modern ideas and in this respect she is different from Sarangan. Her concern is with life and its improvement. She is interested in Sarangan's modern ideas believing that they would produce a new force and rejuvenate the dying tradition. For Lalitha, the value of modern ideas is determined only in relation to their power of changing and making life better.

Jayakanthan deals with the theme of aping the West elaborately. Lalitha points out that Sarangan's habit of drinking is derived from his association with the West. This criticism of Lalitha makes Sarangan highly self-critical and self-reflective. He fully agrees with her critical mode of enquiry. Lalitha says that the concept of imitating should not lead to hollowness in sensibility. Sarangan admits the point that to imitate the West in terms of dress, diet and speech is no imitation but is suicidal and deliberate self-degradation. When people start imitating the West in mere external forms, they lose their roots in their culture and simultaneously they do not get themselves properly rooted in the new culture aped by them. Jayakanthan is of the view that modern ideas are not harmful by themselves. Their value is to be tested in relation to their capacity for improving life. The danger of external imitation is that there is no enduring realisation of the value of anything. Moreover such a mechanical act of aping produces rootlessness.

Jayakanthan remains in the background and makes his characters speak for themselves. Lalitha states that literary taste is not formed by school education. She says that much of what passes in the name of modern writing has no meaning at all. A writer does not write only for the sake of truth, as there are other motives which condition his mind. She says that journals have their set motives and readers have their pet fancies and writers out of their passion for popularity concur with these cheap forces which corrupt mind. A writer is not supposed to provide what the reader wants. He must know and provide what the best thing would be for the reader to know in order to become percipient and lead a meaningful life. The responsibility of the artist is to shape the mind of the reader by determining his taste. Lalitha says that pleasing the superficial taste of the populace should be no part of the artist's aim. That is why Jayakanthan argues in the preface that the duty of the artist is to enable the reader to perceive the right thing in the right way.

Jayakanthan discusses the question of the glory of carnatic music in relation to the value of Western music. The magazine *Manonmani* publishes letters attacking Sarangan's views on music. Lalitha says that Sarangan has a broad base filled with a powerful critical perception. While she pays respect to Sarangan's comparative value-judgement of these two fields of music, Seshaiah raises objection to it. He says that any comparison between the two views of music is irrelevant. Carnatic music is divine while Western music is human. As their purposes are different, comparisons are ruled out and any value judgement is held null and void. But Lalitha is not in agreement with this view of Seshaiah as she thinks that it is not objective criticism.

What Jayakanthan wants to say through Seshaiah is that each music has its own merit and can be appreciated in its own right. But an opposite point is pursued by Lalitha who cites a letter by Sundaram, who explains that religion which inspired the formation of carnatic music has made it static. Any change in the divine quality of music will lead to degradation. He says that for a conservative mind, change means degradation and demoralization. The Indian religion which advocates the concept of Maya attaches no merit to life and in such a scheme change is illusion. The European Enlightenment laid emphasis upon the human dimension of life and consequently there was scope for change in every field of life. Jayakanthan thinks that it is difficult to convince people who think that to continue the old without any alteration is a sign of wisdom.

In his letter to *Manonmani*, Sundaram comments favourably on the new ideas of Sarangan and expresses a radically different point which insists on taking into recognition the time-spirit. Sundaram reminds that Swami Vivekananda stood for a thorough change in all fields of life. The need to reinterpret the old value in the light of modern spirit is what constitutes in one the awareness of the spirit of the times. He says that when an old view is respected and worshipped, it loses its capacity for testing itself in relation to the time spirit. According to him, Sarangan and Lalitha are two great exponents of modern ideas who must remain steadfast in their principles.

Sundaram is an open-minded man whose interest is to reform life. As Sarangan and Lalitha reflect along these lines of reform, they make an appeal to him. Any attempt at reforming life requires an open mind. Sarangan is of the view that Sarangan and Lalitha can so sincerely put forth their plea for modern ideas, that they can change the very perceptions of the people. The greatest creative thinker is one who can elicit the right response from people by enabling them to perceive the truth. It is this yardstick which the novelist applies when he portrays people like Mahalingam, I.alitha, Sarangan and Sundaram. No one can be converted to a new point by force. It is the power of argument based on true perception which becomes an opener for everyone.

Sarangan delivers a lecture on modernity in the school of painting run by Menon. He thinks that ancient foundations need to be made fresh by assimilating the modem idea. The modern outlook of a society is reflected in its literature. (193) Aping the West in external terms and copying it somewhat inwardly is not what is meant by modernity. (194) It is only a profound and meaningful relation to life which makes a man modern. The process of relating the ancient civilization to the present situation is known as the modern way. (195)

Modernity does not mean, according to Jayakanthan, a total rebellion against the ancient civilization. Any interpretation of modernity, in that sense, is the greatest misconception. A real understanding of what is happening in the present with a keen awareness of one's relation to the ancient civilization is what makes a man progressive in his spirit. Sarangan says that a genuine sense of feeling is required in the perception of art, life and literature. (197) It is feeling which adds depth to the power of perception. Jayakanthan rightly points out through Sarangan that modernity does not mean rejecting the past but understanding it in a more meaningful and critical sense for the purpose of creating possibilities which are conducive to a rich growth of life. The advocate of modernity has a greater responsibility of comparing the past with the present and making a meaningful evaluation of it.

It is interesting to find Lalitha, an advocate of modernity falling a prey to the intellectual charm of Sarangan. Intellectual partnership is conceived as a prelude to physical partnership and subsequently both ties are conceived as a preparation for the break of wedlock. Jayakanthan intends to show the dilemma of the modern man whose mind is divided between physical charm and intellectual pursuits. His purpose is not to say that intellectual interest can generate the break of wedlock. As a novelist he is showing the emotional complication of Lalitha which arises out of her longing for intellectual companionship.

Sarangan induces Lalitha to get a divorce from Mahalingam. He impresses upon her the view that marriage is after all a voluntary agreement which can be terminated at any time. (222) According to him the present marriage pattern looks like the framework of jail. Marriage is therefore a kind of key offered by the established institution to get the two persons locked permanently in a jail. In the case of Mahalingam and Lalitha, it is a voluntary entry into the jail.

Now Sarangan argues that voluntary entry into the jail can also imply voluntary exit out of the same jail. (222)

The novelist is not satisfied with the view of Sarangan on marriage and so creates an occasion where Narasaiah on his death-bed is found giving his discourse on wedlock. (265) He says that marriage is a holy relation. The real quality of a good wife lies in her power of understanding and capacity for adjustment. A true wife follows her husband just as waves follow the wind. Marriage is an expression of love and compassion and the two individuals brought together must move on the basis of give and take. Nothing should break the tie of marriage. The love expressed in marriage is identical with charity, compassion and sympathy and so it becomes a source of warmth and inspiration for other people.

Narasaiah indicates that love does not mean possessiveness. (266) The marriage tie becomes weak when love is expressed as a possessive instinct. He says that possessiveness turns into selfishness. Ego and not true love becomes the controller of heart. When love is the basis for marriage, divorce is out of purview. Often possessiveness becomes the building force of marriage and it is at this time that relationship gets distorted and strained. Love ripens into a state of selflessness and there is only a realisation of mutual oneness. This discourse comes from a person who has left his wife and chosen to live with Ganga, a dancer. His own experience is a lesson to him.

Jayakanthan places these two views on marriage in close association with each other. Modernity does not certainly mean acceptance of divorce and thoughtless breaking of wedlock. The novelist makes it clear that true love is understanding. It even rises above the question of intellectual companionship. Lalitha is in a state of dilemma and is not in the right frame of mind to distinguish intellectual companionship from marriage partnership. When Mahalingam speaks disapprovingly of divorce, Lalitha gets herself reconciled with him. The judgement on this question of divorce has been already delivered in this novel which "has a cosmopolitan outlook."[28]

According to Jayakanthan true marriage means love and wrong marriage means possessiveness. The question of divorce arises out of a false understanding of marriage and the failure to develop the right relationship on the basis of love. The novelist says that the admiration for the West should not imply an overturning of values. Any acceptance of new values in the name of modernity must be in relation to their capacity to improve life. Sarangan's trip to Paris is stopped by Sundaram who perhaps believes that the musician's presence is more useful in India than in Paris. What is useful must be learnt from the West for the purpose of ennobling the country to which one belongs. Jayakanthan sums up his debate by saying that the contact with the West is not harmful but that its motive should be to generate fresh insights, which will improve and enrich life.

So Anand and Jayakanthan discuss the relationship between tradition and modernity in different ways. Their way of handling this theme is quite in agreement with their attitudes to life. It is very easy to discover a pattern of conflict between tradition and modernity in Anand. According to him human misery is derived from backwardness which is generated by traditional attitudes to life. He thinks therefore that an organised campaign against tradition is necessary for improving life. Anand's stay in the West results in his rejecting tradition. He is very much influenced by the European Enlightenment which indicates that it is reason which can fully revolutionise life. Therefore religion, tradition and faith block the progress of life.

When Anand assumes that it is religion which has destroyed life, he becomes indirectly an advocate of modernity. He has therefore made a choice. The restructuring of the Indian civilisation is impossible without an active acceptance of this choice. The rebuilding of the nation requires the introduction of modern ideas which, according to Anand, can be imbibed only from the West. He is very clear in his mind that the Western idea of rational reform is the basis for the development of any society. Mere belief in religion and tradition is not a motivating force for the development of human race.

Anand places his absolute belief in modernity and he, without any hesitation, dismisses any form of tradition. The Lal Singh Trilogy is an example of this approach filled with vigour and vitality. The novelist makes Lal Singh the greatest exponent of modernity. There are several instances where he makes his hero steadily oppose tradition. Lal Singh removes his beard and eats in a Muslim hotel. These two acts are forbidden by the Sikh religion. Lal Singh defies the Sikh tradition and embraces the modern idea of brotherhood which goes beyond mere religion. He exposes the false and hypocritical life of Mahant Nandgir who exploits people in the name of religion. When the false religious priest suggests religious incantation as a remedy for diseases, Lal Singh discovers that the ignorant minds of the villagers have no scientific knowledge to realise that a physiological disease requires a physiological remedy. The legitimate role of science is kept out of the reach of people by a tradition which discourages free enquiry. Lal Singh sees that the big dust heap pollutes village and creates many microbes which affect the health of the people. It is the blind adherence to a conservative tradition which does not open their eye to the value of modern ideas.

Jayakanthan has a different way of dealing with the relationship between tradition and modernity. Like Anand, he does perceive that there is a conflict between the two concepts. But Jayakanthan is not prepared to choose one and reject the other. Anand's formal education has brought him under the influence of the European Enlightenment whereas Jayakanthan did not have that environment. This is one reason why Jayakanthan does not become an advocate of modernity in a very partial manner. Most of the prefaces to his novels describe his love of life. His main source of learning comes from life.

Jayakanthan, in the beginning of his career as a novelist, dismissed religion and accepted Marx. He dismissed the kind of religion which does not improve life. He accepted Marx because he thought that human misery requires a remedy and human life needs to be crowned by political and social justice. For Jayakanthan, improving the nature of life is his subject matter. Whoever offers ideas in this matter of enriching life, he accepts. He does not disapprove of a view just because it does not concur with his personal conviction.[29]

Anand is an advocate of modernity in his novels. His aim as a novelist includes the spirit of a social reformer. He believes that a society becomes backward and unprogressive because of its belief in traditional religion. According to him, the value of the European

Enlightenment lies in the efficacious use of reason which does not encourage the unquestioning habit of accepting everything on the basis of tradition and religion. Lal Singh is told by Maulvi that his father will not be blessed with heaven as he happens to be an infidel, a non-believer in Islam. He replies that God does not show favouritism to people. According to him, conventional beliefs like this keep people in abject state of ignorance and despair. Lal Singh feels that, in spite of religion and tradition, people are not human in their understanding of life. The village priest is false, the landlord is jealous and greedy. The moneylender is miserly. Religion has not changed their outlook. Lal Singh becomes a believer in modernity under these wretched social circumstances. Anand thinks therefore that the ignorant minds of the people must be changed by education. There is first a necessity for intellectual change in the minds of people. This is the first condition for modernising life. Then there is the need for building up external life with the help of science.

Anand accepts the value of science and its role of modernising life. This scientific preoccupation of Anand is not shared by Jayakanthan. The fact of having accepted the benefit of science makes Anand an ardent advocate of modernity. Jayakanthan's purpose is different from the preoccupation of Anand. The first premise of Anand is an expression of his interest in intellectual change. Jayakanthan is in agreement with this need for intellectual change. For Anand, intellectual change means a preparation for the mind to free itself from the clutches of tradition and religion.

Jayakanthan accepts this idea but adds a simple rejoinder to this view. He holds the opinion that religion and tradition can be rejuvenated and revolutionised. Anand's interest is not to be dialectical but to be truly related to the condition of the society which is found in a state of backwardness and degradation. Anand believes in the physical change of the society and the tool for external transformation is science. But Jayakanthan's interest is to make life pleasant by making people perceive all ideas in the right manner. This is the purpose of a dialectical thinker. Anand's main interest lies in improving the mind and changing the external conditions of the society.

The five novels of Anand and Jayakanthan analysed here deal with one basic theme which gets expressed in the relation of conflict between tradition and modernity. The theme embodying the clash between tradition and modernity gets unfolded at different levels in these five novels. Anand's Lal Singh suffers on account of a selfish and conservative society described in *The Village*. His *Across the Black Waters* gives Lal Singh's experience of his encounter with the French and the British in terms of their culture, manners and life. *The Sword and the Sickle* raises the rebellion of Lal Singh against the society of feudal aristocracy. The revolution organised to overthrow such a society meets with failure. *The Village* of Anand insists on an intellectual change in the minds of people. *Across the Black Waters* lays emphasis upon the value of a man's exposure to the West and how it makes one aware of reorganizing society, culture, men and life. *The Sword and the Sickle* is an expression of social protest against a corrupt feudal society.

For Anand, the Western intellectual Enlightenment is an antidote to the conservatism and backwardness of the villagers. The use of scientific knowledge in the form of industrialisation and mechanisation is treated as an indispensable factor by Anand for modernizing the Indian Village. Anand's notion of modernity means the creation of an intellectual change and the use of scientific knowledge in removing social evils. In the conflict between tradition and modernity, Anand makes a choice in favour of the latter quite in accordance with his purpose.

But with Jayakanthan, the so-called ideas of modernity and tradition and the unnatural opposition between the two are the consequences of wrong perceptions. He sets things right like a dialectician by placing differing points of view in their right perspectives. The conflict between tradition and modernity is not like a clash between good and evil. Tradition does not mean remaining like a stone and modernity does not mean keeping on changing like a wind. What is valuable can be both traditional and modern.

That is why Sharma appreciates Seshadri and Seshadri respects Sharma. A new way of looking at everything is what constitutes Jayakanthan's conception of modernity. In this conception there is only a debate and not a conflict between tradition and modernity. To sum up one can say that in Anand there is always a clash between modernity and tradition, while in Jayakanthan tradition and modernity are essentially complementary.

## NOTES

1. Jayakanthan, *Jayakanthanin Munnuraikal* (Madurai: Meenakshi Publishing House, 1984), pp. 31-32.
2. John B. Alphonso, qtd. Krishna Nandan Sinha, *Mulk Raj Anand* (New York: Twayne, 1972).
3. K.R. Srinivasa Iyengar, qtd. Krishna Nandan Sinha, pp. 52-53.
4. Jack Lindsay, *The Elephant and the Lotus: A Study of the Novels of Mulk Raj Anand* (Bombay: Kutub-Popular, 1956), p. 15.
5. G.S. Balarama Gupta, *Mulk Raj Anand: A Study of His Fiction in Humanist Perspective* (Bareilly: Prakash, 1974), p. 52.
6. M.K. Naik, *Mulk Raj Anand* (Delhi: Arnold Heinemann India, 1973), p. 57.
7. Mulk Raj Anand, *The Village* (Delhi: Arnold Heinemann India, 1960), p. 58.
8. V.H. Baskaran, *The Theme of Social Justice in the Novels of Mulk Raj Anand and Bhabani Bhattacharya*, Doctoral Thesis, Madurai Kamaraj University, 1987, p. 77.
9. K.N. Subramanian, qtd. Jayakanthan, *Pirammōpatēcam* (Madurai Meenakshi Puthaka Nilayam, 1985), p. 3.
10. Krishna Nandan Sinha, *Mulk Raj Anand*, p. 48.
11. G.S. Balarama Gupta, *Mulk Raj Anand*, p. 59.
12. *Ibid.*
13. V.H. Baskaran, p. 82.
14. Mulk Raj Anand, *Across the Black Waters* (Delhi: Orient Paperbacks, 1980), pp. 92-93.
15. P.P. Mehta, "Mulk Raj Anand: The Novelist of the Underdog," *Indo-Anglian Fiction: An Assessment* (Bareilly: Prakash, 1968), p. 164.
16. Krishna Nandan Sinha, *Mulk Raj Anand,* p. 53.
17. Qtd. Krishna Nandan Sinha, *Mulk Raj Anand*, p. 52.
18. G.S. Balarama Gupta, *Mulk Raj Anand*, p. 64.
19. Krishna Nandan Sinha, *Mulk Raj Anand*. p. 50.
20. *Ibid.*, p. 51.
21. Mulk Raj Anand, *The Sword and the Sickle* (Delhi: Arnold Heinemann, 1984), p. 274.
22. M.K. Naik, *Mulk Raj Anand*, p. 75

23. *Ibid.*, p. 74
24. *Ibid.*
25. G.S. Balarama Gupta, *Mulk Raj Anand*, p. 64.
26. Idhayan, qtd. Arivalakan, *Jayakanthan Āyvatankal* (Cuddalore: Amaravathi Press, 1978), p. 254.
27. Jayakanthan, *Pārisukku Pō* (Madurai: Meenakshi Puthaka Nilayam, 1992), p. 9.
28. Kailasapathy, qtd. Arivalakan, *Jayakanthan Āyvatankal*, p. 261.
29. Jayakanthan, *Pirammōpatēcam*, pp. 5-6.

# Religion, Sex and Society

There are not two worlds, heaven above and the earth below.[1]

Anand and Jayakanthan evolve a new vision of life in their novels. Their endeavour is to free life from all imposed restrictions which curb freedom. In the Western literature, for example, Eliot's vision of life is based upon his belief in the renewal of Christian faith. W.B. Yeats's vision stems from his "Sailing to Byzantium" which represents an integrated civilization. D.H. Lawrence's vision aims at a revival of the pagan antiquity which speaks of the vital force and body-consciousness.

The life scheme of Arnold revives his interest in the Renaissance tradition. Tennyson and Thomas Hardy participate in the philosophy of the Enlightenment while Browning refers to an unbroken arc in heaven. His vision is that God is in His heaven and all is right with the world. Cardinal Newman longs for a new medieval Christian vision of life. He wants reason to be a subordinate instrument of help to Christian revelation. Darwin and Freud liberate the world from religion; while the former speaks of the progressive evolution of the species the latter points out the evil play of libido as an obstructing force to the integration of man's personality.

Virginia Woolf and James Joyce strike a specific atheist note in their vision of life. The complexity found in human consciousness is something that cannot be studied logically. The stream and the flow of consciousness do not create any scope for a rational study and religion and philosophy have side-tracked these mysterious waves and forces. Joyce and Woolf show greater interest in exploring these unorganized zones of human consciousness and so they have openly disavowed their faith in religion.

Anand's vision of life carries a pungent element. When he says that the cat goes on a pilgrimage after having eaten seven mice, his realism and power of perception come to the forefront. Jayakanthan's vision lies in loving men and life. His remark that nothing has jumped from heaven clubs him with Anand in the way of dismissing a supernatural origin of life. Anand's rejection of religion and conventional morality becomes a major force in his vision. Only Jayakanthan's early vision of life involved a total dismissal of religion. Both were Marxist sympathizers with their faith in the reality of the physical world. Later on Jayakanthan's perception of Swami Vivekananda's revolutionary spiritual reform made deep impression upon him. He tends to make a distinction between false and good religion. Further he sees the value of spirituality in improving life. Jayakanthan is a critical realist and his dialectical capacity for objectivity enables him to see the limitations of the false religion and the value of real religion which must aim at spirituality.

Anand's philosophical base for his vision lies in the rationalism of the Enlightenment and so he becomes an uncompromising denouncer of religion. Jayakanthan's early vision is fully comparable to Anemia. But his later vision undergoes certain major changes; he bids farewell to Marxism and does not accept the theory of justifying any form of violence in the name of doing good to society and the human race. The main reason for this motive force comes from the perception that atheism and religion are not enemies but companions working for human progress. Anand's allegiance to the philosophy of the Enlightenment does not work out such a compromise. His vision aims at a large social transformation through belief in science and machines. Anand believes in the real improvement of man through external means like science and technology.

Jayakanthan's vision does not include any external means for producing changes in life. He thinks that man must become more human by turning to his inner self through an active renewal of his interest in spirituality. Anand also speaks of recovering human dimensions in man and social life but he at the same time places his emphasis upon modernity expressed in his belief in science and machines. But Jayakanthan feels that social life will not become cohesive without man's spiritual transformation.

The novels of Anand like *The Village* trilogy, *The Big Heart*, *Lament on the Death of a Master of Arts* and *Death of a Hero* present a powerful vision in which he sees that religion crushes human efforts. Moreover religious hypocrisy has corrupted life. His vision of life is based upon a plea for human liberty and a renewal of interest in life and society. Jayakanthan's novels like *Yārukkāka Alutān?*, *Vālkkai Alaikkiratu* and *Unnaippōl Oruvān* depict a picture of poverty-stricken life where morality and religion are simply out of place. But his later novels like *Vilutukal, Pirammōpatēcam* and *Jaya Jaya Sankara* look for a new spiritual orientation. He is of the view that orthodox religion and spiritual reform is not identical. He believes that spirituality revives the essence of life.

Anand's attitude to love, sex, marriage and morality is shown in the heroines, Maya of *The Village* trilogy and Janki in *The Big Heart*. Anand and Jayakanthan prefer individual freedom and so they make human context more valuable than external ethics. Jayakanthan's novels, *Oru Natikai Nātakam Pārkirāl, Cila Nērankalil Cila Manitarkal, Kokila Enna Ceytu Vittal?* and *Suntara Kāntam* show his views on love, marriage, sex, chastity and morality. For him love is a noble frame of mind identical with charity. Real love means non-possessiveness. He says that love is not romantic idealism but it is a sensible approach to Life with honesty and compassion as the guiding factors. Like Anand, he does not approve of traditional morality. He derives the meaning of anything from the human context. A very deep and meaningful scrutiny of life goes into their vision. Anand visualises a revamping of society through rejection of religion and simultaneous adoption of modernity while Jayakanthan with his critical eye on the false religion looks to the emergence of real and good religion to improve man and society.

Mulk Raj Anand's attitude to religion is shaped by his study of philosophy under the guidance of Professor G. Dawes Hicks. It is the realist tendency in philosophy which attracts him. The German philosophy of Kant and Hegel and the romantic mystical movement make reality abstract. Anand believes that life on earth is concrete reality. Religion, according to him, deals with a supernatural world which is really intangible. The business of science is to examine truth in verifiable concrete terms. Anand sees that science is nearer reality than religion which obscures the significance of life through its reliance on abstractions.

Anand's passion for the realist tendency which comes from his study of philosophy gives a new impetus to him to reexamine abstract concepts like God, Reality and Immortality. He sees that science with its criterion of sensory verification is in disharmony with the abstract postulates of religion. The novelist's nature of mind is in agreement with this realist and scientific temperament which opposes any study of life in abstract terms. A writer who prefers concreteness and exalts the scientific temperament can never admire religion. The reason is that what Anand looks for has no place in religion. His spirit of objective and scientific investigation of things closes the way to the citadel of religion.

Anand's non-metaphysical approach to life can be seen in his illuminating statement, "There is no 'spiritual' world separate from the 'material' world. The soul is body and the body is soul.[2] Anand looks upon human body and soul as inseparable entities. His naturalist cum scientific view of life promotes no dualism between matter and spirit. The main postulate of religion is to hold soul as being to body. But his temperament underscores the traditional dualism between body and soul and rejects the distorted relationship between the two:

> Anand, like Julian Huxley, believes in the evolutionary conception of the Universe and rejects the dualism between matter (or nature) and spirit (or the supernatural) and the body and the mind.[3]

Anand's family background had its impact on his negative attitude to religion. His mother Ishwar Kaur was a pious god-fearing woman. She was in the habit of treating every illness as a mark of supernatural punishment. Anand refers to his mother's peculiar irrational belief in God on the occasion of his illness, " I must get Ali's mother to bring a little goat to sacrifice for you, my son."[4]

Anand puts in the mouth of his mother an explanation for an inevitable sacrifice of goat:

> Yama, God of death wants you—so we must give him another little life to save yours. I will wave the meat over your head and throw it to the vultures. They are Yama's birds.[5]

The novelist makes a distinction between her influence on him as a mother and her attitude towards religion. His father belongs to the reformist movement of Arya Samaj. But he is a careerist who has his own doubts about the supernatural world of religion. His father's materialistic and agnostic temperament shapes the mind of Anand in a liberal mode:

> Anand seems to have inherited from his father an irreligious mind and he used to join his rather in making fun of his mother's idolatrous devotion to all Gods both in heaven and on earth.[6]

Anand's boyhood is characterized by his deep sensitivity. The passing away of some of his close relatives produces a melancholy mood in him. These occasions enable him to turn his searchlight deep inwards. The death of his cousin Kaushalya makes him emotionally unsettled and it becomes a big crisis for him. It also brings before him metaphysical issues which kindle his mind in a new way:

> I could not understand why an innocent girl should be singled out to die. And what was death? Was there survival after the passing away of a person? If not, then life was the only time for happiness. And yet there was pain and suffering in life. Why was all this? . . . No answer came to my questionings but I could see the contrast of life and death.[7]

Commenting on Kaushalya's death and its impact on Anand, Sinha aptly says, "For the first time in his life, he probed into the nature of life and death, pleasure and pain."[8] The subsequent deaths of his uncle Pratap and his aunt Devaki lead to the disintegration of his psyche. For him the reality of life becomes identical with the actual lives of the people. These deaths create in him a philosophic bent of mind. The fundamental belief in the reality of the world becomes an urgent necessity to the passing away of his relatives. All these factors prepare the background for his anti-religious attitude.

Anand and Jayakanthan share their disbelief in the supernatural. They stand on a common platform in voicing forth their disapproval of any form of abstraction which leads to a high sounding idealism. When Anand summarizes the world-view of Iqbal, the Muslim poet, he states indirectly his own position, "The Hegelian Absolute, the Vedantic Brahma and the Sufi God, is a fiction of the mind, a hallucination of the neurotic imagination."[9]

In the same manner Jayakanthan expresses his protest against the idealistic concepts of heaven and hell. In his preface to the collection of short stories, *Inippum Karippum* (Sweetness and Sourness) he states his preference for concreteness and a liking for the external reality of the world:

> Nothing is inside me. Everything lies outside me. The external world is the place for my existence. To think about my soul is like conducting an enquiry upon a dead body.[10]

To think of an ideal heaven beyond human habitation is false. The concept of heaven devalues earthly life. The common point between Anand and Jayakanthan is that a lover of life can never be a lover of imaginary heaven. Like Anand, Jayakanthan is a matter-of-fact man in his own way. Jayakanthan's distrust of a supernatural world is seen in his preface to the collection of short stories entitled *Tevān Varuvārā?* (Will God Come?), "Nothing jumps from heaven. So far nothing has jumped from heaven. Even God has to come in the form of man." (18)

It becomes clear that like Anand, Jayakanthan feels that the history of human life is confined to earth only and that it has no divine background. What is important here is that Jayakanthan treats life as the only text available upon this earth. Like Anand he considers life to be more important than anything else in this world. As religion devalues the significance of earthly life, both are united in their dislike of religion. As novelists, their desire for objectivity, their critical sensibility and a tendency to accept those things which appear before human eye force them to fall into an atheistic cultural mould.

Anand draws his strength as a novelist from his critical observation of human life. In the same way Jayakanthan acknowledges that human life is a vast book to be read from different angles. His keenness of perception is derived from his understanding of life in its various phases. They together develop a belief that human life is a concrete affair and for them as novelists nothing is more important than what they see with their naked eyes before them.

They dismiss supernatural religion and idealistic philosophy on the ground that they exalt abstractions and dogmas at the cost of life. It is nothing but active love of life which brings them together. They are believers in the significance of life. Their standpoint as novelists draws its force from their love of life. The refusal to go beyond the boundary of human life is what distinguishes them. They say that the picture of human misery does not want an idealistic reading of life. For them human issues are so complex that the existence of God becomes a big subject matter of debate. Anand says that the only reality of life and death makes it much more real. Jayakanthan also says that the actual contact with life gave him little opportunity to think of anything other than what he sees or what appears before him.

K.N. Sinha comments on Anand's reliance on life in his own guidance of anything. He points out that for the novelist everything proceeds from the text of life. All Anand's novels are close studies of life without showing any leanings towards religion: "But Mulk Raj Anand is no saint, nor has he the saint's preoccupation with a life-time spent in love, renunciation and self-surrender. . . . He has put what he has known about life in his stories and novels, and if his knowledge is not profound, it is not quite shallow or superficial."[11]

The tendency to adhere to life keeps Anand away from the framework of religion. Therefore his art depends on life and religion has no place in it. The atheistic stance of Anand is seen indirectly when he makes his novels sincere reflections of life. The general tenet of atheism is to reject religion and accept life. Anand conforms to this ethics of an atheist. But what places him above an atheist is his spirit of human sympathy which enables him to understand the suffering which appears in various forms in life. He is more than an atheist as his philosophic bent of mind gives a new dimension to his reading of life.

Jayakanthan shares with Anand his spirit of the atheist's mood in his initial rejection of religion and complete acceptance of life as the only concrete guide. There is a view in religion which says that divine intuition is the origin of knowledge. Anand and Jayakanthan refute this view of religion and consider knowledge to be the product of human experience and observation. Jayakanthan, like Anand, explains that his understanding of life is the basic source material for everything, "The friends who live around me, the men whom I see, have helped me to know and learn the art of speaking, writing and thinking." (8)

Jayakanthan considers average human beings to be his teachers. This passage does not make any reference to any external factor like God and religion as the source of human wisdom. Similarly Anand also does not look to any supernatural source as the origin of human knowledge. Jayakanthan admits the fact that his different levels of relations with life and different kinds of contacts with human beings have ignited his mind and made it fertile. Anand also says that it is his contact with life which makes his art vitally important.

Anand and Jayakanthan are believers in the rich significance of life. They discount religion as it considers heavenly life to be superior to earthly life, "It is not the consciousness of men that determines their existence, but, on the contrary it is their social existence that determines their consciousness."[12]

By quoting Karl Marx, Anand expresses his belief in Marxian postulate which accepts human existence as the sole reality and dismisses all idealistic speculations which devalue the importance of physical life. Like Anand, Jayakanthan believes in physical life as the only easily perceivable and verifiable reality:

> What I have seen or in other words, what the world has shown to me; what I have heard—that is, what life has told or taught me, I show them once again to the world. Once again I tell the same things to you. (118)

This passage shows that life and men provide the material for Jayakanthan's art. When he says that life and human beings teach him, it indirectly indicates that his art does not depend on religion and that his view of life has no relation to it at all. To Anand and Jayakanthan, there are two factors which make religion mechanical and less human. The organizational aspect of religion suppresses the spiritual freedom of man and rituals and ceremonies do not indicate actual refinement as the emphasis upon the external form of observance takes away the inner spirit of man. Anand satirises Pandit Bhola Naths's false religious sanctimoniousness in *The Old Woman and the Cow* when Lakshmi says, "After eating seven mice the cat is going on a pilgrimage." (223)

The contradiction seen by the novelist is that a life-killer appears to be a life-saver. Anand is of the view that a bad man hides his evil nature under the garb of religion. In *The Village* trilogy Lal Singh ridicules Mahant Nandgir, "By going to Benares a dog will not become a holy man."[13]

Anand says in a jovial manner that a man merely going on a pilgrimage does not evolve into a higher nature. So long as a man does not peep into his inner nature all his external behaviour, however refined it appears to be, is of no use at all. For the novelist it is a mark of surprise to see the villains, gluttons and lecherous men thrive in the name of religion. Anand's dislike of religion springs from the perception of these contradictions found in the religious priests. He is in a satirical mood to ridicule them as he sees that the meaning of the real value is totally lost sight of.

Anand's autobiographical account of her mother's ritualistic attitude to religion is important as it shows the emptiness of mere mechanical performance of rituals:

> and in retrospect it seems to me that she merely affected the mumbo jumbo, the incense burning and the holy water-sprinkling of the priests in her worship, while all of us, my father, my brothers and myself, laughed at her as we waited for the time when the ceremonial was finished and we received shares of fruits and other offerings from her.[14]

Anand states that there is no logical link between inner refinement and performance of rituals. It is this false attitude which forces him to reject religion. The spiritual sensibility of man is fully obscured by dogmas and rituals and so Anand is right in rejecting religion and opting for humanism. His main criticism against religion is that it does not make a free enquiry in relation to life. Moreover its dogmas and rituals have no regard for human concerns. Anand feels that religion induces no interest in human dimensions of life. Hence according to him religion is unnecessary, as it is not a life-promoting agent.

*The Village* trilogy of Anand displays his intense anti-religious attitude. Lal Singh is the spokesman of the novelist. A tuft of hair is an important symbol of the religion of Sikhism. Lal Singh makes his major break from the tradition of Sikhism when he gets his hair shorn. This irreligious act provokes the wrath of his father, Nihal Singh. The novelist portrays the emotional reaction of his father who feels that a great sin has been committed by his son:

> With the fury of an old tiger, he fell upon his son, digging his claws into the boy's neck, while Sharam Singh ground his teeth with an 'Ohe! rape mother!' and struck him hard on his head, his neck and on his body . . . son of a 'bitch' shouted Nihal Singh, pushing off Dayal Singh's restraining hands, and, lifting the barber's silver mounted staff that lay by, he struck the bov hard on his neck, his back, his legs and his ribs![15]

The rebellion of Lal Singh against the tradition of a Sikh ritual rouses the anger of his father and others. Anand feels that religion binds itself to meaningless rituals. For Nihal Singh departure from the Sikh convention is an act of sin. But his beating of Lal Singh is only an expression of religious fanaticism which destroys the significance of life. For his father conformity to the ritual is more important than common sense.

Anand explains that the religion of ritualism and fanaticism contains the deposit of mental intolerance which is not a human quality. The reaction of Lal Singh's aunt Ajit Kaur may be noted here, "It is the most shamefullest shame that could be for a Sikh to have single hair of his body shorn. It is the most terrible insult to our religion of the five K's." (93) Anand notices here that the greatest expression of anger is possible in the name of religion. Lal Singh therefore questions the very value of religion as it has not led to any humanizing process of refining the feelings.

Anand feels that religion becomes a kind of cunning strategy in the hands of a false priest like Mahant Nandgir who preaches the divinely ordained theory of social inequality. He presents his peculiar view of religion:

> God has given a place to everyone in this world. You know well that a serf has not the dignity of a farmer like you [Nihal Singh]. Keep your prestige, therefore, but do not set yourself in the same place as other folk. For that would be a sin. This is the true religion that you should not envy your superiors for if you did so, there would be no order in the world. (43)

Anand feels that this advice can have some meaning if it comes from a man of truth. But Mahant Nandgir is false in many respects; he thrives on the wealth of others, receives the gift of clothes, eats like a glutton, drinks without conscience. Lal Singh feels that he can be charged with the act of fornication. He ironically describes him as 'a holy man' the Guru of the community. The priest does not fulfil even the average standards of a human being.

Anand satirizes a very important theory of the Hindu religion and certain connected concepts clubbed with it. The doctrine of predestination, the custom of superstition, the theories of Karma and fatalism mainly flow from a fundamental belief that every event is an outcome of the verdict of God. Lal Singh speaks about this aspect when he refers to his father and brother whose minds have been smothered by custom and superstition. Lal Singh describes their mental state:

> The images of his father and Dayal Singh—seated in the lotus seat, telling beads and mumbling prayers with their heads hung down, their lips trembling as if at the fear of death and abjectly craving a panacea for all the ills of mortality, flashed before him. They seemed base, and contemptible, defeated. They did not want to think, to feel, to do anything, but relegated the responsibility for all their misfortunes, as well as their blessings, on Karma and a God who didn't exist apart from his apostles. (146)

It is unconvincing for Lal Singh to believe like his father that all good and bad things have their own supernatural sanction. Lal Singh bemoans the fact that there is no ray of critical sensibility in them. It is lack of trust in the individual initiative which enables them to think of everything as the fitting verdict of God. Lal Singh asks what God can do when human hands remain idle expecting the descent of divine grace for the betterment of life.

Anand never expresses his faith in God and the hero Nur in *Lament on the Death of a Master of Arts* is the mouthpiece of the novelist. Nur is an atheist and he experiences spiritual discomfort when he must be in the mosque at dawn at the call of the muezzin. He neither understands the Arabic Suras nor does he willingly pray five times a day, "Nur resents the idea of praying in different postures under compulsion. He finds these 'exercises' both irksome and futile."[16] Nur is a philosophical expression of Anand's belief in atheism. Men use religion as a tool for exploiting the ignorance of people. Anand's frontal attack on God finds its vent through Nur:

> Call the faithful to prayer, call them to prayer, you dog. I hate you and I hate your God. I•hate you all! To incur your wrath, I spit on your face—and I spit on the face of your God.[17]

Like Nur, Ananta disbelieves in God and he is not prepared to believe that God is relentlessly watching over man's misfortunes in silence. For him the existence of God is only a matter of ridicule and mockery. He tells his wife Janki in a pungent manner:

> God works in a mysterious way, in such a heartless way that the ominous owl alone has so far taken pains to answer the peasants in the night—God seems to have deserted the world—if ever, he were there helping it along.[18]

Ananta clearly points out that the world does not function under the supervision of God. He says that human happiness is the product of human endeavour alone.

Anand's novel *Death of a Hero* is an example of his strong belief in atheism, secularism and liberty. The novelist points out that organised religions resort to violence in the matter of establishing their faith. The hero Maqubool stands for a united India. He is a nationalist Muslim who takes up the cause of Kashmir Muslim brethren. Ahmed Shah, a Pakistani bigot, wants to force his Government on the people of Kashmir. Anand says that religion does not give freedom to man. The political ideal under the grip of organized religion proves to be a deadly weapon.

Anand believes that real religion must preach love and peace. When violence, war and hatred are accepted in the name of religion the only way to counter it lies in a plan for liberty and secularism. Naturally Anand prefers atheism to religious bigotry. Maqubool is to be taken as a voice of human freedom. He tells Ishaque, another pro-Pakistani, "I am for Kashmir. Not for its usurpation by force but for its freedom to choose where it wants to go."[19]

Freedom or subjection of a nation to religion is the primary question. Religion first and the freedom of Kashmir next, is the cry of Islam. "This controversy leads to bitterness and bloodshed."[20]

Maqubool reviews critically the life of Pakistani Muslim bigots and he feels that their evening prayers have no relation to morning massacre.

Anand has no sympathy for the ways of the terrible aggressors who are fanatical devotees of an organised religion. For such people sentiments like love, pity and compassion have no meaning. Immediately after torturing the people on the previous night they are seen piously "kneeling in the attitude of Sajdah prayer, their eyes closed, their faces turned toward the West." (47) It seems religion lies in their knees and not in their hearts. Their consideration of religion seems to be more important than the value of human life. The greatest irony is that they want to quicken Maqubool's murder in order to capture their regular time for prayers. Anand here points out that organized religion makes one insensitive to the value of human life.

One important thing that the hero notices is the non-resisting nature of the people even when they know that the Pakistani aggressors have destroyed the peace of Kashmir. They simply treat the Pakistanis' encroachment as a mark of divine punishment for the sins. Begum Jilani, Maqubool's mother, reflects on the nature of life in a fantastic manner:

> Life is cruel and as a woman, I have known this truth. We have to accept because in the eyes of Allah, we deserve this punishment. The only way, son, in which this cruelty can be offset is by obedience to destiny. What is written in one's fate will be. (57)

Maqubool is pained to see that people have no independent mind to think that the Pakistani aggression is an outcome of religious fanaticism and that it is certainly not an expression of divine wrath. Even his father sticks to the fatalistic tone when he tells his son that silent submission to the will of Allah is the only way:

> What can we do against such odds, I ask you! The salvation of our souls lies in the hands of Allah and his prophets. If we pray, perhaps Allah will hear our prayers. (63)

Anand raises certain key questions through Maqubool. He feels that religion makes a distinction between soul and body. The soul has a capacity to assert its mastery over body. But this soul is controlled by God. Without divine help this soul cannot be helped. Maqubool strikes at the root of the problem and he says that soul and body constitute one entity. His wise pronouncement is that soul has to be saved along with body. To ignore the reality of human body and pay attention to soul is the work of religion. But for Anand body is the soul and soul is the body. Maqubool concludes that Allah and divine destiny do not create disasters. Every work on earth is the work of man and God is absent and he has no place in human affairs.

Maqubool is created by Anand to be a militant atheist. He says that disbelief in God is the basis for human progress. His letters to his sister explain his attitude. It is lack of pity which makes man monstrous. He says in a very concealed manner that the Islamic fundamentalism implies absence of human pity. He refers to pity as something which possesses a very humanising influence:

> and conscience, however dim, is a great force, and it is the real source of poetry. For, from the obedience to one's conscience, to pity, is but a small step. And pity is poetry and poetry is pity. (92)

Anand clearly says in this passage that organised religion suppresses human pity. Poetry and pity create love of imagination whereas religion and fanaticism invoke the rule of reason and the cruelty of despotism. Anand says that poetry flourishes only on the basis of pity. A wide opening to all aspects of life is barred by reason. It is pity with the background of imagination which opens the door to love. Anand delivers a verdict that religious fundamentalism flourishes on the basis of despotic rule of reason which suppresses pity. Maqubool therefore concludes that the invaders lack human sympathy.

Maqubool dismisses all notions of God. He rejects religion and God if they are put to evil use, "But is there an Allah? Yessuh Massiah was a real person and suffered for mankind—was crucified?" (25) The hero is in a mood to accept the human dimension of Christ without a divine background. He feels that the religiosity of the invaders has no human element. Anand therefore says that any religious scheme of life is bound to collapse if there is no human element in it. Ahmed Shah says that his group will resort to anarchy; Anand says that this anarchy is an expression of the absence of human pity.

Maqubool against all odds says that he puts Kashmir above everything. Does he prefer death in the Islamic court after due trial? Does he prefer life in total obedience to the dictator of Islamic religion? Maqubool does not waver and he honourably chooses death. He nobly thinks that the survival of human liberty requires his sacrifice of his own life. His house is surrounded by raiders and he is shot in the heels while escaping. He raises the question as to why Allah is against the innocents.

Maqubool longs for the day when the religion of fate and fanaticism will disappear and a new religion of love, poetry and pity will come. That, according to him, will be the day of human liberation. His letter to his sister Noor, found in his pocket after his death, says that no one can be human without listening to conscience. Ahmed Shah orders his death and calls him a traitor. Anand says that his religion is a religion of violence and fanaticism, not one of love and sympathy. Maqbool's death is only a symbolic announcement of the novelist that survival of human life requires the growth of five important factors: tolerance, tenderness, love, compassion and pity. As religion negates all these virtues on account of dogmatism, Anand totally rejects it and advocates a plea for humanism and secularism.

Jayakanthan in his early phase attached importance to life and not to religion. He was concerned with genuine springs of life. In his novel, *Yārukkāka Alutān?* he makes Joseph an incarnation of God. This indicates his belief that human beings can have a higher dimension. Joseph finds his own wife Parvathy to be an ill-suited match for him. Even when he finds her in bed with his friend Marimuthu, he condones it on the ground that real relationship is based on mental harmony. He unites them and leaves getting Marimuthu the job of a gardener. Govindasamy Naidu, the clerk in the hotel where Joseph works as a server, is astonished on hearing this rare sacrifice. He points out at his broad heart, saying,

> Joseph, you are not a man—you are a God. Not a Christian but Christ. In this physique of rock, you have a soft, pure heart. I feel I have to worship you.[21]

Jayakanthan's portrait of Joseph shows that he is not so much interested in the questions about God as in the average nature of humanity. According to him, Joseph is a noble man with a good heart and he says that such a man need not be an intellectual giant. He makes this point in a curt way, "Even fools can be Mahatmas, who will find their place near God." (32) Jayakanthan in his early phase as a novelist was interested in the goodness of the human being and did not bother very much about God or divinity.

Jayakanthan in his novel, *Vālkkai Alaikkiratu* talks about people who make use of religion as a cloak for hiding their evil thoughts. Vetachalam Pillai's knowledge of Vedic ideals prevents him from accepting Raja as a suitable match for his daughter Geeta. Gnani refers to his class-consciousness and hypocrisy:

> Vetachalam is a man only of words and not of deeds. He speaks Vedic ideals. But in action, he is mainly after caste and currency. His ego and pride consume his own daughter. His daughter becomes a scapegoat. He never cares for anything.[22]

Sarangan, who is a rowdy supporting the prostitution in Citanallur Chatram, later responds to human sentiments in Raja and Thangam and becomes a better man facing his own death. The humanity in Sarangan is a contrast to the apparent love of divinity in Vetachalam. Jayakanthan finds fault with Vetachalam as he is not a human being despite his talk of Vedic ideals.

The early Jayakanthan was interested in exposing the falsity of orthodox religion. His sorrow was that in religious men human dimension is absent. Anand and Jayakanthan agree that religion without a human element is no religion at all. They reject religion as it is not true to life. The human element in life is a propelling force for Jayakanthan.

In *Unnaippōl Oruvān* he describes Citti as the illegitimate child of Thangam. He sees no logical link between human relations and morals. Thangam lives with Manickam and gives birth to a girl. Jayakanthan does not disregard the so-called immoral women like Thangarn in comparison with Vetachalam. He sees that only a prostitute comes to the rescue of Joseph in *Yārukkāka Alutān?* The humanness in the prostitute is a noble feature for Jayakanthan; religious pretension is worse than prostitution. In his preface to *Unnaippōl Oruvān* he puts this idea:

> All right, where does India live?
> Does it live in the tattered mat of a prostitute?
> Yes.
> There also India lives. The soul is struggling to live there.[23]

Jayakanthan does not want to measure the merit of immoral men and women in relation to religion and morals. The value of life is seen in relation to real human emotions and his rejection of Vetachalam is an indirect rejection of false religion.

Anand is a full-fledged spokesman of modernity in unequivocal terms. His outright condemnation of religion is part and parcel of this modernist faith. Although Jayakanthan started as a denouncer of religion, there is a gradual shift from atheism to belief in spirituality. His prefaces written to the collection of short stories, *Inippum Karippum* and *Tevān Varuvārā?* do contain the seed of atheism. His faith in the reality of the external world, his disbelief in the soul, distrust of anything pertaining to the internal realm of man, his deep interest in life and human beings and his mode of writing by deriving inspiration from human issues propagate his irreligious attitude. Unlike Jayakanthan Anand has not experienced any change in his outlook because his basic faith is rooted in European Enlightenment Movement which speaks of the progress of life only on the basis of reason.

But with Jayakanthan, there is no attachment to any creed. He is a critical realist who keeps his mind open and subject to revision. He has seen and realized that religion in its spiritual form is the basis for the improvement of life. His own involvement in some political activities, his mingling with Marxist friends, and his contact with different men have led him to realize that life can never be improved without the aid of spiritual transformation.

Jayakanthan's later novels, *Piralayam, Pirammōpatēcam* and *Jaya Jaya Sankara* show his slow and gradual shift towards religion and spirituality. His early phase involves a sceptical attitude towards religion. The later phase of his career indicates his change of vision and attitude. It becomes an important duty to distinguish Anand from Jayakanthan in this respect. Anand is not primarily interested in differentiating true religion from its false form. His view that religion has been totally responsible for the degeneration of life remains unchanged. But there is a specific change in the consciousness of Jayakanthan and it forces him to review life from a new angle of spirituality and its role in shaping men.

Jayakanthan delivered a speech on the occasion of Swami Vivekananda's birth anniversary in the year 1977. This spirited speech of Jayakanthan indicates his new analysis of life. Perhaps the creation of Sankara Sharma is partly inspired by his profound interest in Swami Vivekananda as a very great revolutionary spiritual reformer. Jayakanthan's participation in this function provided an opportunity for him to relate life to the concept of spiritual reform. He also develops the habit of separating the essential religion from its many false forms and it helps him in analysing the meaning of life from a fresh spiritual angle.

Jayakanthan turns to religion in the hope that the real progress of life depends on the rise of a new spiritual reformer. He makes a distinction between traditional religion and revolutionary spiritual religion. One great advantage with the reformer is that he is alive to the reality of changes in the world while the man of traditional religion remains stagnant. According to him he who responds to the reality of life in all its forms of change is a progressive reformer:

> Swami Vivekananda calls himself a socialist. He did not call himself so in the manner in which the present day politicians speak of themselves.[24]

Usually a politician has the right to call himself a socialist. But Vivekananda's description of himself as a socialist appeals to Jayakanthan as it has deeper significance. He learnt about socialism from Marxists and Socialists. He never drew any fundamental ideas from them. But his reading of Swami has given a new meaning to the concept of Socialism. In the history of Indian religion, Swami's call for the unity of the human race is significant. His pronouncement that human race is one is a real version of Socialism.

Some of Vivekananda's sayings attract Jayakanthan. He says that a man who wants to improve his life needs to be fired by such ideals. Swami's idea of spiritual revolution gives a new turn to religion. His sayings, 'Wake up', 'Fear is Cowardice, and have faith in one's own inner potentialities' add a new meaning to life. Jayakanthan admires Swami because he thinks of raising life from its fundamental base. His acceptance of religion is also derived from his understanding of Vivekananda. Jayakanthan puts forth indirectly his view of religion in the light of the great spiritual reformer's message.

When some people said that the progress of the country is hampered on account of religious life, it was Swami Vivekananda who made it clear to them that India faced degeneration because it lost its true sense for spirituality. Jayakanthan learnt from the reformer that the genuine form of religion lies in its pursuit of spirituality. According to him organised religion and ritualism play sometimes a negative role. The socialists say that all are one provided all necessities of life are provided. The spiritualist says that all are one at the level of soul and spirit. Jayakanthan feels that the spiritualist's angle is deeper than the socialist's angle and that real socialism comes from the philosophy of spirituality. Mere materialistic change of life is far inferior to spiritual transformation. Jayakanthan says that the spiritualists speak of love of human being while socialists talk about their abstract doctrine of human unity.

Jayakanthan's deep interest in life has enabled him to examine the lives of saints. In *Vilutukal* he develops a new perspective moving closer to the religious lives of saints. He himself says in the preface to the novel that he has no belief in God and has no fanatical devotion for saints. But he says that he is a lover of life. He has enjoyed the company of these saints. According to him a profound form of life is manifested in these saints. He boldly acknowledges in his preface the value of sainthood and its social relevance in these words, "The greatness of life is known through those people who have renounced life. It is a matter of joy to feel that such people teach the essentials of life."[26]

Men in this mode of life are concerned with the welfare of all human beings. Renunciation is shedding narrow restrictions and giving up ego-based barriers. Men know a superior form of life through renunciation. Jayakanthan believes that renunciation aims at a high level of appreciation of life from an impersonal angle fully endowed with love, compassion and joy.

Jayakanthan's hero in *Piralayam* is an idealised pariah man and what he sees and how he comments on men and matters form the substance of the novel. His experience and exposure to life and his profound relation to truth have given him wisdom. He looks like a Vedic master judging life with norms derived from his understanding of life.

Jayakanthan's interest in the truth of Hindu religion is shown through Ammasi Kilavan. There are two passages spoken by him which bespeak his deep and refined religious conviction. He upholds the virtue of hard work and opposes sloth and indolence in this passage, "Whether one is rich or poor, he who does not work hard is a sinner. He is his own enemy."[27] This looks like the voice of a Vedic Guru. He believes in the noble ideal that human beings must earn their living by hard work. Ammasi Kilavan's interpretation of true Dharumam or Charity again puts him in the tradition of Vedic Guru. He thinks that a house of plenty cannot be a house of charity. He points out the real meanings of the words *Dharumam* and *Karumam*:

> Dharumam does not mean getting alms by begging. Karumam does not mean sin. Really their meanings are different. Dharumam means following a discipline of propriety. Karumam means the inevitable duty of performing some work. (78)

Ammasi says that giving food is not identical with Dharumam because it means an ethical discipline involving sacrifice. The capacity to sacrifice what one has is different from what one distributes by way of food from his house of plenty. To illustrate this he recounts the story of Raja Suya Yagam in *The Mahabharat*. Ammasi Kilavan delivers his Vedic verdict that purity of heart with a capacity for sacrifice is superior to mere external display of ceremony. The essence of the Hindu religion is embedded in the speech of Ammasi Kilavan.

Jayakanthan's *Pirammōpatēcam* is the first novel in which he visualises the possible relationship between religion and atheism. Here he does not dismiss religion. On the other hand he is in a mood to see the life-improving possibilities of religion. He has come to realise that it is the orthodox religion which causes damage to human life. He sees that real religion is different from what exists as religion.

When Jayakanthan creates Sankara Sharma, he has in mind Swami Vivekananda. There is a general argument that degeneration in social life as reflected in inequality, caste fanaticism and denial of individual freedom is traceable to religion. The impact of Vivekananda on Jayakanthan throws new light on this controversy. Jayakanthan makes this issue clear in his speech on the occasion of Swami's birthday:

> The progress of this nation is not impeded on account of religious life but because it has lost its genuine spirituality. . . . When the nation faces decline, great Gurus come and guide the destiny of life. Vivekananda who comes in this tradition of Vedic Rishis impresses upon us the need for knowledge, physical strength and perception of spiritual truths.[28]

Jayakanthan in this passage makes a distinction between religion and spirituality. The posture of relating oneself to life in a deep spirit of inwardness is known as spirituality. Jayakanthan has become a lover of spirituality; for him spirituality is a profound expression of life from an impersonal angle in a spirit of love without the disturbing ego.

Jayakanthan does not have a closed mind. In his preface, he says very objectively:

> Just because Sankara Sharma has endorsed some principles contrary to my convictions he need not be made on that ground an object of condemnation. To do so is not a sign of greatness.[29]

Jayakanthan evolves a new criterion in this novel. He says that where there is a true expression of life it must be objectively appreciated. It is this new kind of philosophical objectivity and fairness which opens the way for Jayakanthan's slow entry into the region of religion.

This philosophical objectivity is deeply at work in this novel in his creation of two idealised characters, Sankara Sharma representing religion and Seshadri standing for atheism. There is no conflict but only a debate between these two. Jayakanthan puts forth his argument in the preface:

> Seshadri's atheism will not oppose religion but it will hold a meaningful debate and dialogue with it. . . . Atheism is not modernity. . . . It will not destroy old values. It will generate new ideas with the help of knowledge. It is not a rigidly fixed creed. It will alter the cultural climate and change itself in accordance with the spirit of the times.[30]

Jayakanthan treats atheism as a kind of deeply sympathetic intellectual awareness. He says that atheism is a plea for a renewal of life.

Jayakanthan maintains a fresh and original view that atheism and religion are not opposed to each other. The usual view which prevails in Europe is that atheism involves a clear denial of religion. What the novelist implies here is that there should be an intellectual compromise based on true understanding of life. Jayakanthan's love of fair intellectual enquiries prepares the ground for his smooth entry into religion. He represents Sankara Sharma in a new perspective:

> He is angry with the Brahmin community for its deviation from the high ethics. . . . He wants to revive old values with dedication. . . . No progressivist will contradict his concept of doing intellectual service and developing spiritual perspectives for the uplift of humanity.[31]

Jayakanthan's novel *Jaya Jaya Sankara* shows his full conversion to the genuine Hindu religion. The inspiration for writing this novel comes from the living Guru Sankara Acharya Swamikal. His preface makes a reference to certain holy ideas of the Swamikal.

> When writers begin to write with a passion for developing spiritual exploration, such a taste will be born in the minds of people on its own accord. They must acquire a feeling for a new ethics to raise themselves and also the standards of the readers. Let the writers be blessed with the grace of performing service with a view to improving spiritual welfare, worldly peace and harmony.[32]

Jayakanthan admits that a novelist must develop the habit of writing from the standpoint of a spiritual perspective. He feels that he is blessed with the gift of a spiritual vision and so can fulfil the wish of Sankara Acharya. To review and scrutinize life from a spiritual angle is a new artistic endeavour. The novel, *Pirammōpatēcam* has given him the greatest virtue of intellectual objectivity and fairness.

His mind has become comprehensive enough to include all aspects of life. *Jaya Jaya Sankara* is an imaginative story containing a superior form of truth. Though it is imaginary, it is more real than actual life, as it has a profound relation to truth.

Jayakanthan visualises a simultaneous alliance and cooperation between temple and ashram. He says:

> New experience teaches that temple and ashram must be put together. People must establish an ashram very near the temple. It should be a place for creating Brahmins.[33]

The novelist projects a new idea that religious devotion and spiritual life must go together. He says that religious devotion can become dry and sterile without the real background of spiritual life. It is this insight which enables Jayakanthan to look at religion through the window of spiritual life. He looks forward to the emergence of spiritual activities which will dynamite the old assumptions and create a new zeal for life. When he speaks of their mode of life, he raises certain questions:

> Will these Brahmins embrace marital state? Or will they become Sanyasis? These questions can be settled later. But let them first become Brahmins.[34]

Jayakanthan is on a sound footing when he says that marital state expresses one form of life and renunciation another mode of life. Under the influence of Vivekananda he says that life is seen in marital state and in renunciation also. Both householders and the Sanyasis can do their duty in promoting the significance of life. He is of the opinion that the revival of the old Vedic ideals is crucial in the modern context since they can shape men's minds and ennoble them.

Jayakanthan clearly says that the original Hindu religion has nothing to do with the evil of untouchability. He feels that the Vedic ideals can never be ignored in the building up of life. He appreciates the Vedic doctrine that men must live on a higher spiritual plane with their roots embedded in the practical reality of the world. The three motives of the novel are well brought out by Kalpanadasan in these words: "What he does through *Jaya Jaya Sankara* is a spiritual propaganda. What he wishes to see is the creation of social life on a Vedic basis. The net consequence he expects is something like Sri Ramanuja's creation of New Brahmins."[35]

An unsympathetic reviewer, S. Narmada, is of the view that Jayakanthan's novel *Jaya Jaya Sankara* is inconsistent with his earlier reading of Marx and Lenin. Some objections are raised by her in the following passage: "Why should there be an imposition of the invalidated concept of Brahminism that promotes caste fanaticism and untouchability and it being an instrument for the explicating class in the twentieth century Hindu society which longs for the creation of a new social history?"[36] This is certainly an adverse criticism which misunderstands the purpose of Jayakanthan. No philosophy or concept easily goes out of date. It depends on how men give meaning to things. A critic with Marxist bias and allied atheistic preoccupation may not have the objective frame of mind to appreciate *Jaya Jaya Sankara.* Such a critic is at cross-purposes with the mission of the novelist.

The very purpose of writing this novel is not to reflect the normal reality of life. The novelist here is interested in reassessment and reinterpretation which express a need for a renewal of life in the light of ancient ideals. It is not good logic to say that ancient things are totally bad and that modern things alone are completely good. Sometimes the ancient values are more useful and life-saving than the modern ones.

A critic who wants to understand Jayakanthan's purpose must proceed from *Piralayam* via *Pirammōpatēcam* to *Jaya Jaya Sankara.* These three novels form a logical sequence. In *Piralayam* the protagonist Ammasi Kilavan is an enlightened Harijan found in the tradition of Vedic idealism. The hero Sankara Sharma in *Pirammōpatēcam* is an extension of Ammasi Kilavan. His plea for revolutionary spiritual reform with an unorthodox base is a new one. What he wants is improvement in life.

Jayakanthan feels that atheism is a good corrective to a degenerate religion and a good religion is a good corrective to a degenerate form of atheism. But according to him good atheism can work as an intelligent collaborator with religion. The Marxist critics have failed to see this vision of Jayakanthan. In his grand vision of life atheism and religion are not in a state of opposition with each other but they are in the stage of debate. Jayakanthan's idea that revival of life requires deep contact with the Vedic ideals is not given due weight by these left-oriented critics. Moreover in his vision, Jayakanthan believes that refined atheism and revolutionary spiritual reform are not opposed to each other, but are complementary to each other.

Jayakanthan's *Jaya Jaya Sankara* is a novel which reflects the reality of the Hindu religion and its relation to normal life. The Marxist critics have ignored this motive of the novel on account of their bias. Jayakanthan conceives of an ideal visionary life in which a Brahmin and a Harijan must shake hands with each other. He says that internal reform in the life of a Harijan can take place surely along the Vedic line. Any external change in the life of a Harijan is no permanent solution.

Jayakanthan points out that the spiritual duty of a teacher is great and universal in scope:

> He says that as Jagad Guru he has to shoulder all the sins of those people. . . . It is a public opinion that the Brahmin community has special affinity with him. . . . For the Jagad Guru everyone is the same. (93)

Jayakanthan says that it is a misconception to think that the Hindu religion makes invidious distinction among people. When Swamikal says that for him all human beings are the same it only reflects his universal compassion for all.

Acharya Swamikal severely censures Brahmins and he reminds them of their state: "Brahmins should have a purpose in life. If they are not going to be fruitful to the society, what is the purpose in their existence?" (94) To impart spiritual knowledge to human beings is the duty of a Brahmin. Any failure in this duty lessens his status and takes away the meaning of his existence. Moreover he admits the fact that anyone who does this duty rises to a superior stature.

Jayakanthan points out effectively that character, not caste, is important. How do the Marxist critics fail to see this insight of the novelist? The only answer is that their bias stands in the way. To regard all people in the same perspective is a Vedic concept. Jayakanthan celebrates the Vedic ideal of love of all human beings in his *Jaya Jaya Sankara*.

In his speech on tradition and revolution Jayakanthan hints at a new idea: "To violate a tradition is not revolution; after that a new tradition comes in return. . . . Revolution means new traditions."[37] This speech of Jayakanthan closely reflects the new teaching of Acharya Sankara Swamikal. When he addresses the revolutionary activists he reminds them of their responsibility in this way, "Revolution is construction. It is creation. It is life. It is for the welfare of the world."[38] Jayakanthan categorically points out that revolution is a creative activity. The spirit of the times forces every value to undergo change. Jayakanthan says that the old Vedic ideal admits the possibility of revolution which renews life and aims at the welfare of the world.

There are some common problems which Anand and Jayakanthan handle in their novels. These issues are concerned with their attitudes to society, marriage, love, sex and morality. Anand thinks that society is like a prison dominated by custom, convention and the evil of caste system. In *The Big Heart* the members of the Murli Dhar family think that contact with the high family of Gokul Chand will bring status to them. The novelist puts a pungent remark through Nehru's mother, "The crows are not pigeons and the pigeons are not crows." (160) All the customs and conventions have outlived their usefulness. The age has looked for the formation of a new society. Gokul Chand gives expression to this need for the reconstruction of society, "no one can keep our ancient customs alive without being called a fool by his children." (129)

Munoo faces a class-conscious society while Bakha comes across a caste-oriented society. Munoo is prepared to do anything to the society. What he expects in return from it is the status and the dignity of a human being. But the society withholds the title of a human being to Munoo. Anand thinks that society holds the individual lives of Munoo, Bakha and Ganga at bay. In *Two Leaves and a Bud* the capitalist society oppresses workers and subjects them to severe trial.

The life that the Assam society presents is described by Narain, "This prison has no bars, but it is nevertheless an unbreakable jail."[38] Anand believes that the progress of human life is hampered by the society. When the lovely Leila is about to be raped Gangu's anger knows no bounds. But he is shot dead in the encounter. A trial is held in which the criminal is freed and the innocent is declared guilty. Anand indirectly hints at the fact that the death or the defeat of Gangu is the representation of his poverty and it is also a simultaneous indication of the triumph of capitalism. Saros Cowasjee points out the problems of these two evils, caste and class: "The problems of caste and class are complex and they cannot be solved separately, for they are often linked together and influenced by economic pressure."[39]

Anand sees a conflict between the individual and society. The caste-conscious society reduces Bakha's life to mere sub-human existence. Munoo is not given any relief by the society. It suppresses his inner energy. His life is a trial and a journey to an unknown destination. Anand is of the opinion that society has the claws of tiger to injure human beings. Without a bold fight and revolt against society, life cannot be made comfortable and peaceful for human beings. Anand considers possession of freedom to be the ideal objective of man. The suppression of individual freedom seems to be the one end of society. Nur has acquired academic excellence but still he is a misfit in the society. He does not know the fact that intellectual excellence comes next only to wealth. He avoids Gama his friend on the ground that society considers his co-educated companion to be a man of no rank. But Nur never knows the fact that society has given him a false education and has not trained him in the art of living. Gama rejects this kind of education saying, "What is there in education, brother! Waste of time."[40]

Anand feels that true education is an instrument for the progress of man. The society which is covered with conventions and customs can be corrected only by true learning which comes through education. Moreover society is in the grip of capitalism and money has come to play a major role in human life. Society respects money and refuses to go beyond that narrow concern. Anand thinks that the policy which considers money to be the major motive has no meaning. He takes pains as a novelist to show how society neglects true values, follows false conventions and oppresses individual human endeavour which looks for liberation like a caged bird. Anand is unorthodox in his attitude to love, sex, marriage and morality. He does not treat marriage as a sacred institution because many evils issue from it. Gauri leads a very unhappy married life with Panchi. It is an arranged marriage in which the individuals have not expressed their choice. For example, Maya and Janki strike at the conventional idea of marriage by giving up their vow of widowhood. They decide their fate as individuals and opt for a new life with the men with whom they express their preference to live. Premila Paul observes, "His understanding of man-woman relationship is primarily sexual." (48)

This statement is not fully true because Maya and Janki do not prefer Lal and Ananta just for sex only. They look for deeper relations. Maya admires Lal because he is a fighter against social injustice. Janki likes Ananta as is an idealist. Gauri prefers Panchi despite his habit of manhandling. The reason is that she seeks fulfillment in sex. But Anand shows in Maya and Janki a different level of relation with their heroes. Anand speaks of mental harmony and physical sex is only subordinate to it. The traditional morality disapproves of the relations of Maya and Janki with Lal and Ananta respectively. Anand has scant respect for traditional norms and allows his heroes and heroines to break the existing moral code. Life is more important. He rejects traditional morality, because it denies individual freedom. Anand holds the conviction that without individual freedom human life can never express joy and peace. The new ethics will be built on the basis of individual liberty.

Anand and Jayakanthan do not bring in orthodox canons to judge life. They together feel that all the traditional barriers carry dead weight. Jayakanthan in his early phase adopted a free scheme and did not make much of sexual promiscuity. In *Yārukkāka Alutān?* Joseph gives his wife to Marimuthu on the ground that her choice needs to be respected. Gnani raises the question of traditional morality and argues thus:

> Take Parvathy and Marimuthu. What harm have they done to Joseph? Nothing. Life has made them as they are now; shall we judge them with a yardstick of morality which is above their social set-up? No, it cannot be.[41]

The novelist says that human life must express love and harmony and cannot be produced by moral rules. The goodness of Joseph's heart has not attracted Parvathy. Marriage has lost its meaning because Parvathy's mind moves towards Marimuthu. Joseph makes no formal fuss and simply looks for the joy of human beings. Jayakanthan says that the society is corrupt because a good man like Joseph is accused of theft. No one comes forward to defend him and the critic sees the irony of the situation in this manner, "The prostitute cannot raise her voice in support of Joseph and her attempt becomes futile."[42] A prostitute happens to be good-natured while the so-called virtuous men lack determination to follow truth. Joseph is beaten for his innocence while Gangu is killed for his truth-bearing nature. Jayakanthan admits the fact that the wretched world makes Joseph a scapegoat. He also feels that moral rules leave a hampering effect on the true expression of love.

Jayakanthan in *Vālkkai Alaikkiratu* shows Sithanaloor chatram to be the seat of prostitution. The hero Raja is a man of truth, looking for some employment. He falls in love with Geetha, the daughter of an upper class man, Vedachalam Pillai. He prefers Chidambaram Pillai's son as a good match for his daughter. For them wealth and prestige seem to be more important than man. This conflict leads to the suicide of Geetha. Society is horrid because it does not respect Raja whereas it encourages Chidambaram Pillai's illicit relation with Thangam. Sarangan who lends support to evil, later changes when he accepts the love between Raja and Thangam and drives out Chidambaram Pillai out of the Chatram. Sarangan is killed. Kamatchi who loves Pasupathy shifts her love later to Sarangan, his brother.

Why should Raja marry a prostitute Thangam who is forced into the profession? Why should Geetha commit suicide? Why does Kamatchi shift her love to Sarangan? Is Sarangan a good person? The novelist provides an indirect answer to these questions:

> None can dare to raise his finger at their defaults. They have safeguarded love and Dharma as far as they can. They are destined for mean actions. They are trying to overcome their destiny and preserve their dignity.[43]

Jayakanthan in *Unnaippōl Oruvān* depicts the pathetic life of Thangam and Citti. Thangam's illegal affair with a labourer leads to the illegitimate birth of Citti. Later on Thangam comes across a fortuneteller Kuruvikkaran Manickam. She regards him as her real husband. The novelist refers to their relation in a spirited way, "One morning she gives herself voluntarily to him thinking that such physical union would make both of them cheerful."[44] Jayakanthan feels that such sexual union has a capacity to lessen human strain and tension. While religion advocates sexual restraint as a virtue, he ignores it. Moreover Thangam's intimacy with Manickam is illegitimate.

Kokila breaks the Iyengar tradition and marries an Iyer boy. Ananta Raman's social prestige is a bar to their real union. Their talk of divorce is a threat and their crisis disappears. Jayakanthan's *Suntara Kāntam* describes Sita's problem. She develops love towards men of ideals and conviction. She does not treat sex as a very important affair. But for Sukumaran it is essential. When marriage does not reflect the mental agreeability of the partners, it is bound to be a failure. Marriage must become a meaningful act. In Jayakanthan's *Mūnkil Kāttu Nilā*, Periavar's brother is interested in Nila. At the end they love each other. But caste restrictions do not bring them together. They seek sexual fulfillment. Nila disregards the concept of marriage and social recognition. The reason is that society is not based on righteous principles. Jayakanthan gives greater value to the human context than to mere barren ethical rules.

Jayakanthan's *Pārisukku Pō* expresses his views on love, divorce and marriage. Sarangan in this novel is an apostle of modernity. Lalitha after having married Mahalingam develops love towards Sarangan. He induces her to reject Mahalingam and opt for divorce. The novelist handles this matter carefully. Sarangan argues, "Marriage is just an agreement, not a key to lock the two persons concerned in that jail forever."[45]

Sarangan's modernity tempts him to say that marriage is an agreement which can be terminated at any time. The novelist deliberately contrasts this modern view with the opinion of Narasaiah. He says that real love means a superior mental state. He refers to his concept of love and marriage:

> Marriage is an unbreakable bond. It is a joint life of two individuals, full of love, compassion, sacrifice, tolerance and forgiveness. Actually this life reforms the human beings. (265)

The novelist says that true love expresses charity and compassion. This is a state of selflessness. True love has a purifying effect. The issue of divorce has a wrong background according to the novelist. Usually it is possessiveness which leads to crisis. Possessiveness is selfishness and so love is not identical with it. Narasaiah defines true love in his deathbed: "Here love is wrongly defined as the possessiveness one exercises over the other." (266) Jayakanthan looks upon true love as an expression of a non-possessive instinct. Sarangan's idea of divorce has no meaning in the light of this statement. Jayakanthan develops his new ethics which indicates that human life must be seen in a human context. All human situations have their own background and external standards cannot do justice to them. For example the words of Narasaiah have greater wisdom. But he himself has gone astray and lived with Ganga the dancer after abandoning Balammal, his wife. But his experience is much more profound than Sarangan's Narasaiah argues indirectly that one must learn lessons from one's own life. He regards mutual loyalty between husband and wife as an essential virtue.

Jayakanthan does not approve of divorce or even separation on trivial grounds. All our actions must indicate some meaning. Sarangan's concept of divorce and Sita's creed of separation from Sukumaran are not mature solutions. The feelings of being one with each other comes from selflessness. This does not mean annihilation of self. On the other hand, it implies a higher functioning of the self where ego is absent. For Jayakanthan love is an expression of a noble frame of mind. All inferior feelings which spring from the selfish base can have no place in the manifestation of true love.

Jayakanthan is an unorthodox moralist like Anand. For them, human context is what gives meaning to life and action. Jayakanthan knows that ethics is necessary but he argues that it should be related to complex contexts of life. Mere insistence on ethics will keep one blind to the reality of human context. Anand's women Maya, Janki and Gauri and Jayakanthan's women Kalyani, Kokila, Ganga, Nila, Thangam and Parvathy fulfil a higher expectation of life which cannot be estimated in terms of any ethics without its relation to the human context.

So, both Anand and the early Jayakanthan dismiss religion as it is of no use in their understanding of life. Their main objection lies in the argument that supernatural miracles and blind superstitions have no relation to the actual meaning of life. The life that appears before the human eye becomes much more important than any high sounding idealistic speculations. Anand's interest in Science and Marxism laid the foundation for his rejection of religion. Like Anand, Jayakanthan is a lover of life and the world around. Anything which lessens the dimensions of human living carries no merit. It is his firm belief in the reality of the external world which becomes the motivating force for his perception of the significance of life.

Although Jayakanthan's earlier phase carried a sceptical attitude to religion, there is a change in his mental outlook in his later phase which accepts religion as an important source for transforming life from the standpoint of spirituality. Unlike Jayakanthan, Anand is through and through a denouncer of religion. His faith in the scientific creed of modernity gives him the strength to make a sustained revolt against religion.

Ananta looks to machine for the uplift of humanity and also believes that disbelief in God paves the way for human progress. Maqubool pleads for human liberty. He thinks that the religious fundamentalism is an indirect denial of human freedom. The religious fanaticism of Ahmed Shah look for merging Kashmir with Pakistan while the liberal secularism of Maqubool longs for a united India. His letter written to Noor, his sister, when he is about to die, hints at the fact that religious fanaticism implies absence of human pity.

Jayakanthan sees a new revolutionary spiritual idealism in Ammasi Kilavan, Sankara Sharma and Acharya Sankaran Swamikal. He affirms his new belief in religion and spirituality as a source for enlivening life. Anand and Jayakanthan adopt an unorthodox attitude in their approach to love, marriage, sex, morality and chastity. They together uphold individual human freedom as more important than external ethical standards. Maya and Janki oppose tradition and religion, while Kalyani, Kokila, Ganga and Sita assert their individual rights to determine their mode of life. The human context assumes greater importance than mere morality in the vision of life of Anand and Jayakanthan.

## NOTES

1. Mulk Raj Anand, "Why I write?," *Kakatiya Journal of English Studies*, Mulk Raj Anand Special Number, 2, No. 1 (Spring 1977), p. 253.
2. *Ibid.*
3. G.S. Balarama Gupta, *Mulk Raj Anand: A Study of His Fiction in Humanistic Perspective* (Bareilly: Prakash, 1974), p. 20.
4. Mulk Raj Anand, *Pilpali Sahab* (New Delhi: Arnold-Heinemann, 1985), p. 245.
5. *Ibid.*, pp. 245-46.
6. Premila Paul, *The Novels of Mulk Raj Anand: A Thematic Study* (New Delhi: Sterling, 1983), p. 59.
7. Mulk Raj Anand, "How I became a Writer," *Contemporary Indian Literature*, November-December 1965, p. 13.
8. Krishna Nandan Sinha, *Mulk Raj Anand* (New York: Twayne, 1972), p. 19.
9. Mulk Raj Anand, *The Golden Breath: Studies in Five Poets of the New India* (London: 1933), p. 61.
10. Jayakanthan, *Jayakanthanin Munnuraikal* (Madurai: Meenakshi Puthaka Nilayam, 1984), pp. 8-9.
11. K.N. Sinha, *Mulk Raj Anand*, p. 17.
12. Karl Marx, Qtd. Mulk Raj Anand, *Apology for Heroism* (Bombay: Kutub-Popular, 1946), p. 127.
13. Mulk Raj Anand, *The Sword and the Sickle* (Bombay: Kutub-Popular, 1955), p. 90.
14. Mulk Raj Anand, *Apology for Heroism* (New Delhi: Arnold Heinemann, 1975), p. 30.
15. Mulk Raj Anand, *The Village* (New Delhi: Arnold-Heinemann, 1960), pp. 91-92.
16. Premila Paul, *The Novels of Mulk Raj Anand*, p. 69.
17. Mulk Raj Anand, *Lament on the Death of a Master of Arts* (Lucknow: Naya Sansar, 1939), p. 27.
18. Mulk Raj Anand, *The Big Heart* (Bombay: Kutub-Popular, n.d.), p. 166.
19. Mulk Raj Anand, *Death of a Hero* (Bombay: Kutub-Popular, 1963), p. 51.

20. Premila Paul, *The Novels of Mulk Raj Anand*: A Thematic Study, p. 71.
21. Jayakanthan, *Yārukkāka Alutān?* (Madurai: Meenakshi Puthaka Nilayam, 1986), p. 31.
22. Gnani, *Mārkciyamum Tamil Ilakkiyamum* (Coimbatore: Parinamam, 1988), p. 209.
23. Jayakanthan, *Unnaippōl Oruvān* (Madurai: Meenakshi Puthaka Nilayam, 1991), p. 6.
24. Jayakanthan, qtd. N. Arivalakan, *Jayakanthan Āyvatankal* (Cuddalore: Amaravathy Press, 1978), p. 191.
25. *Ibid.*, p. 191.
26. Jayakanthan, *Jayakanthanin Munnuraikal*, p. 68.
27. Jayakanthan, *Piralayam*, p. 69.
28. Jayakanthan: qtd. N. Arivalakan, *Jayakanthan Āyvatankal*, p. 192.
29. Jayakanthan, *Jayakanthanin Munnuraikal*, p. 30.
30. *Ibid.*, pp. 31-32.
31. *Ibid.*, p. 30.
32. Jayakanthan, *Jaya Jaya Sankara* (Madurai: Meenakshi Puthaka Nilayam, 1992), p. 3.
33. Jayakanthan, qtd. N. Arivalakamn, *Jayakanthan Āyvatankal*, p. 77.
34. *Ibid.*, p. 78
35. Kalpanadasan, *Ibid.*, p. 294.
36. S. Narmada, *Ibid.*, p. 285.
37. Jayakanthan, *Ibid.*, p. 115.
38. Mulk Raj Anand, *Two Leaves and a Bud* (Delhi: Orient Paperbacks, n.d.) p. 40.
39. Saros Cowasjee, *So Many Freedoms* (Madras: Oxford University Press, 1977), p. 131.
40. Mulk Raj Anand, *Lament on the Death of a Master of Arts* (Delhi: Hind Pocket Books, 1967), p. 27.
41. Gnani, *Markciyamum Tamil Ilakkiyamum*, p. 211.
42. *Ibid.*, p. 120.
43. *Ibid.*, p. 210.
44. Jayakanthan, *Unnaippōl Oruvān*, p. 134.
45. Jayakanthan, *Pārisukku Pō* (Madurai: Meenakshi Puthaka Nilayam, 1992), p. 222.

# Summing Up

Anand and Jayakanthan have examined some fundamental issues in their novels. Their rejection of religion and acceptance of humanism form an important phase in their life and literary career although Jayakanthan has changed his outlook in his later phase. Anand hits at tradition as an advocate of modernity while Jayakanthan tries to underplay the clash between the two. Anand and Jayakanthan look at the problem of untouchability from different standpoints. They believe in woman's individual freedom. Anand considers marriage as a legal contract and so gives the freedom to the suffering woman to get separation from man; but Jayakanthan considers marriage as a sacred institution and so desires man and woman to live together with tolerance, forgiveness, sacrifice, love and compassion for each other. Their vision of life has human element as its base which includes their concern for the poor and the downtrodden.

The humanism of Anand and Jayakanthan gets itself expressed in their deep concerns with the lives of poor people. The painful reality of human suffering and a sympathetic portrayal of it is what distinguishes them as humanists. All the five novels, *Coolie, Two Leaves and a Bud. Yārukkāka Alutān? Vālkkai Alaikki:atu* and *Unnaippōl Oruvān* describe their main motives. Explicit denial of God, rejection of abstract philosophical creed, a passion for knowing the sources of human suffering, consideration of society as a monster, a bold dismissal of the traditional morality in the face of the life of the poverty-stricken people constitute their special preference for the category of romantic humanism.

Their humanism lies in an intense perception of the human agony which is expressed in all the novels. The portrayal of human suffering is what is central and common to them. These two writers show their profound interest in an interaction between the characters and the false standards of society. Such a preoccupation emboldens them to endorse their faith in the Marxian ethics which states that poverty and human suffering are artificially engendered by the capitalist structure of society.

Anand and Jayakanthan believe that religion detracts from them their full attention to human life. The valuc of their humanism lies in a profound concern for human life and a simultaneous effort to perceive human pain. Anand's perception of the division between the rich and the poor is an important factor for explaining the human crisis. The society in Jayakanthan's early novels is seen as a prison. These two findings lead to the logical conclusion that their humanism has a predominant Marxian tinge.

Although they are known as two great humanists, their perception of life has some distinct features. Anand in all his novels shows himself as an idealistic humanist tending to believe in the truth that all his protagonists are noble personages. There is no element of evil or villainy in them. The main fact is that Anand as a romantic and idealistic humanist holds the view that man, especially the poor man, is innately good and society is bad and that it corrupts his noble nature. There is no trace of wretchedness in the character of Munoo and Gangu. Only a society built on the basis of wealth, class and capitalism frustrates their hopes. They are profoundly human in their suffering. The poverty of Munoo and Gangu never creates malicious motives. They go out in the world boldly to face all eventualities. Anand's idealistic humanism leads him to draw the premise that it is the corrupt society which is responsible for their suffering.

Jayakanthan also shares Anand's idealistic and romantic humanism. But there is a difference in that there is a desire in Jayakanthan to be a practical and a realist humanist. He makes Joseph a Mahatma and an incarnation of goodness and love. He dissolves his marriage and allows his own wife Parvathy to live with Marimuthu. Raja is a noble character. But Citti in *Unnaippōl Oruvān* and Sarangan in *Vālkkai Alaikkiratu* are characters of imperfections. Citti keeps company with a wayward group and Sarangan is the active promoter of prostitution in Sithanaloor Chatram.

Anand and Jayakanthan take immense care in laying emphasis upon the tremendous mental power and the fierce individuality of the protagonists. The crisis of Bakha comes from the caste-fanaticism of the society. His accidental touch of a person provokes anger and censure. For the caste-Hindus, the touch and sight of an untouchable is a mark of pollution and a sign of sin. Bakha is aware of this peculiar injustice. Pandit Kalinath makes an attempt at molesting Bakha's sister Sohni and shifts the blame onto her by saying that he is polluted by her touch. Bakha's anger knows no bounds but he realizes his helplessness on account of his social inferiority. Bakha's individuality emerges from his perception of the awareness of human inequality.

Unlike Bakha, Āti is an enlightened intellectual who has come under the influence of the revolutionary spiritual leader Satasiva Iyer. Bakha is hurt when people dishonour him whereas Āti remains unperturbed by people's attitudes and reactions. Āti's learning has endowed him with freedom of perception and the courage to place faith in his own choice of life. He discourages the idea of temple-entry on the ground that God can be found in any place and not necessarily in a holy temple. This is a bold line of thinking which shows that he has liberated himself from backward mentality. Āti is different from Bakha because the former is a learned individual who has gained enormous intellectual power to resist any conservative type of mentality. Bakha is conditioned by the currents of the society while Āti looks forward to the shaping of a new order of life.

Anand and Henry are high idealists. They are lovers of life and human beings. Their common mission lies in doing service to society. Ananta is a disbeliever in God and religion and gives credit to human effort. He disregards people's belief in fate. His ideal is to reflect along the line of improving the human race through the power of the machine. Ananta is comparable to Henry in his love for fellow human beings. Henry, like Ananta, respects life and ignores religion. For them life and human beings matter primarily. Henry's love of human beings is so great that he thinks that it is an offence to dismiss the views of others. He feels that it is not a sign of good culture to wound people's feelings.

Ananta and Henry are not after wealth and possession. Their main motive is to serve humanity in some capacity or other and not to accumulate wealth. Ananta is an uncompromising idealist, in his rejection of religion and acceptance of machine as salvation for humanity. Henry's character, unlike Ananta's, lies in showing his capacity for flexibility. He does not want to disagree with anyone for he thinks that such an act does not make him human. He wants to be human and lovable. Both Ananta and Henry identify love as their major principle of life. They look alike in their magnanimity and unselfish nature. Ananta is a man of determination because he is an advocate of modernity. Henry is a man of free will and has no determination like Ananta because he is not a strong advocate of anything. But he has a purpose as an Idealist and it lies in accepting human life in all forms.

Anand and Jayakanthan tend to treat the evil of untouchability as a complicated problem. But they work under different premises when they trace the origin and history of this evil. Anand is an advocate of modernity who has come under the influence of the European Enlightenment. Therefore it is nothing but a logical necessity for him to blame the Hindu religion for the existence of the evil of untouchability. Jayakanthan has no occasion or condition to work under this kind of logical obligation. His perception of Swami Vivekananda's place in the spiritual reform has inspired Jayakanthan to reassess the role of the Vedic religion. He sees that the Vedic religion in its pure form speaks of its concern for the world welfare. But in its degenerate form it has led to many wrong notions. Unfortunately untouchability is an anomaly in the Hindu religion.

Anand elaborately describes the pernicious effect of caste fanaticism, as he is concerned with the actual state of affairs. The behaviour of the caste-Hindu becomes the greatest subject matter of study for the novelist. Anand feels that almost all the caste-Hindus behave like monsters who treat men like Bakha as animals. Much of the effort of the novelist moves in the direction of showing how a character like Bakha suffers and faces humiliation and shame. Jayakanthan's purpose is different from Anand's. He is of the view that these untouchables must evolve themselves into higher nature through learning and become men of self-assurance and independent judgement.

Jayakanthan is of the opinion that the state of lowborn nature comes from the feeling of ignorance. It is only knowledge which can remove this psychological defect. Anand suggests a solution which is different from Jayakanthan's. He feels that dung and latrine cleaning bring indignity to men like Bakha. The only way to remove this dishonour is to introduce a scientific device whereby the life of the untouchable will undergo a sea change. The indignity comes from the work they do. Anand's solution is that the introduction of flush system changes the character of work. Anand adds another point and he says that gaining of economic freedom will modernise their life and make them respectable human beings. Jayakanthan argues that knowledge and learning will open the door to the gateway of emancipation much more quickly than any other external agency. Unless a man learns to fight for his own right and equips his mind with good insights it is impossible for him to achieve dignity and self-respect. For eradicating untouchability Anand seeks solutions 'from without' while Jayakanthan suggests remedies 'from within'.

Anand and Jayakanthan believe that real human freedom comes when women enjoy equality with men. But they know that this state is not so easy to be attained. Therefore they create certain revolutionary women characters to achieve their special motive which lies in human equality. There are two factors which make Maya a great revolutionary. She ignores her family background of wealth and rank. Her choice of a poor peasant as a lover is a mark of her simplicity. She nullifies her previous marriage, rejects her widowhood and boldly contracts a runaway marriage with Lal Singh.

Janki plays the same role as Maya. She gives up her widowhood and chooses to live with Ananta. Maya sees in Lal Singh the figure of a fighter for justice and this becomes a source of attraction for Maya. Similarly Janki sees in Ananta the mark of a high idealist whose interest is to serve people and improve their lot. Her special sidelight as a new woman is that she puts Ananta in touch with the reality of human life. She gives due balance to the excessive emotional idealism of Ananta by reminding him of the actual problems of life like famine and starvation. She knows that Ananta's mission of improving the lot of the human race through machine is admirable. But his emotional enthusiasm is inadmissible according to Janki and so she insists on his ability to pay attention to all problems of life without any bias.

Jayakanthan, like Anand, respects the individual freedom of woman. He knows that marriage is a peculiar emotional tie which arises from mental harmony. Kalyani chooses a married man Ranga as her life partner. This is nothing but an expression of her individual freedom and personal taste. Kalyani's attitude to love makes her a new woman. She is against all Petrarchan and Romantic tradition where high emotions are involved in the expression of ideal love. She thinks that love must express a calm balance of mind. Love as sentimentalism or emotionalism or idealism is untrue to the facts of life. Ranga does not appreciate Kalyani in this respect. Kalyani holds her flag as a new woman and she says that any individual must respect the right to retain the difference of opinion. This staunch difference of opinion leads her to temporary separation from Ranga. But she endures the pang in a bold manner.

Kokila is less sophisticated but more courageous than Kalyani. She breaks the Iyengar tradition and marries an Iyer boy. This is her initial victory as a new woman. The greatest crisis comes in her life when Ananta Raman suspects Kokila's love on the ground of the visit of her mysterious friend to their house. He is not able to resolve this dilemma and it reaches a climax where he suggests his idea of remarriage. Kokila remains undaunted as a new woman and she does not bother about his remarriage. She tells him firmly that such a threat is fruitless. A declaration is made by her that she will remarry a person of her choice. She says that when men behave ruthlessly, woman has the right to check and resist it boldly.

Ganga is a lonely individual. The mysterious rape incident in the car becomes a great crisis in her life. Her uncle Vengu Iyer holds the opinion that any proposal of her marriage after the rape incident in the car is a sin. This puts her in search of identifying the person. She discovers that it is Prabu who is a married man. The situation becomes more complicated. She can neither marry him nor can she have any kind of relation with him. But her continued meeting creates a new dimension of relation with him and it goes beyond all the rage of physical passion. She develops a kind of enlightened friendship with him. She becomes an emancipated woman when she prefers to sacrifice the idea of marriage and remain alone. She finds solace in helping all people.

The case of Sita as a new woman is interesting. Her marriage with Sukumaran is an outcome of avoiding a big financial crisis. Sita's marriage is worse than an arranged one, because there is an element of force and compulsion. She is not able to endure her agony like an ordinary woman. There is no common tie between Sita and Sukumaran. Sita's intellectual bent of mind makes her relation with Sukumaran disagreeable. Later on she comes away from him and lives a life of separation.

Both Anand and Jayakanthan plead for woman's equality with man. With regard to man-woman relationship in the context of marriage, Anand considers marriage a mutual convenient arrangement, and so when it turns out to be inconvenient, a woman, according to Anand, has the liberty to break the arrangement and lead an independent life of her own. But Jayakanthan feels that man and woman are born and made for each other and that the marriage, being a sacred bond is unbreakable for it sustains spiritual order.

Anand and Jayakanthan disapprove of blind religious conservatism and they accept the spirit of objective rational criticism as the basis for progress and improvement in life. Lal Singh in *The Village* trilogy of Anand becomes the real spokesman of modernity. He says that chanting a religious Mantra is not a medicine for any disease. Lal Singh's father Nihal Singh regards machine as a devil and Science as a giver of darkness. The hero feels that only an intellectual awakening can remove the conservative mentality. Lal Singh sees that backwardness in social life is engendered by religion and tradition.

The novel *Across the Black Waters* suggests a remedy for this evil of conservatism. For Lal Singh the European nation is a heaven as it has vastly improved itself on the basis of industrialization and mechanization. The stench in the village reminds Lal Singh of the hygiene and sanitation seen in France. He sees that the first step to progress lies in the recognition of the necessity for an intellectual awakening and that the second step to any social reform comes through an open acceptance of modern scientific outlook. Anand does not stop with the second step but suggests a third step in the novel *The Sword and the Sickle.* The message of the third novel is that the corrupt order of society can be resisted by an organized rebellion. Intellectual change, scientific outlook and Marxian mode of protest against social injustice through organized resistance become the themes of the three novels.

Jayakanthan shares these preoccupations of Anand in his two novels *Pirammōpatēcam* and *Pārisukku Pō*. Sharma is a religious revolutionary who believes in improving the welfare of the human race by imparting knowledge. He considers this to be the Dharma of a true Brahmin. Seshadri differs from him and he says that the conditions of social life must be changed by adopting atheism and Communism. These are the two claims of Sharma and Seshadri. Sharma says that atheism destroys life and that no civilization has ever made any progress without religion as a true base. Seshadri is a refined intellectual and so he does not disrespect his view. As a communist he thinks of changing the external order of the society while Sharma thinks of internal mental maturity as a sign of progress. Jayakanthan therefore says in his preface to the novel that real religion and atheism work in close co-operation with each other. The novelist perceives Sharma and Seshadri in their idealized form where each makes his contribution to the building up of social life in a worthwhile manner. Jayakanthan sees the importance of Sharma and Seshadri in relation to each other. For Seshadri the new Veda is communism. Sharma acknowledges the fact that he prefers true atheism to a corrupt form of Brahminism. Jayakanthan feels that a better flowering of social life depends on an alliance between reason and religion.

What brings the two novelists to the framework of comparison is their rational spirit. For example, Lal Singh, Seshadri and Sarangan share a common scientific outlook and look forward to deep changes in the society. Sarangan believes in aesthetic appreciation as a mark of good culture. Lal Singh and Seshadri place their faith in the Marxian dogma of economic and social justice. Without a change in the external conditions of social life, social reform is meaningless. Sharma and Narasaiah plead for a revival of the old values which still have their own relevance and significance. A sacrificial spirit is what makes life noble. Lal Singh struggles to improve his village and Seshadri evinces his interest in labour union activities and Sharma does the job of a head cook. Sarangan's proposal of divorce does not reflect a sacrificial spirit. Narasaiah's definition of love and his plea for true spirit of sacrifice and his talk about mutual adjustment among married partners constitute a new attempt at seeing the right relation between tradition and modernity. So in the clash between tradition and modernity, Anand is definitely on the side of modernity while Jayakanthan attempts at a healthy alliance between tradition and modernity.

Anand and Jayakanthan project a new vision of life and each derives his meaning from a particular logic of his own. Anand's search for the realist tendency in philosophy has brought him into contact with only concrete reality of things. His perception of degeneration in life on account of conservatism of religion and backwardness of tradition has led him to place faith in the creed of humanism.

Jayakanthan is identical with Anand in his vision of life in many ways in his earlier phase. But one thing is common between them, that is, they remain unorthodox till the end in their approach to life. The only difference lies in Jayakanthan's reinterpretation of the Vedic ideal in the light of the distinction he makes between religion and spirituality. In *Vilutukal* he says that Sanyasis offer a genuine appreciation of life which is useful to all people. Jayakanthan perceives that these saints have no worldly obligation and so relate themselves to life. In a more fundamental way, the novel *Piralayam* shows Ammasi Kilavan as an excellent judge of life. He speaks in terms of low and depressed people gaining maturity as a representative of his class.

Jayakanthan thinks that gaining inwardness is an important act of a human being. His two novels *Vilutukal* and *Piralayam* give genuine and dispassionate criticism of life and thereby they prepare the preliminary background for Jayakanthan's entry into the world of religion and spirituality. Jayakanthan believes under the inspiration of Swami Vivekananda that the spring of true religion must lead one to the fountain of spirituality. He slowly realizes that the loss of spirituality is the genuine reason for all the degradation in life and the need of the hour is to revive it.

Anand and Jayakanthan are opposed to a conservative outlook of life. The existing mode of marriage, morality, sex and chastity carries no value for Anand. As Anand gives importance to individual freedom, all traditional rules become null and void. Jayakanthan also agrees with Anand that it is human context which is more important than traditional ethics. As Jayakanthan gives due credit to real religion, he does not accept any indiscriminate violation. Kalyani and Kokila do not break the framework of marriage in spite of their crisis. Sita opts only for a life of separation like Gauri. But Anand's heroines Maya, Janki and Gauri defy tradition and believe that life can be renewed only by dispensing with the canons of religion. Jayakanthan does not go that far and pleads for a balance between individual freedom and general social outlook.

There is plenty of scope for further research so far as the study of Anand and Jayakanthan is concerned. The theory of art in Anand and Jayakanthan is a rich subject. Anand is of the view that art is not a propaganda machinery though it can be used as an instrument for social transformation. What is the real relationship between thought and feeling in the works of Anand?

Anand starts with the conception that man is good by nature. Jayakanthan has similar sentiments but with a rider. His conception is that man is a bundle of complexities and contradictions. Artists are basically propagandists but mere propaganda does not become art. For this study Anand's *Apology for Heroism*[1] and *Jayakanthan's Prefaces*[2] provide basic materials. Anand's "Why I Write?"[3] *Author to Critic: The Letters of Mulk Raj Anand*[4] edited by Saros Cowasjee, "Creative Process"[5] and Asnani's "A Critique of Mulk Raj Anand's Literary Creed"[6] and *Jayakanthanin Munnurai Ilakkiyam*[7] written by Tamizhannal and Thirumalai are the other source materials that are of immense use.

Existentialism in Anand and Jayakanthan is another viable area of research. As existentialists, both express their concern for human life. Existentialism in Europe is an expression of despair. It expresses in Anand and Jayakanthan its relation to poverty and suffering of human life. There is no pessimism but only an element of realism. Their existentialism is not nihilism. They discover meaning in life. They look at the survival of human life with love and joy as optimists although they see agony in life and give expression to it in their novels.

The study of Marxism in Anand and Jayakanthan is another interesting area. For Anand the greatest division between the rich and the poor is the greatest anomaly causing suffering in human life. Jayakanthan illustrates the same lesson that economic impoverishment is the root cause of the tragic suffering of Citti and Raja. Both believe that capitalism breeds imperialistic domination and it generates exploitation of the poor. They give importance to human life and external world. For them life on earth is the only reality. One may note the change in Jayakanthan's outlook and contrast Anand's commitment to Marxian ideals with Jayakanthan's novel idea of co-existence of Marxism and spiritualism. The concept of change which is fundamental to Marxism attracts the two novelists. They believe in the Marxian dogma of economic justice. Their plea for human equality makes them fully Marxians in their attitude to life. G.N. Agnihotri's "Mulk Raj Anand: His Progressive Proletarianism"[8] and Marlene Fisher's "Mulk Raj Anand: The Novelist as Novelist"[9] are useful sources of information on Anand, Arul Rathinam's chapter on communism in his doctoral dissertation[10] can be the starting point for a discussion on Jayakanthan's attitude to Marxism.

Anand and Jayakanthan probe the question of Brahminism. Anand condemns unsparingly the Brahmin priesthood and attacks the counterfeit sainthood. Jayakanthan attacks Brahmins but in his later phase launches into a strong defence of Brahminism. For him real Brahminism involves renunciation and greater ethical responsibility of guiding and shaping the world.

## NOTES

1. Mulk Raj Anand, *Apology for Heroism: A Brief Autobiography of Ideas* (New Delhi: Arnold Heinemann,1986), pp. 7-203
2. Jayakanthan, *Jayakanthanin Munnuraikal* (Madurai: Meenakshi Puthaka Nilayam, 1984), pp. 5-238.
3. Mulk Raj Anand, "Why I Write?" *Indian Writing in English*, ed. Krishna Nandan Sinha (New Delhi: Heritage, 1979), pp. 1-9.
4. Mulk Raj Anand, *Author to Critic: The Letters of Mulk Raj Anand*, ed. Saros Cowasjee (Calcutta: Writers' Workshop, 1973), pp. 1-125.
5. Mulk Raj Anand, "Creative Process", *Littcrit*, Vol. 4.1 (1978), 1-3.

6. M. Shyam Asnani, "A Critique of Mulk Raj Anand's Literary Creed", *New Dimensions of Indian English Novel* (Delhi: Doaba, 1987), pp. 116-31.
7. Tamilannal and Thirumalai, *Jayakanthanin Munnurai Ilakkiyam* (Madurai: Solai Noolakam, 1977), pp. 10-118
8. G.N. Agnihotri, "Mulk Raj Anand: His Progressive Proletarianism", *Indian Life and Problems in the Novels of Mulk Raj Anand, Raja Rao and R.K. Narayan* (Meerut: Shalabh, 1984), pp. 28-60.
9. Marlene Fisher, "Mulk Raj Anand: The Novelist as Novelist", *Marxist Influences and South Asian Literature*, ed. Carlo Coppola (Delhi: Chanakya, 1988), pp. 67-82.
10. Rethinam Arul, "Communism and Naturalism, Emile Zola and Jayakanthan: A Comparative Study of their Portrayal of Social Problems in Select Writings," Doctoral Thesis submitted to Madurai Kamaraj University, 1980, pp. 276-99.